WORD MEANING AND LEG

AN INTRODUCTORY GUIDE

Word Meaning and Legal Interpretation

An Introductory Guide

By

Christopher Hutton
School of English, University of Hong Kong

First published 2014 by
PALGRAVE MACMILLAN

Palgrave Macmillan in the UK is an imprint of Macmillan Publishers Limited, registered in England, company number 785998, of Houndmills, Basingstoke, Hampshire RG21 6XS.

Palgrave Macmillan in the US is a division of St Martin's Press LLC, 175 Fifth Avenue, New York, NY 10010.

Palgrave Macmillan is the global academic imprint of the above companies and has companies and representatives throughout the world.

Palgrave® and Macmillan® are registered trademarks in the United States, the United Kingdom, Europe and other countries.

ISBN 978–1–137–01614–0

This book is printed on paper suitable for recycling and made from fully managed and sustained forest sources. Logging, pulping and manufacturing processes are expected to conform to the environmental regulations of the country of origin.

A catalogue record for this book is available from the British Library.

A catalog record for this book is available from the Library of Congress.

Typeset by MPS Limited, Chennai, India.

Printed and bound by CPI Group (UK) Ltd, Croydon, CR0 4YY

Contents in Detail

Part II   Case Studies

List of Figures and Tables

Figures

Tables

Acknowledgements

I should like to thank my colleagues in the Emerging Strategic Research Theme: Law, Literature, Language at the University of Hong Kong, in particular Elaine Ho, Janny Leung, Scott Veitch and Marco Wan. Marco Wan and I originally devised and co-taught the undergraduate course Law, Meaning and Interpretation, and I am grateful to him for introducing to me to two of the cases discussed in this book. Patrick Jiang provided excellent feedback on an earlier draft. My thanks go to Kelvin Au, Frederick Blumberg, Noël Christe, Frank Dikötter, Adam Jaworski and Julia Kuehn for helpful suggestions, to Adrian Pablé for many discussions about word meaning, and to Kimberly Tao for discussions about transgender issues in law and society. I should like to thank the editorial staff at Palgrave Macmillan for their support and help throughout, in particular Anna Marie Reeve the original commissioning editor, Aléta Bezuidenhout for the production, Paul Stevens whose support was crucial in bring this project to completion, and David Stott and Catherine Minahan for their work in the final stages. I hereby acknowledge the support of Hong Kong RGC GRF award HKU 745412H, in particular in relation to Chapters 1–3 and 13.

Note on Conventions

Key specialist terms in the study of law or of meaning are presented in bold: **semantics** when used for the first time. General terms, categories, and words and phrases at the centre of the cases are presented in italics: *vehicle*. Meanings or **glosses** are given in inverted commas: 'self-propelled means of transport'. Inverted commas are also used for 'scare quotations' and for direct quotations, except for displayed quotations which appear without inverted commas. Secondary sources are cited using the 'author, date: page number' convention: Durant, 2010: 27. Law cases are cited by party names and date in the body of the text: *Smith v US* (1993). This is not the conventional way to cite legal cases, but it avoids the need for footnotes. Page and paragraph numbers for quotations from law cases are given using the convention 'at 56', or 'para. 5'. Full case citations and bibliographical references are given at the end of the book. Cases from a range of jurisdictions are included, in particular England and Wales, the United States and Hong Kong. Since 2009 the judicial functions of the House of Lords have been vested in the Supreme Court of the United Kingdom. It should be clear from the context whether *Supreme Court* refers to the UK or the US.

Abbreviations

ADA	Americans with Disabilities Act (1990)
AFDC	Aid to Families with Dependent Children
AG	Attorney-General
Anor	Another
Art.	Article
Arts	Articles
c.	chapter
Cap.	chapter
CFA	Court of Final Appeal of the Hong Kong Special Administrative Region of the People's Republic of China
CJ	Chief Justice
CR	Congressional Record
ECHR	European Convention on Human Rights
GID	gender identity disorder
HK	Hong Kong (Special Administrative Region of the People's Republic of China)
HKRPA	Hong Kong Racing Pigeon Association
HMRC	Her Majesty's Revenue and Customs
HTSUS	Harmonized Tariff Schedule of the United States
ICCPR	International Covenant on Civil and Political Rights
J	Justice, judge
LJ	Lord Justice
MR	Master of the Rolls
NYT	*New York Times*
OED	*Oxford English Dictionary*
PAC	Political Action Committee
para.	paragraph
paras	paragraphs
per	in the judgment of; according to
PRC	People's Republic of China
Pt	Part
REOP	reasonable expectation of privacy
s.	section
Sch.	Schedule
ss.	sections
SRS	sex reassignment surgery
TSUS	Tariff Schedules of the United States
UK	United Kingdom of Great Britain and Northern Ireland
UP	University Press
US	United States of America
v	versus
VAT	value added tax
VP	Vice President

Introduction

This book is about word meaning, linguistic categories and the classification in law of objects, events, actions and people. It is concerned with how words at issue in legal cases are assigned interpretative meanings. The aim is to give the reader a strong sense of the texture of legal problems, and to that end this book presents actual cases, analyzed so as to be comprehensible to someone without legal training. It analyzes legal **meaning troublespots** (Durant, 2010: 27) such as: Is a bicycle a *carriage*? Are Sikhs a *race*? Is a company a *person*? These involve ordinary words, commonsense categories and problems of classification: 'Meaning troublespots are less about understanding something that seems out of reach than about settling on a meaning for something understood in too many different ways right in front of us' (Durant, 2010: 31). If the statute states that 'No games are allowed in the park', a judge may have to decide whether playing an electronic game on an I-pad is against the law, i.e., whether the e-game is a *game* for the purposes of the legal rule. Law must reach decisions in relation to individual people and concrete circumstances against a background of a dynamic socio-cultural order, and yet justify those decisions in terms of abstract legal categories and impersonal rules. This is a basic human dilemma in relation to moral principles, as well as the crux of the interpretative problems that confront law.

The book is divided into three parts. Part I, 'Meaning and Interpretation' (three chapters), reviews approaches to word meaning and interpretation in linguistics, philosophy and law. Part II, 'Case Studies', consists of 10 chapters and makes up the core of the book. The cases discussed are drawn from common law jurisdictions, primarily those of England and Wales, the United States and Hong Kong. They turn on the meaning of a particular word or phrase and the classification of an object, event, person or group. Readers should note that these cases are drawn from different time periods and social contexts, and the explanations are not intended to state definitively the current state of the law. In Part III, 'Concluding Remarks', the fundamental issues are identified and reviewed.

It should be stressed that there are many interpretative issues in law concerning word meaning not covered by this book. It does not deal with specialized topics such as legal translation, defamation law, hate crimes, obscenity law and trademark law, nor with evidential texts, such as confessions, witness statements, suicide notes and so on. It is confined to genres of text defined by law, primarily statutes, but also contracts and wills. The reader is referred to standard introductions to law such as *The Law-Making Process* (Zander, 2004), to legal reference works on statutory interpretation (e.g. Bennion, 2010; Scalia and Garner, 2012), and to general studies on language and law such as Tiersma (1999) and Solan (2010).

Issues concerning linguistic categories and systems of classification (**taxonomy**) permeate specialized discourses such as natural science or anthropology, bureaucratic and administrative regimes, as well as everyday talk about the world and the mundane things, people and events observed within it (Jaworski and Coupland, 1999: 3). Legal decisions belong to the social history of classification and can reflect deep-seated tensions in intellectual culture and social organization. The issue in the New York case of *Maurice v Judd* (1818) was whether a tax that applied to *fish oil* also applied to *whale oil*. This question was staged as a confrontation between an emergent but unstable scientific taxonomy, according to which whales were *mammals*, and the traditional Biblical order, whereby living beings were classified according to their domain: 'the fish of the sea', the 'fowl of the air', and living things that move 'upon the earth', according to which whales were *fish* (Burnett, 2007).

Modern social theorists regard categories and classification systems as **social constructs**. In this book the related term **fiction** is used at various points. Fictions operate within law in various ways, for example to maintain the coherence of legal discourse or to fill an evidential gap (Fuller, 1967). Other forms of legal fiction involve stipulating the nature of an entity, for example the idea that a registered company has **legal personality** or is a **legal person** (see Chapter 14). An example of a fiction as to fact is the rule that where two people die together in unknown circumstances, the younger one is deemed to have survived longer. The 'fact' that the younger survived the older is treated 'as if' it has sufficient existence for law to operate upon it (see Chapter 5). More fundamentally, many of the forms of authority, evidential assumptions, classification schemas and interpretative methodologies on which law draws have been characterized as fictions. The category is intrinsically contentious (Smith, 2007). One question that this book raises is the status of two concepts fundamental to legal interpretation, namely **decontextual (abstract) meaning** and **ordinary meaning**. Both can be seen as fictions or constructs, and 'ordinary meaning' is arguably a key legal fiction. Using the term 'fiction' or 'construct' does not necessarily provide the answer to a set of intellectual problems; rather it is an invitation to look behind the category in order to understand the role it plays in the interpretative culture of law.

The interdisciplinary study of law has a number of potential aims. It might seek to apply frameworks from disciplines outside law into the study of law, in order (i) to impact directly on the practice of law, including decision-making by judges; (ii) to influence legal education (see Dorato, 2013) and academic debates in legal theory; and (iii) to inform non-specialist readers about law, and thereby contribute to public understanding of legal topics. A further interdisciplinary aim, with scrutiny directed in the reverse direction, would be (iv) to use the study of law to reflect critically on the concepts and methods of academic disciplines such as linguistics and the philosophy of language.

If we put linguistics into the scheme above then the aim of legal linguistics might be (i) to change how judges make decisions about meaning and interpretation in actual cases. Since the medium of law is primarily language, expertise about language, it is argued, is relevant to the ways in which judges make decisions about what words mean. This would suggest that linguists can teach lawyers how better to perform the linguistic tasks of law. More modestly, the aim (ii) might be to transpose or translate the linguistic and interpretative culture of law into the conceptual framework of a discipline such as linguistics or anthropology. This would be done not with the aim of correcting the interpretative culture of law, but of understanding legal interpretation as a set of cultural and institutional practices. This might extend to (iii) popular discussions of meaning and interpretation in law. To scrutinize linguistics through the lens of law (iv) would involve using law as a critical testing ground for the models of meaning and interpretation proposed by linguists. It might be argued that the study of language has much to learn from the study of law, since law is a social domain in which linguistic issues with which all members of society have to deal are treated in a hyper-explicit or **reflexive** manner (Hutton, 1996). It has been argued by linguists that law's dealings with meaning and interpretation are problematic; yet, from the point of view of law, it might be argued that linguistics is itself naive about the nature of language and interpretation, in particular the kind of contentious and strategic decisions that are made by judges.

A claim to know what words mean represents a claim to a specific kind of intellectual or institutional authority. While language is a social institution, no one has ultimate authority or control over it. No theory of meaning allows the analyst, as a matter of incontrovertible method, to determine what a word means in the abstract or in a particular context. Language is best understood as an open-ended and disorderly participatory democracy. Yet linguistics seeks to identify an underlying order in the form of stable sets of form-meaning pairings that make communication possible. It claims a particular form of authority in relation to its statements about language. Law involves the institutional creation, recognition and application of its own specific forms of authority, and within law, interpretation is a highly specialized domain for the exercise of that authority. However, while law has multiple discourses about categories and classification, it has ultimately 'no all-purpose theory of things' (Madison, 2005: 382). And while law claims authority over interpretation within its domain, it equally has no 'all-purpose' theory of language and interpretation.

The dilemma that haunts all interdisciplinary discussions is that intellectual questions frequently make sense only within a certain disciplinary framework. To bring two or more frameworks together risks creating a conceptual clash. But one question the reader should be able to ask is: Does this idea from linguistics or philosophy offer useful insights when applied to problems of legal interpretation? Even if the answer is ambivalent or negative, the reasoning process is itself highly revealing. It is conceptual tensions such as these that make the topic of language and law such a fascinating one.

PART I

Meaning and Interpretation

CHAPTER 1

Linguistic Meaning

The discussion below reviews in brief approaches to the study of linguistic meaning or **semantics**. The word **meaning** is notoriously difficult to define (Ogden and Richards, 1923), as is the word **word** itself (Hanks, 2013: 25ff.). There is little agreement about the questions to be asked, let alone the answers (Stout, 1982), and the student is confronted by a bewildering array of terminology and frameworks. Two points should however be kept in mind. First, there is an underlying ideal of **one word–one meaning**, to which at some level every theory of meaning is responding. Secondly, each language user has the extensive resources of his or her linguistic and interpretative experience on which to draw.

Basic terms and concepts

The term **linguistic meaning** implies that there are particular properties that words (phrases, sentences, etc.) possess and by virtue of which they function as signs. One common way to explain the meaning of a word (**lexical meaning**) is by the identification of a **synonym**, that is, a word with the same or a similar meaning. Synonyms are used, for example, when an unfamiliar or difficult word is explained with reference to a familiar one. A student of Latin who looks up *arbor* in a Latin–English dictionary will find it defined or glossed as 'tree'. If we look up *unctuous* in a monolingual English dictionary, we find that it means 'oily, greasy' and that it can be applied to people, with the implication that they are smooth-talking, affected, insincere and untrustworthy. In these cases the dictionary explains the less familiar by reference to the more familiar. However, basic words such as *oily*, and even simple words such as *mouse*, *the* and *in*, also appear in standard dictionaries, and have to be explained with reference to less basic or more difficult words.

   A second semantic function of the dictionary is to provide authoritative generalizations about the meanings of a word, including organizing these into sub-categories. In semantics the distinction is made between **polysemy** (where a word has a range of distinct but related meanings) and **homonymy** (two words which have the same form but a different meaning), and this is also reflected in the structuring of dictionary entries. **Hyponymy** is a semantic relationship of inclusion: *cat* is a **hyponym** (or subordinate category) of *animal*, and *animal* is a **hypernym** (superordinate term) of *cat*.

Dictionary entries tend to deal with polysemy by arranging meanings from the more common to the less common, and from the **literal** to the **figurative**. The *Oxford English Dictionary*'s entry for *rose* begins with a section of meanings under 'flower or plant' ('flower or a flowering stem of any of numerous wild and cultivated plants of the genus *Rosa*'); section 2 of the entry gives the 'allusive, emblematic, or figurative' meanings, especially metaphorical meanings. This corresponds to the intuition that the concrete or literal meaning – in this case also the botanical – is more basic than the figurative. In the *Oxford English Dictionary*'s on-line definition for *female* there is the same emphasis on biological reality (<oxforddictionaries.com>):

- of or denoting the sex that can bear offspring or produce eggs, distinguished biologically by the production of gametes (ova) which can be fertilized by male gametes: a herd of female deer
- relating to or characteristic of women or female animals: a female audience; female names
- (of a plant or flower) having a pistil but no stamens
- (of parts of machinery, fittings, etc.) manufactured hollow so that a corresponding male part can be inserted.

Definitions come in many styles. Charles Dickens (1812–70) in his novel *Hard Times* parodied a soulless form of pedagogy in the figure of the teacher Mr Gradgrind. For Gradgrind, the word *horse* is properly defined in terms of facts about horses (Dickens, 1854: 16):

> Quadruped. Graminivorous. Forty teeth, namely twenty-four grinders, four eye-teeth, and twelve incisive. Sheds coat in the spring; in marshy countries, sheds hoofs, too. Hoofs hard, but requiring to be shod with iron. Age known by marks in mouth.

(*Graminivorous* means: 'eating grass or the seeds of grass'.) In terms of lexicographical theory, Gradgrind prefers so-called **real definition** (encyclopedic definition of things, people or events) to **lexical definition** (definition in terms of conceptual meaning) (see Harris and Hutton, 2007: 37ff.).

Metaphor is the most familiar category of figurative language. According to an influential definition, its essence is to be found in 'understanding and experiencing one kind of thing in terms of another' (Lakoff and Johnson, 2003: 5). A celebrated literary metaphor is 'All the world's a stage', from Shakespeare's *As You Like It* (Act 2: vii). Theatrical metaphors are commonly used for the courtroom trial (Friedman, 2000) and even the legal process as a whole: 'All the law's a stage' (Ball, 1999). Metaphor involves a tension between perceived similarity or **analogy** and perceived deviation from the norm or **anomaly**. The phrase *justice is blind*, for example, brings to mind the female figure of justice (often called Lady Justice), carrying a sword in one hand and a pair of scales in the other. This is a visual metaphor based on **personification**, in that an abstract idea, 'justice', is depicted in terms of a human figure. The figure is frequently, though not always, blindfolded. This loss of vision represents, by analogy, the idea of impartiality or objectivity. By virtue of being unable to see, the figure is freed from the biases of ordinary perception. The blindfold further represents self-restraint, since the figure could see, but elects not to. In addition, there is a second analogy between weighing and judging. A scale, like justice, should be objective; it is a public instrument of measurement, used as a comparative reference point.

But there is also an anomaly in the way we read the figure of Lady Justice, and in the related phrase *justice is blind*. Justice, after all, is not a person; weighing goods on a scale is very different from evaluating evidence or assessing arguments. Furthermore, vision (rather than its absence) can also represent understanding and insight. When the figure is blindfolded, we interpret this as representing impartiality; yet when the figure is not, we still read the figure as representing law's impartiality. Both the ability to see and the inability to see can stand for similar metaphorical meanings. Conversely, the phrase *justice is blind* can be used to praise law's impartiality, or to bemoan its inability to get at the truth.

Contemporary theorists of metaphor stress the essential role it plays in our understanding of self, society, culture and nature, as well as of basic processes and categories such as causality, time, and space (Lakoff and Johnson, 2003). Metaphor, they argue, is grounded in our bodily experience, and is integral to the fundamental ways in which we make sense of the world. Yet the metaphors we use are always contentious, or potentially so. One person's insightful metaphor is another's manipulative rhetoric. Metaphor highlights or proposes sameness (analogy), but it simultaneously conceals or downplays incompatibility and difference (anomaly). The boundary between analogy and anomaly is at stake in our most profound disagreements. Is it a helpful analogy or a linguistic anomaly to call the brain a *computer*? Is a nation a *family*? Should we conceptualize official action against illegal drugs as a *war*? Is a foetus a *person*? In what sense is the *pain* of animals like (or unlike) the pain of human beings? What does it mean to say that God is *happy* or *angry* (Kołakowski, 2012)?

The relationship between literal and figurative meaning plays a fundamental role in the study of word origins and history known as **etymology**. The etymology of a word is understood as a relationship between different stages of the history of a word (x becomes x^1), and among words in languages that are related or in contact (x is related to y). But etymological meaning is not simply a historical curiosity. Modern linguistics has rejected the relevance of etymology for current meaning (the **etymological fallacy**), arguing that words mean what people take them to mean in current usage. *Prestigious* means 'having high status' not 'full of trickery' (its etymological meaning), since that is how ordinary speakers of English now use the word. The origin of a sign is not necessarily relevant to its meaning. For example, a woman in Tokyo carrying a handbag with a Union Jack design is presumably not making a statement of loyalty to the British flag. Yet in asking for the literal meaning of a word, we often look for the historical and usually more concrete meaning that is felt to underlie it. Since literal meaning is profoundly important as a frame for thinking about word meaning, etymology can be used as an analytical tool where peripheral and contingent meanings of a word are stripped away in order to reveal the original, core concept. To invoke the literal meaning therefore often involves appealing (explicitly or implicitly) to the etymology; further, etymological analysis is frequently exploited for a variety of rhetorical purposes, including in legal interpretation.

In their search for an understanding of word meaning, linguists, literary critics and philosophers tend to draw a distinction between **ambiguity** and **vagueness**, though they make the distinction in a variety of ways (see Schane, 2006: 12ff.; Solan, 2012; Poscher, 2012). In general a sentence is said to be ambiguous if there are two (or more) distinct readings that can be offered of it. An example would be: *The chickens are ready to eat*, which can mean 'The chickens can now be eaten' or 'It is time for the chickens to be fed'. A vague sentence would be one such as *Sam bought a lamp*, since it is not specified how much the lamp cost (Lakoff, 1970). On the level of words, *bank* would be ambiguous, since it can refer either to a financial institution or to the shore of a body of water; the word *friend* might be considered vague, since it covers a wide range of relationships. But, arguably, *The chickens are ready to eat* represents two distinct sentences, just as there are two distinct words (homonyms) spelled *bank*.

As for vagueness, there is always potentially a fuzzy edge to any identified meaning. A sentence that is ambiguous out of context might be perfectly clear in context. In a discussion of the scope of the word *knowingly*, the court in *US v Jones* (2002) stated that: 'Although the language was ambiguous, the potential for confusion was not realized' (at 750). Conversely, a sentence that appears unambiguous in the abstract might be ambiguous when used on a particular occasion. The literary critic William Empson (1906–84) effectively merged ambiguity with vagueness when he defined ambiguity as 'any verbal nuance, however slight, which gives room for alternative reactions to the same piece of language' (Empson, 1953: 1). For Endicott, a word or expression is vague 'if there are borderline cases for its application' (Endicott, 2000: 31). This suggests that all language is ambiguous or potentially so, and moves close to the position that language is **indeterminate** (see 'Indeterminacy' below).

Negotiating the semantic maze

In semantics there are three basic modes of explanation for the meaning of a word or phrase (Harris, 1980). These are:

(a) conceptual or cognitive;

(b) referential;

(c) interactive.

On the first view, meanings are concepts that 'reside in people's heads, as part of words' (Elbourne, 2011: 156). These meanings may be realized in the form of **intentions**. On the second, words possess meaning in virtue of referring to objects, states of affairs and facts. Children are often taught words by having objects pointed out to them (so-called **ostensive definition**). Children's reading primers traditionally present words organized alphabetically, with the name of the object accompanied by a picture: 'A is for Apple', 'B is for Boy', etc. In Genesis, God brings the animals before Adam and 'whatsoever Adam called every living creature, that was the name thereof' (2:xix). The basic picture is one word–one meaning–one object (or object-class). On the third view, meaning arises out of interaction and communicational behaviour. It is a contextual phenomenon which needs to be understood in terms of language's role in maintaining social cohesion, focusing social action and achieving practical ends: 'Meaning is not what happens in our individual, monadic minds; it is something that is constructed within the discourse' (Teubert, 2010: 7). One consequence of this 'construct view' is that meaning cannot be identified solely, if at all, with the communicative intention of the speaker, since it arises in the course of the interaction itself.

The idea that meaning is primarily conceptual ('in the head') is associated with the Swiss linguist Ferdinand de Saussure (1857–1913). Saussure rejected the idea that meaning was a relationship between the word and the world outside the human mind. Words for Saussure did not stand directly for things; a language was not a **nomenclature**, that is, a list of labels for things in the world (Saussure, [1916] 1972: 97–98). Meaning was best understood as 'difference in value' in a relational system (*langue*) that existed as a set of form–meaning correlates in the minds of the speakers of a language (Saussure, 1972: 155ff; 2002: 28). On this model, each part of the vocabulary of a language might be understood as a conceptual space structured by interdefining sub-fields. Examples of such sub-fields would be colours, cooking terms, kinship terms and other **semantic fields**. For Saussure, the primary reference point is the **language system** or *langue* itself, understood as a set of conceptual structures (largely) shared as a social fact by members of the speech community.

These conceptual structures have been analyzed through the postulation of underlying atomic elements of meaning known as **semantic features** or **components**. In **componential analysis**, the words *father* and *child* would both be defined by the component [+ HUMAN], but differ in the presence or absence of the feature [ADULT]; *father* would be [+ MALE], whereas *child* would be +/– i.e. neutral with respect to this component (see Lyons, 1968: 470ff.). A more recent framework, known as **Natural Semantic Metalanguage** (NSM) (Wierzbicka, 1996), analyzes word meaning by means of **reductive paraphrase**. Here is a definition of the word *women* following this technique (Goddard, 2012: 722):

a. people of one kind

b. someone can be someone of this kind after this someone has lived for some time, not for a short time

c. there are two kinds of people's bodies, people of this kind have bodies of one of these two kinds

d. some parts of bodies of this kind are not like parts of bodies of the other kind

e. the bodies of people of this kind are like this:

at some times there can be inside the body of someone of this kind a living body of a child [m]

'[m]' refers to a so-called **semantic molecule**. These are held to be ultimately 'decomposable' into **semantic primes** (Goddard, 2012: 720). Both componential analysis and the NSM approach seek a more fundamental level at which meaning can be unambiguously represented: one component–one meaning.

Linguists and philosophers debate the level of the primary unit of linguistic analysis. Is it the word? The sentence? Or do we have to begin at the level of the paragraph, the conversation, or the text? For the lexicographer, the unit of analysis is normally the single word. The meaning of complex phrases and sentences is, on this view, best understood as derived from the meaning of the parts (primarily words), together with the rules of combination: 'words are atomic elements' (Katz, 1964: 742). This is known as the **principle of compositionality** (Grandy, 1990: 557). But for many philosophers of language and logicians, the basic unit of analysis is generally the sentence (or more precisely, the proposition expressed by the sentence). The philosopher J.L. Austin (1911–60) saw word meaning as essentially derivative from sentence meaning: 'It may justly be urged that, properly speaking, what alone has meaning is a *sentence*' (Austin, 1979: 56). Language users had various ways of finding out the meaning of a word, such as looking in a dictionary, giving examples of possible sentences in which it might be used, or by offering real or imaginary experiences or situations. But 'concepts' or 'abstract ideas' were 'fictitious entities' (Austin, 1979: 60). For Austin, *the meaning of a word* was a spurious phrase (1979: 75). A range of theories in philosophy and sociology have focused on **utterance meaning**, and on the inferences that speakers make from the conventional or literal statement ('It's cold in here!') to arrive at the contextual meaning ('Please shut the door!'). Two important exemplars are the philosopher H. Paul Grice's (1913–88) pragmatic **theory of implicature** (Carston, 2013) and the sociologist Harold Garfinkel's (1917–2011) **ethnomethodology**. For such theorists, people do not and cannot say exactly what they mean, since they and their listeners draw on an unspoken (and largely unconscious) reserve of background assumptions and principles.

An explanation in terms of components of meaning looks like a classic **regress**: how do we know what the components themselves mean? They look like ordinary English words dressed up as universal components. The philosopher Hilary Putnam decisively rejected the idea of cognitive meaning: 'Cut the pie anyway you like, "meanings" just ain't in the head!' (Putnam, 1973: 700) Others deny that word meanings exist at all, at least not 'inside' the words of a language: 'meanings are not somehow contained in language' (Threadgold, 1997: 103). Similarly, if the sentence, rather than the word, is the primary unit of meaning, surely it must in turn derive its meaning from higher units of discourse such as the paragraph or the conversation?

Yet the questions 'What does this word mean?' and 'What does *this* word mean *here*?' are an inescapable part of our linguistic practices, and central to the culture of law. We cannot avoid thinking about what words mean, even if the harder we think, the deeper we enter the philosopher's maze. One way out of the maze was proposed by the philosopher Ludwig Wittgenstein (1889–1951): 'For a *large* class of cases – though not for *all* – in which we employ the word "meaning" it can be defined thus: the meaning of a word is its use in the language' (Wittgenstein, [1953] 1978: para. 43). But **use in the language** suggests that each word follows a stable pattern of use and that the pattern can be observed over time and across different contexts. This raises the problem of the observer's point of view: where should one stand in order to observe linguistic usage objectively?

One way to access usage might be through introspection or observation, or a mixture of the two. Wittgenstein evidently drew on a mix of intuition and observation in explaining his notion of **family resemblance** (1978: para. 66):

> Consider for example the proceedings that we call 'games'. I mean board games, card games, ball games, Olympic games, and so on. What is common to them all? Don't say, 'There must be something common, or they would not be called "games"' – but look and see whether there is anything common to all. For if you look at them you will not see something common to all, but similarities, relationships, and a whole series of them at that. To repeat: don't think, but look!

There is no single feature or set of features that all games have in common; rather, if we look at all the phenomena we call *games*, we find an open-ended set (1978: para. 66): 'And the result of this examination is: we see a complicated network of similarities overlapping and criss-crossing: sometimes overall similarities, sometimes similarities of detail.'

Following Wittgenstein's idea of family resemblance, **prototype theory** proposed an influential modification of the one word–one meaning framework. This rejected the so-called 'classical' view of categories, attributed to Aristotle (384 BCE–322 BCE), based on *per genus et differentiam*. If we take a word that represents a category or class of objects, then defining that word involves identifying the fundamental category (*genus*) to which the object belongs, and the feature by which it is distinguished from other members of the same category. The example often given is the sentence: *Man is a rational animal*. It is in virtue of being rational that man is distinguished from other animals, and in virtue of being an animal that man is distinguished from plants, gods, natural phenomena, etc. Categories have features which (i) are individually necessary and, in conjunction, sufficient to differentiate each from the other categories; (ii) are purely binary, that is, 'yes/no' features; (iii) have clear boundaries; and (iv) have members that are of equal status (Taylor, 1995: 22–24).

For the prototype theorist, by contrast, *bird* is not a 'yes/no' category. Some birds are more 'bird-like' than others. If one asked a hundred people to list the 10 species of bird that come most readily to mind, one can show that some birds are more salient or core members of the category (*wren, robin, sparrow*), and others more marginal (*ostrich, penguin*). The meaning of the word *bird* is not a single unitary concept but includes the awareness of a category with a range of meanings and with a fuzzy boundary. Categories are 'networks with prototypical members clustered in the center [...] with less prototypical members at various distances from the central members' (Johnson, 1987: 192). One could study the fuzzy boundary between categories such as *cup* and *mug* from the point of view of conceptual variation (Labov, 1973; Kempton, 1978).

Prototype theorists reject the idea that word meaning is disordered or unstructured. Given that 'we form our concepts the same way', there will be within a speech community a 'relative consensus about the application of words to situations in clear cases' (Solan, 2010: 41). Prototype effects result primarily in different judgements at the margins of linguistic categories, whereas there is agreement at the core, the so-called **core meaning** (Schane, 2006). In this way, prototype theory seeks to reconcile the idea that meaning is primarily conceptual or 'mental', with the variation in the intuitive judgements that people make about meaning.

A second, related modification to the one word–one meaning ideal stressed the social rather than psychological nature of categories. This might involve the study of **stereotypes** (Geeraerts, 2008: 24; Vilinbakhova, 2013). However, any study of categories must deal with the effect of different methods of elicitation and analysis. This may be hard to distinguish from variation as a result of personal and group identities or arising in different institutional and occupational domains. Put simply, the word *tree* might mean something different to an urban teenager, a villager and a forester. Literary critics have likewise stressed that for both individuals and groups, words have associations, connotations or particular affects. There are 'feelings in words', to use a phrase from William Empson (Empson, 1985). Ullmann (1966: 10–11) speaks of the **associative field** of a word. The associative field is 'an unstable and highly variable structure: it differs from one speaker to another, from one social group to another, and possibly even from one situation to another'.

Some linguists have sought to make systematic use of their own intuitions and those of 'native speakers' (Chomsky, 1965), and various proposals have been made to deal with the methodological problems this raises (Schutze, 1996). But for more sociologically oriented linguists, what was needed was objective observation. There was no way to measure intuition or ensure consistency in introspective judgements. The 'intuition of the theorist' should be replaced by 'observation of language in use' (Labov, 1973: 370). In contemporary sociolinguistics there is a wide range of approaches focusing on actually occurring texts, that is, on discourse, and the social relationships and interactional strategies embedded within it. Examples would be conversations, media products (films, websites, chatrooms, etc.), interaction in the classroom or the court, and so on.

'Observation of language in use' now can be carried out with the aid of large databases of texts. A **corpus** is a database of primary texts (e.g. transcribed speech, newspaper articles, literary texts, etc.). Some corpora are **marked up**, that is, they are coded for various kinds of grammatical or semantic information. The World Wide Web itself can also be thought of a vast, disordered and open-ended corpus, and the entire Web, or a subset of it, can be searched for data about linguistic usage. Corpora are now essential to lexicographical practice. Resources such as these provide an enormous amount of information about how words and phrases are used, or have been used in particular periods, especially the types and frequencies of word combinations or **colloca-tions**. The on-line *Oxford Collocations Dictionary* (<www.ozdic.com>) allows one to identify the most common adjectival **collocates** for a noun like *rejection* (e.g. *blanket, outright, total, wholesale*), and identifies *decisively, emphatically, firmly, roundly, strongly, vehemently, vigorously* among others for the verb *to reject*. This is sometimes termed *lexical priming*: 'As a word is acquired through encounters with it in speech and writing, it becomes cumulatively loaded with the contexts and co-texts in which it is encountered' (Hoey, 2005: 8). The **co-text** is the immediately adjacent words. While a massive corpus gives the researcher access to aggregated information on a scale previously impossible, the mode of storage, the kinds of information it includes (and excludes) and the boundary of the corpus are determined by its animating purposes (Toolan, 2006: 177). A corpus aggregates many different forms of knowledge, points of view, usages and experience. For these reasons, no corpus (and no diction-ary) can be said to represent the ordinary linguistic knowledge of an individual speaker or community. However, the corpus extends the linguistic horizons of the researcher in ways that can be exciting and stimulating.

Decontextual (abstract), contextual and interpretative meaning

Words and their meanings are frequently spoken about as if they possessed an autonomous identity. We talk of words as 'being in the dictionary' or 'having' meanings. Dictionary definitions are general statements intended to capture the essential attributes of a word's meaning. This can be described as the **abstract** or **decontextual meaning** of a word, phrase or sentence. If someone asks for the meaning (definition) of the word *mortgage*, or the French equiva-lent (translation) of *cat*, then that is primarily a question about this **decontex-tual** meaning. So when we talk of abstract meaning we are talking **meaning potentials** (Hanks, 2013: 73): meaning across the actual as well as foreseeable and imaginable contexts of use. Schauer speaks of the **semantic autonomy** of a word, that is, the way that language 'carries something by itself, independ-ent of those who use it on particular occasions' (Schauer, 1991: 56; Endicott, 2000: 18).

When we read a text or take part in a conversation, the individual words that we encounter have a co-text and a particular context, that is, the particular time and place, participants, setting, etc. While we often focus our analysis on a single problematic crux expression, meaning is more realistically understood as 'diffused across an utterance or text' (Durant, 2010: 6). In our individual and social existence we are immersed in a stream of language, whether it is our own thoughts, the radio in the background, overheard conversations, interac-tions with family or co-workers, signs in the street, newspapers and texts of all kinds. The meanings of these events, utterances and stretches of text can be referred to as **contextual meaning**. A person engaging with language in context experiences **meanings as events** (Hanks, 2013: 73). Contextual meanings involve **first-order** engagement in communication. For example, watching a film involves following a narrative that draws on images, dialogue, music and other modes (e.g. sub-titles). Our on-going real-time experience of the film is a first-order one, in that we are absorbed in the unfolding story. Similarly, as participants in a conversation we generally respond in rapid sequence to the remarks of others. Abstract, decontextual meaning, by contrast, is a **second-order** phenomenon.

When we ask 'What does this word mean?' this may be a request for a synonym or a definition, i.e. a question about the decontextual meaning. But, alternatively, it may involve the request for the explanation of a particular word in a particular text. The question is now a different one: 'What does *this* word mean *here*?' Asking what a particular word or phrase meant on a particular occasion involves a confrontation with the contextual meaning. If I ask a friend 'What did Jon mean when he said that he was bitter about what happened', I am asking for the motive behind what was said, not a dictionary definition of the word *bitter*. A request for a definition can often represent a highly aggressive challenge. The more specific, time-bound and contentious the question about meaning we are asking ('What did you mean by saying *that* to *me now*?'), the less relevant the abstract definition generally will be.

Defining the decontextual meaning of a word is quite distinct from using a definition for rhetorical effect. If in the course of a discussion or debate a word is defined for the purposes of the exchange, this is termed **stipulated definition**. In a speech before the US Congress, Sherrod Brown declared that the public should pay 'fair prices' for prescription drugs ([CR], 2000: 2069): 'For the sake of argument let us define "fair" in this case as necessary to continue a brisk pace of research and development.' Clearly this is not the kind of definition that a dictionary would provide. In the 'Which is to be master' scene in *Through the Looking-Glass* (Carroll, [1871] 2012: c. 4), Humpty Dumpty takes the technique of stipulated definition to a surreal extreme. There is this famous exchange over the meaning of the word *glory*:

'I don't know what you mean by "glory,"' Alice said.

Humpty Dumpty smiled contemptuously. 'Of course you don't – till I tell you. I meant "there's a nice knock-down argument for you!"'

'But "glory" doesn't mean "a nice knock-down argument,"' Alice objected.

'When I use a word,' Humpty Dumpty said in rather a scornful tone, 'it means just what I choose it to mean – neither more nor less.'

'The question is,' said Alice, 'whether you CAN make words mean so many different things.'

'The question is,' said Humpty Dumpty, 'which is to be master – that's all.'

Lawyers are very fond of making reference to this scene. For example, Lord Atkin invoked it in a famous dissent in *Liversidge v Anderson* (1942) (see Chapter 2).

The mainstream view both within law and linguistics is that there are qualities of language that can be identified out of context and remain invariant across all contexts. Words 'have a central core of meaning that is relatively fixed' (Williams, 1945: 191). Thus, for Solan, a sentence like *The guard was taken from the courtroom to the prison* establishes a set of meanings that are independent of real-world context: 'Anyone saying or hearing this sentence will understand the relationships among the various phrases and words strictly by virtue of the grammatical roles that they play in the sentence' (Solan, 2010: 39). This assertion assumes that:

(a) this sentence possesses a stable set of qualities which are found in each of its instances, including its structure and meaning;

(b) there is a community of language users for whom this sentence possesses these qualities; and

(c) there is an identifiable and stable entity or language (English) to which this sentence belongs.

However, the linguistic context for each word is unique, in that the written text or spoken discourse in which it is embedded will not recur. It also follows that (in some sense) 'each word when it is used in a new context is a new word' (Firth, 1957: 190; Hutton, 1990). For more discourse-oriented linguists it is the co-text and the context that focuses meaning and makes understanding achievable, since the interpreter is able to choose a particular meaning from the range of possible abstract meanings: 'in ordinary language the sense of a word is governed by the context and this sense normally excludes all others from the mind' (Lewis, [1967] 1990: 11). A sign about 'wines and spirits' would not normally lead us to think of 'angels, devils, ghosts, and fairies – nor about the "spirits" of the older medical theory' (Lewis, 1990: 11). Durant argues that, for most utterances, 'there is commonly one main meaning, or primary focus of meaning, that presents itself as relevant and will usually be derived by most people in the target audience, albeit it with a penumbra of local interpretations and associations around it' (2010: 87).

Asking for the meaning of a word is not a single activity; it is a bundle of interlocking and often contradictory social and institutional practices. In daily life, much linguistic business passes by without explicit questions about meaning being raised. Where there is an explicit question about contextual meaning and a conscious (or **reflexive**) process of deliberation, then the outcome can be termed the **interpretative meaning**. In reaching an interpretation, we reach a contextually relevant determination of what the word (phrase, text, …) meant. In general, how a word (phrase, text, etc.) is interpreted on a particular occasion is in the first instance a question for the participants. But observers, those given second-hand reports, readers of newspaper accounts, etc. of an incident will also form an opinion.

Interpretative meaning is at stake, for example, in controversies about the meanings of particular words in sacred texts such as the Bible. In Matthew (10:xxxiv) Jesus declares that he comes to bring 'not peace' but 'a sword'. Is *sword* a reference to violence, or does it express a non-violent determination to transform radically the existing order? The same issues arise in literary interpretation. Critics concerned with Shakespeare's understanding of sexuality and gender debate the interpretative meaning of the term *master mistress* in Sonnet 20 ('A woman's face with nature's own hand painted / Hast thou, the master mistress of my passion').

Linguistic categories and the classification of things

Many of the cases discussed in this book concern the relation between a linguistic category, a classification system, and a legally relevant definition or category. Whether the classification of things reflects the 'natural joints' found in reality (so-called **natural kinds**) has been debated since antiquity (Campbell et al., 2011). If creation is the work of God then the boundaries between the species belong to the natural order of things. The idea that all of creation is a hierarchy of natural kinds (God, angels, humanity, animals, insects, plants, minerals) is summed up in the phrase 'the great chain of being' (Lovejoy, 1964). In Enlightenment science, exemplified by the systematizing works of Carl Linnaeus (1707–78) and Georges Cuvier (1769–1832), the ideal was a single system of classification, a taxonomy, that would encompass all of nature by reference to an objective set of criteria. Modern evolutionary biology, especially in the wake of Charles Darwin's (1809–82) *Origin of Species* (1859), depicted a world where natural categories such as *species* are in a state of flux. This does not necessarily imply that the classification of natural phenomena is a fiction created by the observer, since species and similar categories are relatively stable. In contemporary sociology and anthropology, however, the idea that reality and its categories are socially constructed has become almost an unchallenged principle (Hacking, 1999).

One of the historical origins of the idea of the 'social construction of reality' (the title of a famous book by Berger and Luckmann published in 1966) is Karl Marx's (1818–83) notion of the **fetishism of the commodity**. Put simply, Marx asserted that the categories of our commonsense perceptions, in particular our sense of the solidity and economic value of an object, are the products of ideology. It is not the intrinsic properties of a commodity such as gold or of a manufactured object such as a table that creates its value; rather, it is the underlying social relations (Marx, [1867] 1962: 85–88). Since our perceptions of the world and the things in it are not grounded in external reality but in the dynamism of social relations, in late capitalist modernity '[a]ll that is solid melts into air' (Marx and Engels, [1848] 2012: 38).

One of the many variants of social constructionism is found in linguistics. This is the view that the everyday vocabulary of a language embodies the worldview of its speakers. The classification systems used by a society depend 'on the type of language used' (Sapir, 1994: 87). More strongly formulated, the idea is that linguistic categories condition how speakers experience the world: 'Human beings do not live in the objective world alone, nor alone in the world of social activity as ordinarily understood'. Rather they are 'very much at the mercy of the particular language which has become the medium of expression for their society' (Sapir, 1962: 68–69). In linguistics this is known as the **linguistic relativity principle** (Lee, 1996: 84–159).

At an even deeper level, Emile Durkheim (1858–1917) and Marcel Mauss (1872–1950), in their anthropological classic *Primitive Classification* ([1903] 1963), argued that 'the classification of things reproduces the classification of men' (Bloor, 1982: 267). The organization of things into categories reflects the way people are categorized. This theory, which is not so far from Marx's understanding of the commodity, is no longer accepted in anthropology; but most social scientists would accept that 'the organization of a classificatory system is not, and cannot be, determined by the way the world is' (Bloor, 1982: 269). The boundaries between categories do not inhere in the phenomena themselves but reflect a complex of inherited modes of thought, as well as conscious and unconscious assumptions and purposes. While human beings reproduce biologically in the same way across different societies, they vary dramatically in their understanding of the structures of kinship and the boundary of the family, including permitted categories of marriage partners (Radcliffe-Brown, 1965: 51).

Even if we grant the constructed nature of categories, there remains the question of their shared nature and stability within a particular community or society. Categories like *table*, *cat* and *mother* have an intuitive grounding in everyday reality. Common sense intuits the meanings of individual words as 'the level of communication at which people tend to place most faith in stable meaning' (Durant, 2010: 70). Boundaries are 'central to the common-sense picture of the world' and yet 'deeply problematic' (Varzi, 2012: para. 2). Some social science discourse seems to imply that all members of a society agree where the boundaries between categories lie. For example, for Alfred Schutz (1899–1959), informal knowledge is **typified** in 'the vocabulary and syntax of everyday language' (Schutz, 1962: 14). Ordinary, non-scientific language is the primary mode of typification and generalization, it is 'a language of named things and events' reflecting the speakers' collective 'relevance system', that is, socio-culturally salient categories:

> The pre-scientific vernacular can be interpreted as a treasure house of ready made pre-constituted types and characteristics, all socially derived and carrying along an open horizon of unexplored content. (Schutz, 1962: 14)

If linguistic categories are the key to social classification then, given that individual languages are held to represent distinct modes of understanding and perception, i.e. the worldviews they express are **incommensurable**, there is no question of categories reflecting natural kinds. Language is not a nomenclature, a list of names for pre-existing and pre-defined phenomena. If this is correct, then language is a poor guide to reality. However, the close relationship between language and social classification suggests that members of a speech community live in a shared, albeit constructed, reality. They inhabit a world of shared basic concepts. Prototype theory, for example, while it rejects the idea that speakers of the same language share identical categories, nonetheless offers reassurance that there exists an underlying coherence and order.

However, things are not quite so straightforward. The languages we call 'English' or 'Cantonese' are not well-defined social objects. Alongside this informal system of commonsense classification (with categories such as *cat, table, shop, taxi, woman, cloud*) there exists a profusion of specialized discourses and classification systems, associated with different trades, sub-cultures, professions, institutions, academic disciplines, scientific frameworks and so on. Traditional or pre-modern taxonomies persist and interact with those of modernity. For example, there exists a plethora of ways available for describing human personality types. These include the traditional theory of the 'humours' (*phlegmatic, bilious*), Freudian terms (*anal retentive, neurotic*), the Jungian (*introvert, extrovert*), psychiatric concepts (e.g. *Type A* versus *Type B* personality), and our everyday vocabulary available for describing disposition and character.

Theorists who emphasize the role of language and ideology in the creation and maintenance of categories sometimes refer to **naturalization**, that is, the way in which social systems create and maintain the 'taken-for-grantedness' of commonsense assumptions. Categories that seem natural are beyond reflexive awareness or criticism. One powerful example of this is the idea that human beings belong to distinct races. Critical philosophers, such as Michel Foucault (1926–84), have sought to **denaturalize** Western orders of knowledge and systems of classification, making them as strange or as alien as so-called exotic worldviews. The opening paragraph of *The Order of Things* (Foucault, [1966] 1994: xv) quotes a passage from a Jorge Luis Borges (1899–1986) essay (Borges, 2001; Duszat, 2012). This essay quotes from a (fictional) Chinese encyclopedia in which animals are divided into:

> (a) those that belong to the emperor; (b) embalmed ones; (c) those that are trained; (d) suckling pigs; (e) mermaids; (f) fabulous ones; (g) stray dogs; (h) those that are included in this classification; (i) those that tremble as if they were mad; (j) innumerable ones; (k) those drawn with a very fine camel's-hair brush; (l) etcetera; (m) those that have just broken the flower vase; (n) those that at a distance resemble flies.

For Lakoff, this mimics 'the impression a Western reader gets when reading descriptions of nonwestern languages and cultures' (Lakoff, 1990: 92). More precisely, it paints a caricature of the alleged exotic nature of unfamiliar classification systems. In so doing it asks us to scrutinize the rationale underlying our own 'commonsense' worldview.

In our own familiar world, mundane categories and relationships are salient and apparently grounded in the intrinsic qualities of phenomena. Other categories, modes of classification or potential correlations are unseen, marginalized or repressed. One position that follows from this is postmodern anti-foundationalism, with its 'making strange' (**denaturalization**) of commonsense oppositions and questioning of conventional boundaries between machines, people, animals, objects, as well as of the central category of the *human*. But even if we reject this as an intellectual project, it is undeniable that, on occasion, 'things fall apart' and all that is solid melts into contention and discord. Law often provides examples where the most straightforward of categories breaks down under the pressures of adjudication. How should we understand these situations where categories seem to 'run out' or become enmeshed in meaning troublespots (as in law)? How can we know whether the objects that we perceive, the categories that we employ and the correlations we observe are the products of ideology or not?

Indeterminacy

One key position in anti-foundationalism is the denial that there exists a shared language with common meanings that underwrite social order. Such approaches to language are based on the idea of **indeterminacy** and reject the notion of stable, decontextual (abstract) meanings. *To determine* is to 'fix', 'resolve', 'regulate', 'ascertain', or to 'draw a boundary', 'assign a value', 'bring to a closure'. Indeterminacy is the inability to assign, or to justify the assignment of, a value to some element of a system: words, phrases and texts do not have meanings that can be objectively established or 'determined'. It follows that decontextual, abstract meanings are second-order **constructs** or **fictions**. The decontextual meaning of a word is a 'fiction which represents many […] acts of speech' (Richards, 1962: 104); any attempt to grasp decontextual meaning involves the aggregation of countless contextual meanings. A word 'becomes something that a million people use on the same day, and that successive generations go on using through hundreds of years' (Richards, 1962: 104). **Indeterminacy** implies the absence of any fixed decontextual features, beyond those assumed or created by interactants themselves in particular contexts.

Indeterminacy is associated with the literary movement known as **deconstruction**. This movement was centrally concerned with the nature of authority over meaning and interpretation. Deconstructionists denied that the author's intentions were a reference point for the interpreter, asserting that the language of a text was open to multiple and potentially contradictory readings (see Culler, 1982). This movement had an important influence on radical legal theory, given that legislative intent is a traditional point of reference for legal interpretation. More broadly, indeterminacy involved the denial that linguistic meaning provided a stable reference point for interpretation. The literary theorist Stanley Fish argued that 'words alone', taken in the abstract, 'without an animating intention', have no linguistic or semantic qualities, in that they 'do not have power, do not have semantic shape, and are not yet language' (Fish, 2005: 632). In other words, the sign 'does not pre-exist the communicational context' (Wolf, 1999: 28); in this sense 'the meaning is always "now"' (Toolan, 1996: 125). There is no stable linguistic-semantic framework to which parties to a dispute about word meaning can appeal. Whatever stability is found is created by the participants or other interpreters themselves against the background of uncertainty and indeterminacy. Words do not exist as 'fossilized exhibits like dead butterflies in the entomologist's glass case'; if they have any real existence, 'it must be in the day-by-day exchanges of actual speakers and hearers' (Harris, 2006: 213). The intuition of stability in relations between words, ideas and objects or between names and places (Pablé, 2009; 2010) is fragile, and can break down in the face of a wide range of contextual factors. At such moments, it might be argued, the fictional status of decontextual meaning is revealed.

Belief in indeterminacy involves primarily an assertion about the nature of signs. It is the rejection of abstract, decontextual meaning (**semantic indeterminacy**). If signs are indeterminate in the abstract, then it must be the participants in a communicational exchange that create, impose or find a shared meaning. Against the background of semantic indeterminacy, linguistic communication can be understood as 'the reaching of agreement by verbal signs in particular interactional contexts' (Harris, 1988: 120). To borrow a phrase from the poet, participants 'give shapelessness a form' ('Fray', in Phillips, 2007: 184). However, in cases of controversy, where there is no agreement among the participants about how to reach an authoritative interpretation, we encounter a further level of indeterminacy. If there is no agreed point of reference for determining what a word or text means, then all meanings are subject to potential objection, and are created, or imposed, by one or more interpreters whose authority is of a contextual or social or ideological nature. This **interpretative indeterminacy** may be resolved by virtue of the fact that one of the participants has the institutional authority to determine the interpretative outcome. In that sense, law produces determinate outcomes, since the legal system endows decisions with coercive force. But for sceptical commentators, this reveals that coercion rather than interpretative order represents the essence of law.

Conclusion

Most linguists and philosophers of language reject the idea of indeterminacy, and see words as having relatively constant meanings across the different contexts of their use. There are nonetheless profound disagreements about how these meanings should be retrieved and represented. Most theorists of meaning would accept that co-text and contextual factors can influence meaning in unpredictable ways: what a word means in a particular context is largely but not fully determined by its decontextual or abstract meaning. This implies a strong, but not absolute, correlation between decontextual meaning and interpretative meaning. While the correlation is subject to contextual and idiosyncratic factors, it holds good across the vast majority of instances. But indeterminacy theorists reject this position. They argue that in literary or legal interpretation, what emerges as the interpretative meaning reflects the underlying interpretative politics at work. The way questions of meaning are framed reflects underlying socio-political or cultural tensions, and appeals to decontextual meaning are simply one strategy among many.

Summary points

- The ideal of one word–one meaning is a fundamental reference point in semantics.

- Everyday experiences of language use can provide a rich resource for thinking about meaning.

- There is no single authority over meaning, either institutional or intellectual.

- Scholars disagree about: what constitutes meaning; the basic unit of linguistic analysis; how to study meaning.

- In semantic analysis, literal meaning cannot be neatly distinguished from etymology.

- Metaphor involves a tension between analogy and anomaly.

- We need to distinguish decontextual (abstract), contextual and interpretative meaning.

- A wide range of theories in social science see linguistic categories and social classification as constructs.

- Indeterminacy involves either or both (i) the general assertion that signs lack a stable decontextual meaning (semantic indeterminacy), and (ii) the denial that there exists a single definitive source of authority for arriving at an interpretative meaning (interpretative indeterminacy).

CHAPTER 2

Word Meaning and Interpretation in the Law

The discussion below examines some of the key debates within legal interpretation and explains the terms in which interpretative questions are generally discussed, focusing in particular on word meaning. Taken in its widest sense, any interpretative act carried out within the frame of law involves legal interpretation. For example, it is often forgotten that the police 'act as the first line of statutory interpreters' (Solan, 2010: 7). This book is more narrowly concerned with the adjudication by judges of word meaning in statutes, contracts and wills.

Fidelity to the legal text

Judges are required to show fidelity to the texts that constitute the law. Fidelity to law implies fidelity to the language of law, i.e. the wording of statutes, contracts, wills, etc. Questions of word-meaning and textual interpretation are therefore fundamental to common law practice and legal theory. Under a system of **binding precedents**, judges are also required to follow the decisions of superior courts. The legal doctrine is called *stare decisis* (Tiersma, 2007; Wan, 2012). *Stare decisis* involves respect for the legal principle established by an authoritative judgment (the **ratio** or **ratio decidendi**). Where a decision is by majority vote, the judge or judges who disagree may set out the grounds for their disagreement in a **dissenting judgment** or **dissent**. Older decisions generally become less authoritative over time (Black and Spriggs, 2013), but some emerge as so-called **superprecedents** which are fundamental to a particular legal domain. One example would be the House of Lords decision in *Salomon v A Salomon* (1897). *Salomon* is central to company law as it developed in the UK and related jurisdictions (see Hutton, 2012).

Proponents of the rule of law see the sanctity of the legal text and interpretative fidelity to its wording as standing between social order and chaos. A classic case where fidelity to legal language was at stake is *Liversidge v Anderson* (1942). In World War II, emergency regulations were introduced under the Emergency Powers (Defence) Act 1939, to give the British Government special powers. Rule 18B of the Defence (General) Regulations 1939 allowed the Home Secretary to intern (i.e. imprison) someone if he had 'reasonable cause' to believe that that person had 'hostile associations'. In this case, Robert William Liversidge (1904–94, formerly Jacob Perlsweig) had filed an application asking the Crown to justify his detention. The House of Lords ruled in favour of the Home Secretary. Their Lordships upheld the detention, together with the refusal to give reasons for the detention. (Liversidge was in fact released a few weeks later.)

Lord Atkin, dissenting, argued that this decision involved a strained interpretation (construction) of the statute. It had the effect of giving an uncontrolled power of imprisonment to the Home Secretary. Laws spoke 'the same language in war as in peace'. The war was precisely being fought over 'one of the pillars of freedom', the principle that 'judges are no respecters of persons and stand between the subject and any attempted encroachments on his liberty by the executive, alert to see that any coercive action is justified in law'. The decision amounted to accepting that the Home Secretary could make the words *reasonable cause* mean whatever he wanted them to mean. The decision implied that the Home Secretary had reasonable grounds for detaining someone if he believed he had reasonable grounds. Lord Atkin then quoted from Lewis Carroll's *Through the Looking Glass*:

> I know of only one authority which might justify the suggested method of construction; 'When I use a word,' Humpty Dumpty said in a rather scornful tone, 'it means just what I choose it to mean, neither more nor less.' 'The question is,' said Alice, 'whether you can make words mean different things.' 'The question is,' said Humpty Dumpty, 'which is to be master – that is all.'

Lord Atkin concluded:

> After all this long discussion the question is whether the words, 'If a man has' can mean 'If a man thinks he has.' I am of the opinion that they cannot, and the case should be decided accordingly ... (at 245)

Interpretation and intentional meaning

The idea of meaning as **intention** is widely accepted across a range of disciplines (law, philosophy of language, literary theory), but it has also been the subject of extensive criticism. A nineteenth-century legal classic defined interpretation as 'the art of finding out the true sense of any form of words', that is, 'the sense which their author intended to convey' (Lieber, 1839: 23). Similarly, legal interpretation is 'a search for the meaning intended by the authors of legislation' (Posner, 2008: 365). The interpretative task of the judge is frequently seen as requiring respect for the intentions of the lawmaker or legislature: judges should not **make law** but rather **declare** or **apply** the law that has been enacted. One approach to statutory interpretation makes this explicit, drawing on the specifically legal notion of **agency**. The **principal** (that is, the instruction-giver) is the legislature, the **directive** is the statute and the **agent** is the judge: 'Interpretation can be viewed as an honest effort by an "agent" to apply the principal's directive to unforeseen circumstances' (Eskridge, 1994: 125). This analogy assumes that when faced with a particular problem, the agent does not or cannot contact the principal directly for advice.

The interpretation must reconcile the lawmaker's intention with the unique set of circumstances (**factual nexus**) that has given rise to the case.

While the legislature's intentions must be respected, it is the judge (the agent) who makes the determination of the law in relation to the particular facts of the case. Whether a court may look behind the law at the legislative history, that is, at policy papers and speeches made in parliamentary or congressional debate, is a matter of debate. Traditionally this was not formally permitted in the United Kingdom courts, but the House of Lords decision in *Pepper v Hart* (1992) overturned established practice, allowing a judge to consult statements made by the minister promoting the legislation or other relevant parliamentary materials, if it was considered that this would shed light on the issue at hand. This was controversial because the intention of the legislature was traditionally held to be expressed definitively by the words actually used in the statute. In the United States it has been common practice for judges to look at the legislative history, but this is strongly opposed by advocates of **textualism** for whom the purpose (or intention) of a law is to be found in the wording agreed by the legislature and the surrounding legal texts alone (Scalia and Garner, 2012). Fidelity to the language of the statute in its immediate legal context is the key to the textualist approach, rather than the attempt to reconstruct the legislative intent (Scalia, 1997). By contrast Solan (2005b) argues that courts should make use of any materials that might assist in ascertaining legislative intent.

In practice, the boundary between judges applying the law as opposed to making it is very hard to maintain. Judges do not always agree about the precise nature of their jurisdiction. For Lord Mansfield (1705–93), 'the common law, that works itself pure by rules drawn from the fountain of justice, is for this reason superior to an act of parliament' (*Omychund v Barker* (1744) at 23). Yet for the textualist Supreme Court Justice Antonin Scalia, fidelity to law implies fidelity to the precise words used, if judges are not to violate the democratic order that puts them in a subordinate position to the will of the legislature (Scalia and Garner, 2012). In addition, it is sometimes argued that modern, extremely detailed legislation is incompatible with an active style of judging (see Solan, 2010: 1–5; Kennedy, 1997: 23ff.). The Companies Act 2006 (UK) has 1,300 sections; by contrast, the Chartered Companies Act of 1837 had a mere 32.

The language of adjudication

Legal interpretation is conventionally presented in terms of **maxims** (or **canons of construction**). The three most basic are:

(a) the **literal rule**, which is commonly cited in this form: 'If the words of an Act are clear, you must follow them, even though they lead to a manifest absurdity' (Lord Esher, in *R v Judge of the City of London Court* (1892) at 289);

(b) the **golden rule**, according to which the judge is 'to give to the words used by the legislature their plain and natural meaning, unless it is manifest from the general scope and intention of the statute injustice and absurdity would result from so construing them' (*Mattison v Hart* (1854) at 385);

(c) the **mischief rule**, according to which it is the role of the judge to identify the specific object or target of the legislation and 'to make such construction as shall suppress the mischief, and advance the remedy' (Lord Coke, in *Heydon's Case* (1584) at 7b).

In legal theory debates about legal interpretation are frequently expressed in binary oppositions. **Literal** or **plain meaning** approaches are contrasted with **purposive** styles of adjudication (Zander, 2004: 193ff.).

One common set of terms invokes meaning as a conceptual space: **narrow** versus **broad**; **narrow** versus **expansive**, **overbroad** or **facially overbroad**: 'Where a statute is susceptible of a narrow construction, we must apply that narrow construction rather than find the statute facially overbroad' (*Modavox, Inc. v Tacoda, Inc.* (2009) at 534). In addition to metaphors that evoke conceptual space, there are those involving ideas of self-restraint versus generosity, such as **strict** versus **liberal**. In *McGilley v Chubb & Son, Inc.* (1987), the court had to decide what it meant to *occupy* a vehicle. There was a choice between 'a strict definition of the term', which required 'physical contact with the vehicle', and a 'liberal approach', which focused on whether the 'claimant was performing an act normally associated with the immediate use of the vehicle' (at 555). (This issue typically arises when someone is found drunk inside a stationary car.) A more traditional pairing, which evokes Biblical interpretation, is that of **letter** versus **spirit**: 'It is a familiar rule that a thing may be within the letter of the statute and yet not within the statute, because not within its spirit nor within the intention of its makers' (*Church of the Holy Trinity v US* (1892) at 512).

As mentioned, another important term often contrasted with **literal** is 'purposive'. In the Hong Kong case of *Ng Ka-ling v Director of Immigration* (1999), the court set out its basic approach to interpreting the Basic Law (Hong Kong's so-called mini-constitution): 'As to the language of its text, the courts must avoid a literal, technical, narrow or rigid approach. They must consider the context' (at 340). This meant that 'interpretation should be purposive, that is, it must be governed by the underlying principles of the Basic Law, rather than through a literal focus on a particular provision in isolation from its context' (at 364). 'Purposive' is used in legal theory to refer to a philosophy of adjudication, which argues that the judge should give effect to the overall purpose or **normative message** of the legal text (see Barak, 2007).

Ideas of the **ordinary** or **natural** play a central role in binaries of legal interpretation, in particular when juxtaposed to interpretative meanings that appear distorted or forced. Ordinary (or **plain and ordinary**) is set against **forced**, **unusual**; similarly, **natural** is often juxtaposed to **artificial** (*Roman v CIA* (2002) at 1367). All kinds of combinations are used: 'When no statutory definition exists, we presume that the legislature intended terms to have their plain, natural, and ordinary meaning' (*State v Reynolds* (2011) at 26). Judges sometimes also talk of **first impression** meanings, as well as of **common**

meaning or **common and ordinary meaning**: 'Throwing a toy at a baby's face and injuring the baby constitutes abuse, within the common and ordinary meaning of the word' (*Doe ex rel. Hansen v Thorin* (2012) para. 9). One relatively rare phrase is **intuitive meaning**, in spite of the importance that intuitions about meaning play in legal judgments.

As mentioned above, word meanings are frequently presented metaphorically as spaces. In legal discourse, the ideal of one word–one meaning generates a rich visual imagery of margins, borders, borderlines, boundaries, overlappings, etc. Advocating increased US federal regulation of economic activity, the law professor Walton Hamilton (1881–1958) proclaimed: 'The word "commerce" has no natural boundaries' (Hamilton and Adair, 1937: 14; Natelson, 2006: 792). A meaning or an object can be said to **fall within** or **fall outside** a particular legal category. For example, in *Figas v Horsehead Corporation* (2008) (at 13) it was argued that 'not every form of protective equipment necessarily falls within the meaning of the word "clothes" simply because it covers, or is somehow in close proximity with, an employee's body'.

In a case concerning a disputed insurance contract, *Tektrol Ltd v International Insurance Co of Hanover Ltd* (2005), at issue was the interpretative meaning of the phrase 'erasure loss distortion or corruption of information' (at 342). Sir Martin Nourse wrote that these were 'overlapping words' used to cover every possible case where the information on computer systems might be 'interfered with by electronic means'. Elsewhere in the judgment (at 345), Buxton LJ quoted a comment on this drafting style from Lord Hoffmann (*Tea Trade Properties Ltd v CIN Properties Ltd* (1990), a case that concerned a lease): 'The draftsmen traditionally employ linguistic overkill and try to obliterate the conceptual target by using a number of phrases expressing more or less the same idea.'

Another common set of metaphors involves ideas of flexibility or malleability, e.g. the **stretching** of meaning. In *People v Kloosterman* (2012), the defendant had been convicted under a Michigan law which targeted anyone 'employed by, or associated with' a racketeering enterprise who knowingly participated in its affairs. The case involved a single individual involved in a pattern of criminal activity (retail fraud). The court commented that *to associate* required that 'a person must necessarily align or partner with another person or entity'. The meaning of the word was not 'ordinarily interpreted to mean that a person associates with him or herself'. It 'would stretch the meaning of the word beyond reason to conclude that the Legislature intended such an unusual usage' (at 3). The conviction was reversed. A person could not be said to associate with himself or herself.

A further visual-spatial metaphor is **scope**. The scope of a legal category refers to the set of phenomena that it picks out. For example, in *Wingrove v Secretary of State for Communities and Local Government* (2009), the court rejected the appellants' appeal against denial of planning permission. The appeal relied on the appellants being classified as *gypsies* or *travellers*. The court ruled that they 'fell outside the scope' of the definitions of *gypsy* and *traveller*, defined as people 'of nomadic habit of life whatever their race or origin' (para. 7). Another use of 'scope' is in relation to the interpretative problems raised by the ambiguous application of adverbs such as *knowingly* and *willfully* (see Chapter 3).

Etymology in adjudication

In a discussion of the word *felony* ('a serious criminal offence'), the American judge James Wilson (1742–98) argued that the key to its 'true meaning' was to be found in its 'true etymology' (Wilson, 1804: 17). Today judges make reference to etymology much less frequently than in the past (Watt, 2013: 571). Yet one can see a certain kind of word analysis as etymological in spirit, especially where it involves breaking down a word into its component parts and analyzing the basic or literal meaning of each. For example, in *Lukhard v Reed* (1987), the distinction between *income* and *resources* took on a particular importance for recipients of federal welfare (Aid to Families with Dependent Children, AFDC). The State of Virginia was treating personal injury awards as *income* rather than *resources*, which led to a reduction in the entitlement to the AFDC benefit. A narrow reading of the term *income* favoured the welfare recipients in excluding these awards from the calculation. In the lead judgment, Justice Scalia pointed out that both general and legal reference works 'commonly define "income" to mean "any money that comes in"' (at 375). While this is not strictly an etymological analysis, the framing of the word meaning in terms of *in + come* is etymological in spirit. The Court opted for the broad meaning, suggested by this etymological framing, by a majority of five to four.

Metaphor and legal interpretation

In the domain of law, questions about metaphor arise in a number of forms (Schane, 2006). Legal theorists see the misuse of metaphor as the clearest example of how linguistic categories are capable of distorting the reasoning process (Probert, 1972). Metaphors operate on this view as a kind of formulaic language, like the spells of 'word magic': 'Metaphors in law are to be narrowly watched, for starting as devices to liberate thought, they end often by enslaving it' (Justice Cardozo, *Berkey v Third Avenue Railway Company* (1926) at 61). *Berkey* concerned corporate **legal personality** and the liability of the parent company for the acts of its subsidiary: 'The whole problem of the relation between parent and subsidiary corporations is one that is still enveloped in the mists of metaphor' (per Cardozo, at 61). What was needed was careful legal analysis of the factual basis of the relationship between subsidiary and parent.

In many domains of law a particular metaphor serves as the key to legal doctrine. The First Amendment of the US Constitution prohibits 'the making of any law respecting an establishment of religion'. This is often expressed through the metaphor of a **wall of separation** that marks off religion from the domain of the state (*McCollum v Board of Education* (1948); Driesbach and Whaley (1999)). But according to one commentator, this is a metaphor that has failed: 'Metaphors do create law, and poor metaphors inhibit law's progress' (Sirico, 2011: 489). In debates about the nature of property, the

bundle of sticks (or **bundle of rights**) metaphor plays an important role (Cardozo, 1928: 9). This metaphor expresses the idea that property is a set of interpersonal relationships, not a simple right in relation to a thing: 'property constitutes a legal complex, of various normative relations, not simply rights' (Penner, 1995: 712–13). The 'legal meaning' of *property* is quite distinct from the 'common meaning' (Sprankling, 1999: 1). However, metaphors, 'unlike synonyms, are invariably inexact and therefore potentially misleading' (Ellickson, 2011: 215); the 'bundle of sticks' metaphor has been criticized for encouraging too fragmented a view of property rights (Merrill and Smith, 2007).

One contemporary challenge for law is whether its conceptual infrastructure, core categories and interpretative strategies are adequate for the digital age. Terms such as *space, storage, file, email address, website*, draw on a metaphorical analogy between physical space and virtual space. In terms of our experience of it, the Internet is 'a physical place', even though 'the idea that the Internet is a place in which people literally travel is not only wrong but faintly ludicrous' (Lemley, 2003: 523). The key question for law is not the plausibility of the analogy itself but the legal effect of adopting a particular metaphorical framework. Some commentators fear that the application in law of place/space metaphors for cyberspace will lead to its privatization: 'the progression of property interests over the past five hundred years shows that places tend to be enclosed and privately exploited' (Hunter, 2003: 443). For example, the *cybersquatting* metaphor relies on an analogy between the unlawful occupation of land and the misleading use of a domain name. The term refers to the 'bad faith' registering of a domain name, usually in order to sell it to the presumptive owner. This may include *typosquatting*, where a range of spelling variants is registered. In *TOYS "R" US, Inc. v Abir* (1997), one domain at issue was www.toysareus.com (Look, 1999: 56).

Madison (2003: 437) argues that the 'Internet-as-place metaphor' should be interpreted so as to be consistent with 'user experience of the Internet', rather than 'via formal, abstract, and absolutist notions of "property"'. If, for example, we criminalize hate messages on signs and billboards in the *visible environment*, should the same rules apply to the Internet? Sumner rejects the analogy: 'only by stretching the metaphor to the breaking point is it possible to say that Internet hate sites are "part of the visible environment"' (2013: 383). In *US v Carey* (1999), the court rejected the analogy between, on the one hand, looking for documents in a file cabinet and finding evidence of a crime in plain view, and, on the other, searching files on a seized computer (see Gore, 2003: 417). But would user experience lend credence to these decisions?

For consumer law, one question is whether it will be 'online or offline law' that determines 'consumers' rights over property and data' (Fairfield, 2012: 59). Buying a hardcopy book and an e-book are legally quite distinct, even though the same everyday terms for the transaction are used: 'If you purchase a book offline, you own the book. If you purchase an e-book, you own nothing' (Fairfield, 2012: 59; Laughlin, 2010). In insurance law, the status of computer data is unclear: do they fall under the category *property*? The court in *American Guaranty and Liability Insurance Co. v Ingram Micro, Inc.*

(2000) said yes; in *State Auto Property and Casualty Insurance Co. v Midwest Computers and More* (2001), the answer was no (see Marble et al., 2002).

Critics of dominant or paradigm metaphors argue that these exacerbate law's tendency to rely on slogans and reductive formulae. In United Kingdom sentencing law, the phrase **custody threshold** has been used to refer to the point at which an act of offending becomes serious enough to warrant prison. Padfield (2011: 611) terms this an 'unhelpfully deceptive, but popular metaphor', concluding that the multidimensional issues involved 'exceed the carrying capacity of the metaphor'. Through 'word magic', complex multidimensional problems are reduced to imagery that fails to represent the underlying doctrinal complexity. Nuanced historical readings and close textual analysis, however, can reaffirm or rediscover these underlying complexities: law strives to be 'black and white', but 'for all its efforts, it cannot but express itself in all the colors of the human imagination' (Winter, 2008: 376). Debates about metaphor reflect a longstanding tension between law's reliance on formulae and the **realist** demand that categories be constantly interrogated for their underlying substance.

Word meaning, co-text and legal maxims

All questions about word meaning in legal interpretation must at some level involve consideration of the co-text (and context), even if the explicit focus is on an individual word. In statutory interpretation, there are a number of specific maxims that apply to word meanings and their relation to co-text. One maxim states that 'every word of a statute must be given significance; nothing in the statute can be treated as surplusage' (Posner, 1983: 812). In applying this maxim, problems can arise because of law's characteristic use of **doublets**, i.e. pairs of near-synonyms in the same phrase or the same section. Examples are phrases such as *goods and chattels* or *terms and conditions*. Article III of the US Constitution, which concerns the jurisdiction of the Supreme Court, uses both the term *cases* as well as *controversies*. A great deal of constitutional argument has been devoted to whether these terms should be given separate meanings (Pennington, 2009). Posner rejects reliance on such canons on the grounds that they falsely imply that there is 'legislative omniscience' behind the drafting (Posner, 1983: 812). That is to say, the text is treated as if an all-knowing intelligence endowed with it just those meanings that an ideal statutory interpreter would be able to find there.

The maxims (canons) remain an integral part of the interpretative culture of law, despite these and other cogent criticisms (see Llewellyn, 1950; Hutchinson, 2000). For example, the maxim of *ejusdem generis* states that where there are two or more specific terms followed by a more general term, the meaning of the general term should be restricted to the same general kind or class of the preceding terms. To apply this maxim the court still needs to decide what essential feature (or features) defines the general term. The problem can be seen in a phrase such as *oil, gas and other minerals*, found in land grants. Does *mineral* include coal (Strong, 1989)? In *Mack Oil Company v Mamie Lee Lawrence* (1964), an agreement to sell land reserved rights in 'oil, petroleum, gas, coal, asphalt and all the other minerals of every kind or character' (para. 3). It was held not to cover water, which was 'fluid and mobile' (para. 27, citing *Erickson v Crookston Waterworks, P&L Co.* (1907), at 485; see Schane, 2006: 39–40). A contentious case where the maxim was debated is *Ali v Federal Bureau of Prisons* (2008). At issue was the immunity for negligence granted by statute to 'any officer of customs or excise or any other law enforcement officer'. The case concerned a prisoner's lost property. The Supreme Court ruled by a majority of five to four that *any other law enforcement officer* should be given its broad meaning, and the immunity was held to cover an official unconnected with customs duties, such as a prison officer. The *ejusdem generis* rule was not applied.

In and outside the text

Courts often speak about legal texts such as statutes and contracts in terms of an inner (textual) and outer (social) reality. Reference to the **four corners** of a text implies that everything necessary for the interpretation of the document is found on that piece of paper. In *South Eastern Electrical Plc v Somerfield Stores Ltd* (2001) (at 1), Judge Wilcox agreed with the arbitrator that the case allowed for 'construction within the four corners of the contract' without an analysis of the contract's 'factual substrate', though an explanation of the agreed 'factual background' was helpful. By contrast, in *Investors Compensation Scheme Ltd v West Bromwich Building Society* (1998), Lord Hoffmann argued that contracts should be interpreted in a way similar to 'the common sense principles by which any serious utterance would be interpreted in ordinary life', that is, against the background knowledge and assumptions available to the parties, what he termed the 'matrix of fact' (at 912). Similarly, Neuberger LJ argued that a commercial contract should not be interpreted 'purely by reference to the words the parties have used within the four corners of the contract'; rather, the court would need to make reference 'to the factual circumstances of commercial common sense' (*Skanska Rashleigh Weatherfoil Ltd v Somerfield Stores Ltd* (2006) para. 21).

In statutory interpretation we can find similar imagery. In *US v Great Northern Railway Co.* (1932), Justice Cardozo made this claim: 'We have not travelled, in our search for the meaning of the lawmakers, beyond the borders of the statute' (at 155). He noted, however, that the court was 'at liberty, if the meaning be uncertain, to have recourse to the legislative history of the measure and the statements by those in charge of it during its consideration by the Congress' (at 155–56). This suggests that aspects of the context can be treated as an optional extra or a discrete, well-defined stage in the interpretative process. (As noted above, the method of consulting the legislative record to retrieve legislative intent is controversial.)

Social change and word meaning

In addition to the co-text and the immediate factual matrix, context can include factors such as socio-cultural background, standards of conduct and morality, as well as the technological and institutional infrastructure with which law and the wider society operate (see Tiersma, 2010). The last 50 years has seen the transformation of social attitudes to fundamental aspects of social and family organization, lifestyle, sexual behaviour, and the role and status of women. Technological change is a sub-category of social change, and often a catalyst for it. For example, with the advent of Facebook and other social media, words like *friend* and *to like* have acquired a new complex of associations and practices. A *click farm* (a fraud involving paying workers to endorse a product on line) is a long way from cows and crops. More fundamentally, new techniques in reproductive medicine have evolved in tandem with ideological change in relation to the family (see Lévi-Strauss, 2013: 45ff.). Words like *family, parent, relative, spouse, child* have been subject to quite dramatic shifts within a fairly short period of time (on the definition of *parent* in the Federal Family and Medical Leave Act of 1993, see Radoff, 2010).

In relation to social change, courts have used the test of whether 'an ordinary man addressing his mind to the question' would recognize someone as falling into the category at issue (*Brock v Wollams* (1949) at 395). In *Gammans v Ekins* (1950), the question was whether a man who had lived ('cohabited') with a woman for 21 years could take over a statutory tenancy. Lord Evershed commented that it was 'difficult to imagine any context in which by the proper use of the English language a man living in such a relationship with her could be described as a member of the tenant's family' (at 141). However, in *Dyson Holdings Ltd v Fox* (1976), James LJ affirmed that where there had been a significant 'change in social conditions', the court was not bound by previous decisions. The 'popular meaning' of the word *family* was not fixed once and for all time (at 511). Lord Bridge concurred. If it was recognized that a word could 'change its meaning to accord with changing social attitudes' then the new meaning should be applied. Decisions that applied the previous meaning 'should not continue to bind thereafter, at all events in a case where the courts have consistently affirmed that the word is to be understood in its ordinary accepted meaning' (at 513) (see Barlow, 2012).

The court in *Dyson* presented this as interpreting words according to their current meanings, rather than as importing social change into the law. This approach was strongly criticized in *Helby v Rafferty* (1979): 'change in social habit' could not have the 'effect of changing the meaning of the word enacted and re-enacted in successive Acts of Parliament'. Judges did not have the authority to interpret the meanings of ordinary words in this way, and the majority judges in *Dyson* had 'formulated a canon of construction which is novel to me and for which I know no previous authority' (per Cumming-Bruce LJ, at 25).

In *Fitzpatrick v Sterling Housing Association Ltd* (2001), the House of Lords held, by a majority of three to two, that 'a same-sex partner of a tenant was now to be recognised as capable of being a member of the tenant's family', for the purpose of inheriting a tenancy. This was not a usurpation of the powers of Parliament; rather the framework for understanding the family had changed:

> It is not an answer to the problem to assume (as I accept may be correct) that if in 1920 people had been asked whether one person was a member of another same-sex person's family the answer would have been 'No'. That

is not the right question. The first question is what were the characteristics of a family in the 1920 Act and the second whether two same-sex partners can satisfy those characteristics so as today to fall within the word 'family'. An alternative question is whether the word 'family' in the 1920 Act has to be updated so as to be capable of including persons who today would be regarded as being of each other's family, whatever might have been said in 1920. (per Lord Slynn of Hadley, at 35)

The question before the UK Supreme Court in *Yemshaw v London Borough of Hounslow* (2011) was whether the definition of *violence* (Housing Act 1996, s. 177(1)) was 'limited to physical contact' or whether it included 'other forms of contact' (para. 1). The case concerned the link between the definition of *violence* and that of *homelessness*. A person who left accommodation to which he or she was entitled would not be classified as *homeless*, unless it was 'not reasonable' for that person to stay. It was not *reasonable* in particular where it was 'probable' that to stay would 'lead to domestic violence or other violence'. In *Danesh v Kensington and Chelsea Royal London Borough Council* (2006), the Court of Appeal had found that *violence* 'means physical violence'. On its own, the word did not include 'threats of violence or acts or gestures, which lead someone to fear physical violence' (para. 14). In criminal law, *assault* included not just physical contact but 'a threat or a hostile act'; but it would be wrong to read this meaning into the word *violence* in the Housing Act. While the 'acontextual meaning' of a word was not 'an entirely safe basis for interpretation', in the case of an ordinary English word 'one is entitled to assume that, in the absence of good reason to the contrary, it should be given its primary natural meaning, and to my mind, when one is talking of violence to a person, it involves physical contact' (per Neuberger LJ, para. 15). This decision had been followed by the Court of Appeal in *Yemshaw v London Borough of Hounslow* (2009).

In the *Yemshaw* appeal before the UK Supreme Court, Lady Hale, writing the lead judgment, accepted that the natural meaning of *violence* involved 'physical contact'. But it was not the 'only natural meaning', and violence could include non-physical forms of abuse (paras 19–35). Since the original enactment in 1977, a range of British agencies and international bodies had recognized this wider meaning. This was an example of a statute where, as Lord Steyn had argued in *R v Ireland* (1998), it was right to construe the wording 'as if one were interpreting it the day after it was passed' (at 158). As with *family* in the *Fitzpatrick* case, it was legitimate to recognize that the meaning of *violence* could change over time. This was necessary in order to give effect to the statutory purpose, that of 'providing a secure home for those who share their lives together' (para. 27). The term *domestic violence* should be read as 'physical violence, threatening or intimidating behaviour and any other form of abuse which, directly or indirectly, may give rise to the risk of harm' (para. 28). *Danesh* was overruled and the Court of Appeal decision in *Yemshaw* reversed.

These decisions, it should be stressed, remain confined to their immediate legal context, and do not create a newly definitive legal meaning for all purposes and for different statutes. While one might argue that these decisions reflect the fact that the ordinary meaning of *family* has changed, it would be extremely difficult to give empirical substance to that claim, given the diversity of contemporary opinion about the nature of the family.

Technological developments provide an analogous set of problems. The California appeal case of *Ni v Slocum* (2011) concerned the validity of an electronic signature on a citizen's initiative petition. At stake was the meaning of the phrase *personally affix*. From an on-line legal dictionary (Merriam–Webster's *Dictionary of Law*) the judge identified two potentially relevant meanings of this phrase (at 629): (i) 'to attach physically'; (ii) 'to attach or add in any way'. The court had to choose between 'construing the statute to require the endorser to write his or her signature and other information directly on a paper copy of the petition', or allowing any form of attachment, including an electronic signature. 'Use of a writing utensil' was 'the intuitive meaning' of the phrase *to affix a signature*. The court concluded that the plain meaning did not permit the court to 'legislate' so as to allow this new technology. The section 'means what it says and does not suggest that virtual electronic signatures are the legal equivalent of the required handwritten process of the Elections Code' (at 636).

If the words of the statute have acquired new meanings, it might seem logical that the court be required to follow them. In one sense, the very linguistic substance of the statute itself has changed, with the result that the ordinary language of the statute must now be read in the light of the new, popular meanings. Statutes are frequently said to be 'always speaking' and 'not tied to the circumstances in which they were passed' (Steyn, 2001: 68). In theory the application of this principle is to be distinguished from the court simply recognizing changes in social morality or popular standards of justice. In *R v R* (1992), for example, the court refused to apply the common law rule that a husband could not commit the crime of rape against his wife. But the line between recognizing a new meaning and reforming the law is frequently blurred, to say the least. Some judges reject any updating of this kind. For the textualist Scalia, words 'must be given the meaning they had when the text was adopted'. He does, however, accept that judges need to take account of technological changes (Scalia and Garner, 2012: 78, 85–86).

Public official and defamation law

If a category defines a right or a liability, then one party to a legal dispute will have an interest in widening its scope and the other an interest in minimizing it. In defence of free speech under the First Amendment, US courts have placed great emphasis on the role of criticism and scrutiny of public officials in promoting good government. Following J.S. Mill (1806–73) in *On Liberty* (1859), even a false statement 'may be deemed to make a valuable contribution' (cited in *New York Times v Sullivan* (1964), at 279, fn. 19). In this sense, 'there is no such thing as a false idea' (Justice Powell in *Gertz v Robert Welch Inc.* (1974) at 339). For that reason, in defamation law, public officials must meet a higher evidential standard than private citizens when suing in defamation. They must demonstrate that there was 'actual malice' in what was said or written about them (*New York Times v Sullivan* (1964)). Case law, however, has extended the category of *public official* in the direction of the more general category of *public figure* (*Curtis Publishing Co. v Butts; Associated Press v Walker* (1967)), and even to cases where the plaintiff was not a public figure and was involuntarily involved in a public controversy (*Rosenbloom v Metromedia Inc* (1971) at 896). A person who comes to prominence in relation to a particular controversy is known as a *limited purpose public figure*.

The question of classification has thus become crucial to the outcome in many defamation cases (Kaminsky, 1982: 804). The category of public figure is 'both problematic and hotly contested' (Schauer, 1984: 906): 'Defining public figures is much like trying to nail a jellyfish to the wall' (*Rosanova v Playboy Entertainments Inc.* (1976) at 443). One view is that courts have allowed the definition to expand beyond its original 'archetype' (or prototype), that is, 'the public figure who was closely analogous to a public official or who had some significant effect on the determination of public policy' (Schauer, 1984: 914). This archetype could encompass captains of industry, heads of trade unions, archbishops; it would include 'the publisher of the *New York Times*; the anchorman of the CBS Evening News; the chairman of the Democratic National Committee; the president of Harvard University; the head of the Ford Foundation' (Schauer, 1984: 916). But if we add to this concept the idea of 'general fame or notoriety' (*Gertz*, at 351–52), the list could be expanded to admit 'actors, singers, musicians, professional athletes, comedians, game show hosts, painters, sculptors, poets, authors of mystery novels, dancers, television chefs', as well as that 'amorphous category' known as 'personalities' (Schauer, 1984: 916).

For Schauer, this shift in the underlying archetype distanced the category from its constitutional grounding in state–citizen relations. He accepted that legal categories 'are rarely neat' and 'have fuzzy edges', but 'the existence of close cases at the edges of legal categories should not lead us to ignore important and obvious differences between the predominant portions of legal categories'. The distinction between *public official* and *public figure* was potentially important, and it was not necessarily advisable to set the same standard for both (Schauer, 1984: 935).

A relatively recent decision in this area is *Hatfill v New York Times Co.* ('*Hatfill III*') (2008). There the court gave 'an expansive application of the limited-purpose public figure doctrine to dismiss a defamation claim against a major media organization' (Ferguson, 2008: 724). The *New York Times* had published a series of articles criticizing the FBI for not pursuing the scientist Steven Hatfill in relation to anthrax sent through the US mail. Hatfill was never charged with any such offence, but his classification as a *public figure* denied him the chance to seek redress for a series of serious and apparently unfounded allegations. For Schauer, the drift away from a core policy concern observable in the case of *public figure* is attributable not to the fuzzy edges of concepts, but to the fuzzy reasoning of legal professionals.

An analogous set of problems arise with the definition of *journalist* in US law (Calvert, 1999). Different US state laws offer a variety of so-called **shield laws** that protect journalists who refuse to reveal the identity of informants to the police or in giving evidence in legal proceedings. The Supreme Court's decision in *Branzburg v Hayes* (1972) has been understood to give journalists **qualified privilege** under the First Amendment. State laws vary not only in the nature of the privilege, but also in how they determine '*who* is a journalist or *what* qualifies as journalism' (Pieroni, 2009: 812). In the draft Free Flow of Information Act (defeated in the Senate in 2008), *journalism* was defined as (s. 8(5))

> the regular gathering, preparing, collecting, photographing, recording, writing, editing, reporting, or publishing of news or information that concerns local, national, or international events or other matters of public interest for dissemination to the public. (<www.govtrack.us/congress/bills/111/s448/text>)

However, the rise of on-line news blogs, cyber activism as journalism, 'info-tainment', Youtube, Facebook, Twitter, Wikileaks, etc., means that potentially 'we are all journalists now' (Gant, 2007). The legal system must deal with social change as it applies 'decades-old legal concepts and doctrine to cutting edge technology' (Purvis and Greer, 2012: 107; Carr, 2013).

Indeterminacy and legal interpretation

Legal theorists associated with **Legal Realism** and **Critical Legal Theory** (CLT) have regarded the linguistic and interpretative culture of law as muddled at best, and open to opportunistic exploitation at worst. One expression of legal scepticism is the argument that words lack stable decontextual meanings and that, given the fundamental indeterminacy of its medium, law must be inde-terminate in some important sense (see Endicott, 1996). This argument goes beyond the identification of problems of vagueness in different areas of law (Endicott, 2000). If words, phrases and texts do not have meanings that can be objectively established or 'determined', then the language of law lacks the nec-essary qualities of objectivity and autonomy to perform the role that law assigns it (Langville, 1988; Manderson, 2012: 77). Interpretation, it is argued, does not proceed with the judge directly engaging with the text alone; rather, the role of interpreter, and the way the interpretative task is understood, arise out of the particular context. It is interpreters who give meanings to words, since 'words in themselves have no meaning' (Corbin, 1965: 164). If a court declares that the written words of a contract 'are so plain and clear and unambiguous that they need no interpretation' and that extrinsic evidence is not admissible, it is drawing on 'the extrinsic evidence of its own linguistic experience and educa-tion', of which it merely takes judicial notice (Corbin, 1965: 189).

To put the point more generally, many academic critics of law's interpre-tative practices distrust the idea of self-evident meanings. The immediately available, commonsense, intuitive answer to an interpretative question may also be the most theoretically dense and difficult to justify (Fish, 1987: 403):

> A meaning that seems to leap off the page, propelled by its own self-sufficiency, is a meaning that flows from interpretive assumptions so deeply embedded that they have become invisible.

For those who see indeterminacy as an ineradicable feature of language in general (semantic indeterminacy), it follows that law cannot rest its claims to justice on the stability of legal language. Law on this view masks and manages social coercion and retains elements of the Hobbesian dystopia 'where every man is Enemy to every man' (Hobbes, 1651: 62) and the domination of the strong over the weak.

However, semantic indeterminacy, it might be argued, is not fatal to law, since law itself is a social mechanism for achieving interpretative determinacy. On this view, meaning is indeterminate, but law has the legitimate authority to impose interpretative form on semantic shapelessness. Law takes the multidimensional complexities of the human social world and reduces them, if so required, to outcomes such as 'guilty' or 'not guilty'. Law, if asked, can decide (i) whether, or to what extent, nude dancing is a form of protected *speech* or *expression* for the purposes of the First Amendment (*Barnes v Glen Theatre, Inc.* (1991); Bernardin, 1992); or (ii) whether *exotic dancing*, i.e. erotic dancing, constitutes a *choreographed performance*, and therefore whether a business providing it should be exempt from sales and use taxes (*677 New Loudon Corporation v State of New York Tax Appeals* (2012)). The answers in these cases were: (i) only to a limited extent, and not so as to require that the state prohibition be struck down; and (ii) no. One might well disagree with these decisions (and there was a dissenting judgment in each) and assert quite plausibly that there are no facts about word meaning or about the world to which law can appeal in such cases. But one might argue nonetheless that law is here performing the socially essential function of mediating between conflicting interests (e.g. taxpayers versus tax authorities) and ethical principles (freedom of expression versus the right of the community to regulate public conduct on moral grounds).

For some commentators, however, the kind of definitional and semantic indeterminacy found in such cases points to a more fundamentally problematic level of interpretative indeterminacy. Law is seen either as arbitrary and capricious, or as a mask for special interests and authoritarian social control. The interpretative indeterminacy view has been characterized as follows: 'In any set of facts about actions and events that could be processed as a legal case, any possible outcome – consisting of a decision, order and opinion – will be legally correct' (Solum, 1996: 488). Law can be understood as indeterminate 'to the extent that legal questions lack single right answers' or 'to the extent that authoritative legal materials and methods permit multiple outcomes to lawsuits' (Kress, 1989: 283).

If one believed in the divine right of kings then the interpretative determinacy supplied by a monarch with absolute adjudicative powers would be unproblematic. If law is a legitimate social institution then its interpretative decisions may, like those of the judge-monarch, be understood to supply the determinacy that society needs. But law is required also to justify its decisions. It is not acceptable in a democratic society that the interpretative outcomes of law are perceived to be capricious or distorted by extra-legal ideologies or systems of power (Durant, 2010: 128–29). It is for this reason that the notions of semantic determinacy and decontextual meaning are central to the ideal of the rule of law. Without a stable grounding in language, the legal theorist is lost in the labyrinth of political theory and the task of legitimizing the coercive nature of law becomes immeasurably more difficult.

Conclusion

The debate over indeterminacy in law highlights two crucial categories that underpin of mainstream legal theory. The first category is decontextual (abstract) meaning. The second is ordinary meaning. Ideally, legal interpretation operates as far as possible with publicly available meanings. Not only are these meanings perceived to be highly stable (in that they are abstract), they are deemed to be shared by the community of ordinary speakers within the jurisdiction (in that they are ordinary). In a court case, what is at stake is how the law applies to (categorizes, labels, …) a set of circumstances that arose *after* the legal text was drafted. But it should be possible in principle to work out the relation between what the law says in general and how it applies in practice to a particular act or event. For this reason, legal interpretation assumes as a default position the **plain meaning** or **ordinary meaning rule**: 'Words are to be understood in their ordinary everyday meanings – unless the context indicates that they bear a technical sense' (Scalia and Garner, 2012: 69). This is by far the most important principle of legal interpretation, and is the subject of more detailed analysis in Chapter 3.

Summary points

- Interpretation is often understood as a search for the intentions of the author of the text.
- The judge interpreting a statute has been compared to an agent carrying out the directive of a principal.
- Judges and legal theorists disagree about whether the judge should consult legislative materials and debates prior to the enacting of the statute.
- Textualists oppose this practice, stressing the need to interpret the publicly available meanings of the legal text.
- Word meanings are often understood metaphorically as spaces.
- Many of the key terms applied to legal interpretation are in binary oppositions, such as literal versus purposive interpretation.
- Many problems of legal interpretation can be framed as questions about metaphor; some legal metaphors are criticized for simplifying or misrepresenting the underlying issues.

- Questions of co-text and context pervade legal interpretation; some scholars stress that the interpreter is a fundamental part of the context.
- Technological change and shifts in socio-cultural values raise difficult questions about the interpretative autonomy of the judge in relation to the legislature.
- All legal categories operate under complex pressures; some may widen over time to include further categories of people or things.
- Scepticism about the interpretative culture of law focuses primarily on the idea that words lack stable meanings and that language is indeterminate.
- The plain meaning or ordinary meaning rule is the most important rule of legal interpretation.

CHAPTER 3

Ordinary Language and Legal Language

This chapter examines the tensions that surround the notions of ordinary language and ordinary meaning in law. As noted in the previous chapter, in legal interpretation, words are to be understood in their ordinary meanings, unless the context indicates otherwise. It should be stressed that in cases where the statute has defined a particular term or an authoritative case law decision has laid down a particular definition, legal definition trumps ordinary meaning. In theory, 'the mind must always be ready to discard an accepted definition of a word symbol for the particular legal effect which the circumstances demand' (Levin, 1934: 1088). Yet it is almost impossible to banish the established associations of the word, especially where the statutory definition of a familiar word 'strays too far from its common or established meaning' (see Price, 2013: 1038–39).

Historically and in interpretative practice, the boundary between legal and ordinary meaning is frequently problematic. In the well-known case of *Fisher v Bell* (1961), a shop owner who had a flick knife displayed with a price in his shop window was found not to have contravened the Restriction of Offensive Weapons Act 1959. Under s. 1(1) of that instrument, it was a criminal offence to *offer for sale* such a knife. In contract law, the display of goods with a price is not a contractual *offer for sale* but rather *an invitation to treat*. In other words, the display of goods is in law not a formal offer, the acceptance of which would lead to a contract binding on both parties. The shop keeper can refuse to sell an item in the shop, even if the customer offers the price on the label. Since other criminal statutes avoided the contract law term by using terms such as *to expose for sale*, the court felt justified in applying the technical contract law meaning, rather than the ordinary meaning, even in the context of the criminal law (Munday, 2013).

In the English law of marriage, *cruelty* has traditionally been a ground for divorce. But it was defined by the courts in a highly specific, technical sense as involving 'words of menace, intimating a malignant intention of doing bodily harm', but not 'want of civility, or rudeness, or insult, or bad language, or abuse'. Transmitting a venereal disease was *cruelty*, but not putting one's spouse at risk of this (see Hurst, 1983: 39). *Cruelty* in other words was a legal term of art. However, by the 1960s, judges were 'treating cruelty as a word to be read in the ordinary and popular sense, not as a technical term' (Hurst, 1983: 39–40). A whole range of behaviours, including a husband's requirement that his wife tickle his feet (*Lines v Lines* (1963)), has been found to amount to *cruelty* (DiFonzo, 1997: 105).

The conclusion might be that there is a broad trend for ordinary meanings to be preferred to legal meanings in a range of legal domains. If there is such a trend, it is highly uneven. In *Perrin v Morgan* (1943), the House of Lords ruled that the phrase *all monies* in a will should include all personal property. This broader reading was closer to the popular meaning and was also the most reasonable interpretation of the intent of the testatrix. This was in spite of a line of decisions affirming that the phrase *all monies* should be interpreted narrowly to mean 'cash'. However, in *Re Rowland* (1963) the Court of Appeal preferred the strict legally mandated meaning rather than the apparent intention of the testator (see Chapter 5).

Statutory definition and ordinary meaning

The issue of statutory definition arose in *Morris v Revenue and Customs Commissioners* (2006). At issue was a camper van in relation to the category *car*. Mr Morris used the camper van for travelling to and from the business premises, but it served primarily as his office. The authorities argued that it was a *car* within the meaning of the Income and Corporation Taxes Act 1988, s. 157. There, *car* was defined as 'any mechanically propelled road vehicle', and the main exceptions were for vehicles used in construction, motor-cycles and invalid carriages (s. 168(5)). Finding against Mr Morris that a camper van was a *car*, the judge (Park J) evidently felt obliged to apologize for the discrepancy between the ordinary meaning of *car* and its statutory definition. The decision might seem strange 'to someone who is unfamiliar with the way in which statutory definitions can stretch the meaning of words so as to embrace matters which would normally be outside the ordinary sense of the word defined'. However, as a matter of law, 'definition sections can have effects of that sort and not uncommonly do' (para. 14). As a further illustration of the problem, the judge cited the decision in *Savoy Hotel Co. v London County Council* (1900), in which the Savoy Hotel was held to be a *shop*. That decision was reached 'because of the remarkable breadth of the statutory definition of that word'.

Common sense would suggest that there is a limit to the distance between a word's ordinary meaning and its stipulated legal definition. But there is no way of knowing in advance where the boundary between the plausible and the implausible lies. Endicott claims that when a child calls a kitten a *puppy*, 'it is not just unusual, it is wrong' (2000: 23). But, one might object, it is wrong for the adult, not the child. What is right for one user may be wrong for another. Unless one knows the legal background, the idea of a corporation as a *person* is no less exotic than calling a kitten a *puppy*. The US Congress recently declared that pizza was a *vegetable* for the purposes of school meals (Winstead, 2011). In *State ex rel. Miller v Claiborne* (1973), the court ruled that a rooster was not an *animal* under an animal cruelty statute, since the legal rule had previously been applied exclusively to four-legged animals. Scalia and Garner label this decision 'perverse' for its wilful disregard of ordinary usage. In *Knox v Massachusetts Society for the Prevention of Cruelty to Animals* (1981), by contrast, the court held that a law forbidding the giving away of *live animals* as prizes did apply to goldfish (see Scalia and Garner, 2012: 72–73, fn. 72).

Just how contentious the issue of legal versus ordinary meaning can be is shown by Justice Frankfurter's dissent in *Commissioner of Internal Revenue v Acker* (1959). The question was whether the failure to file an income tax return should attract the additional penalty for substantially underestimated income. Was the failure to file equivalent to underestimating one's income as zero? The majority decided that there was no explicit language authorizing this punitive interpretation, and reversed the lower court ruling. However, Frankfurter in dissent argued that, contrary to English legal practice (at that time), American courts should take account of all relevant statements of Congress: 'If [the United Kingdom] Parliament desires to put a gloss on the meaning of ordinary language, it must incorporate it in the text of legislation'. But 'the process of statutory construction practiced by this [Supreme] Court over the decades in scores and scores of cases' was quite different. It was open to Congress to be the 'glossator of the words' used in legislation, 'either by writing its desired meaning, however odd, into the text of its enactment, or by a contemporaneously authoritative explanation accompanying a statute' (at 94). Even if the proposed reading was unlikely when set against ordinary English, if that was what Congress intended, it was 'not for this Court to frustrate its purpose'. The Court was 'to construe not English but congressional English. Our problem is not what do ordinary English words mean, but what did Congress mean them to mean' (at 94–95).

The dictionary and beyond

Judges move to and fro between, on the one hand, evoking ordinary English within a commonsense world where words 'mean what they say' and refer to familiar concepts or things, and, on the other hand, an insistence that legal interpretation is an autonomous activity in which word meanings are created and maintained as a matter of law. In *Brutus v Cozens* (1973) the issue was whether the interruption of a tennis match by a political protest constituted *insulting* behaviour under the Public Order Act 1936, s. 5. Lord Reid made this oft-quoted statement: 'The meaning of an ordinary English word of the English language is not a question of law'. If the context revealed that a word was being used 'in an unusual sense', the court could determine what that sense was. But for the judge, in the case at hand, *insulting* was being used in its usual sense: 'It appears to me [...] to be intended to have its ordinary meaning' (at 861). In *Cabell v Markham* (1945), Justice Learned Hand argued that it was a sign of 'a mature and developed jurisprudence not to make a fortress out of the dictionary'. It was necessary 'to remember that statutes always have some purpose or object to accomplish, whose sympathetic and imaginative discovery is the surest guide to their meaning' (at 739). Similarly, Lord Edmund-Davies in *R v Caldwell* (1982), discussing the relation of the legal meaning of *recklessness* to its ordinary meaning, stressed that the law over time 'compiles its own dictionary' and 'what was originally the common coinage of speech acquires a different value in the pocket of the lawyer than when in the layman's purse' (at 23). Law on this view has its own linguistic values – in effect, its own semantic currency.

'Ordinary language' suggests an identifiable language user. But, like the famous **reasonable person**, the speaker of ordinary language is a convenient fiction. One way in which courts feel they can access the ordinary language user's point of view is through dictionary definitions. In *Lock v State* (2012), the category at issue was *motorized bicycle*. The court saw the case as turning on 'how an ordinary person would interpret the statute', so resort to 'legal definitions and scientific sources' was 'less desirable than consultation of standard language dictionaries' (at 3). Dictionary definitions showed that 'a person of ordinary intelligence would interpret this statutory definition of "motorized bicycle" to exclude any devices whose highest possible speed – as conceived of, planned, or devised – is more than twenty-five miles per hour' (at 3). In *Edwards (Inspector of Taxes) v Clinch* (1982) (at 870), Lord Lowry appealed to the 'ordinary user of English' in deciding that the appellant, who was an engineer employed from time to time to hold public inquiries on behalf of the Secretary of State for the Environment, did not hold an *office* for tax purposes.

In an insurance case, *Sher v Lafayette Ins. Co.* (2008), arising out of the 2005 Hurricane Katrina disaster in New Orleans, the question arose as to how to define the word *flood*. The court rejected any attempt to distinguish between artificial and natural floods, and to impose a technical meaning on the term. The 'plain, ordinary and generally prevailing meaning' of the word *flood* was 'the overflow of a body of water causing a large amount of water to cover an area that is usually dry' (at 193). This definition did not vary according to 'locality, culture, or even national origin'. Rather 'the entire English speaking world' would accept that definition.

In seeking the ordinary meaning of a word, judges may have recourse to intuitions, dictionary definitions, or a combination of both. For judges, the dictionary offers a conceptual map, within which the judge can locate the definitional or interpretative problem at issue (Hutton, 2009: 85–101). Traditionally, consulting the dictionary was understood as a way for judges to refresh their memory of word meanings and take **judicial notice** of ordinary usage (Onstott, 2007). Judicial notice involves the legal recognition of basic facts and states of affairs that do not have to be proven in court. The dictionary is not directly determinative of the relevant legal meaning (*Nix v Hedden* (1893) at 306–07):

> Of that [ordinary] meaning the court is bound to take judicial notice, as it does in regard to all words in our own tongue, and upon such a question dictionaries are admitted not as evidence, but only as aids to the memory and understanding of the court.

The rise of an explicitly textualist jurisprudence, in which dictionaries play a highly significant role, has led to increasing academic controversy (Garner, 2003). For the textualist, the dictionary entry provides an authoritative guide to the ordinary and publicly available meanings on which law is based. However, the line between the judge being reminded of the ordinary meaning and the dictionary strongly influencing the legal decision is difficult to draw at best.

Criticism of the overreliance on dictionaries has come from both legal scholars and linguists. One line of argument is that judges engage in 'dictionary-shopping', choosing the dictionary or the definition that suits their legal point of view (Aprill, 1998). A second criticism is that there is no proper theory of adjudication underlying this practice (Werbach, 1994; Thumma and Kirchmeier, 1999). Hoffman rejects the focus on word meaning that resort to dictionaries represents, arguing that judges should focus on syntactic relationships at the level of sentence and the meanings of phrases (Hoffman, 2003). One further line of criticism is that the primary focus on word meaning and dictionary definitions obscures the underlying legal framework and policy issues. In *Muscarello v US* (1998), the key meaning at issue was *to carry* in relation to a firearm. The statute (18 USC s. 924(c)(1)) imposed mandatory minimum sentences on drug offenders who *carried* (or *used*) a firearm while committing a drug trafficking offence. But what if the firearm was in the locked glove compartment or the trunk (boot) of the vehicle? The court used a combination of dictionary definitions and literary quotations in arriving at the conclusion that *to carry* included 'transporting in one's vehicle'. For one legal commentator, the underlying policy goals with regard to sentencing and deterrence 'got lost in a whirlwind of nit-picky dictionary definitions and outdated literary references' (Giroux, 1999: 365–66). The legal complex around this statutory provision dramatizes the tension between word meaning-based approaches (an unstable mix of intuition and dictionary definitions) and policy analysis, based on the detailed analysis of the circumstance of the offence, the logic of deterrence and the theory of sentencing. Among the key cases in this area are *Smith v US* (1993) and *Bailey v US* (1995) (see Bettenhausen, 1998; Jaffe, 2009).

Some academic linguists see dictionaries as inferior to the more systematic tools offered by modern linguistics. Slocum points to 'the subjective nature of commonsense-based judicial assertions of meaning' and criticizes 'the flawed nature of dictionary usage by the judiciary' (2012: 41). The corpus offers one example of a more precise tool (Cunningham et al., 1994: 1563). In criticizing the dictionary, some scholars offer particular linguistic theories as a superior alternative: Slocum makes the case for generative lexicon (GL) theory (2012). Cunningham et al. (1994: 1563) reject dictionaries as a 'crude and frequently unreliable aid to word meaning and usage', favouring 'analysis of a particular textual problem by a trained linguist'. They seek to identify ways in which judges could be assisted 'in identifying and choosing among possible interpretations in a principled and objective way that remains grounded in the textual language' (Cunningham et al., 1994: 1561). In particular, they believe that linguistics can make a 'potential contribution' to solving 'the apparent problem of the "fuzzy boundaries" of categories referenced by words in legal texts' (1994: 1588). A further objection to the use of dictionary definitions is that the neutrality of the dictionary is both its most essential but also its most artificial feature: 'Generalized focus makes no more semantic sense than private property that belongs to no one' (Harris and Hutton, 2007: 212). This objection would also apply to the semantic analyses offered by linguists. One possible response would be that legal rules are abstract in this sense, that is, they are intended to have generalized focus, and therefore this objection misses the point.

One case that figured prominently in these debates was *National Organization for Women v Scheidler* (1994). This centered on the question of whether PLAN, an anti-abortion activist group that used threats of violence, or actual violence, to disrupt the work of abortion clinics, could be considered an *enterprise* under the Racketeer Influenced and Corrupt Organizations Act ('RICO') (1970). RICO allowed special punitive methods against organized crime, including the seizure of assets. There were two basic meanings at stake in this case: one narrow, one broad. The first understood *enterprise* to refer to an organization engaged primarily in economic activities; the second referred to any collective endeavour or organization. Cunningham et al. (1994) undertook two surveys. They consulted usage in the NEXIS database, in order to 'enlarge the linguists' database beyond whatever examples might have been available by simple introspection' (1994: 1596). They then carried out a follow-up survey based on a questionnaire, asking for feedback as to whether particular entities or organizations might be termed an *enterprise*. The authors stressed that such research could not pre-empt the role of the judge in determining the application of statutory terms, and that legal meaning was not something that could be 'determined by an opinion poll' (1994: 1600). Rather, such surveys and the resulting analysis could raise linguistic awareness and augment linguistic intuitions, and in the authors' view should be taken into account by judges when deciding cases (Kaplan et al., 1995). A corpus analysis of the collocations of *enterprise* can be found in Mouritsen (2011).

Criticism of judges' use of dictionaries is often embedded in a wider distrust of the way that judges approach ordinary language. For Solan (1993), judges frequently treat ambiguous language as if it had a single, plain meaning. They thereby conceal the fact that there is a plausible alternative interpretation to the one proposed (Soboleva, 2013). One special class of legal problems where linguists have been critical of judges relates to the interpretation of adverbs such as *knowingly* and *willfully* (Tiersma, 1999: 60–61; Solan, 2012: 89; Scalia and Garner, 2012: 309–12). These cases challenge our understanding of the boundary between ordinary and legal meaning. If a statute states that to be punishable the act must be committed *knowingly*, how much of the offence must the accused be aware of? In *Liparota v US* (1985), a case which concerned the buying of food stamps 'in any manner not authorized' (7 USC s. 2024(b)(1)), the defendant admitted buying the food stamps at less than their face value, but denied that he knew this was unauthorized. Applying the **rule of lenity** (that the defendant should be given the benefit of any ambiguity in the construal of criminal statutes), the Supreme Court found by a six to two majority that the prosecution had to show specific intent to commit the act while knowing that it was unauthorized. It was not enough to show intent to commit the act. In effect, the prosecution were required to show that the defendant knew that the transaction was illegal. If knowledge of the law is an element of the intent to commit a crime (i.e. is a constituent of the **mens rea)** then the question naturally arises as to how specific that knowledge must be.

In *US v X-Citement Video, Inc.* (1994), at issue was Title 18 USC s. 2252(a)(1) (1988), which criminalized

[a]ny person who [...] knowingly transports [...], any visual depiction, if (A) the producing of such visual depiction involves the use of a minor engaging in sexually explicit conduct; and (B) such visual depiction is of such conduct.

The question was whether the statute criminalized any transportation of such materials, or whether it was necessary to show that the defendant knew the content was obscene or that the defendant knew the content was both obscene *and* involved minors. The lack of a requirement of conscious knowledge of wrongdoing (*scienter*), it was argued, would make the law unconstitutionally vague, since anyone who innocently forwarded such material would be criminally liable. The Court of Appeals (9th Circuit) reversed the original conviction on these grounds. The Supreme Court, however, reinstated the conviction, arguing that there was a way to interpret the statute so as to make it constitutional, namely, that the scope of *knowingly* included (A) and (B). (The defendant had in fact known that the materials were obscene and involved minors.) In dissent, Scalia argued that the Court of Appeals' reading was the only possible construction.

One further case that has drawn considerable comment is *Flores-Figueroa v US* (2009). The statute created a class of aggravated identity theft, when, in the commission of certain crimes, someone 'knowingly transfers, possesses, or uses, without lawful authority, a means of identification of another person' (18 USC s. 1028A(a)(1)). The question was whether the defendant would have to know not only that a particular social security number was not his own, but also specifically that it belonged to someone else. Federal courts were divided on this question. The Supreme Court held unanimously that in 'ordinary English' it seemed natural 'to read the statute's word "knowingly" as applying to all the subsequently listed elements of the crime' (at 650). In ordinary English, listeners would 'in most contexts' understand *knowingly* to apply to 'how the subject performed the entire action, including the object as set forth in the sentence' (at 650).

A brief submitted by four linguists argued that there was no ambiguity as to the scope of *knowingly* in the statute (Ernst et al., 2008). It modified 'the predicate in its entirety', that is, all the words governed by the transitive verb (at 6). This reflected the 'ordinary meaning' of the statutory language, that is, 'the way that the statute is likely to be understood by an ordinary native speaker of English' (at 1). On a related matter, it has been argued that judges, in their interpretation of the Americans with Disabilities Act (ADA) (1990), have missed multiple ambiguities in unfair dismissal cases (Anderson, 2008). In the Act, disability is defined as '(A) a physical or mental impairment that substantially limits one or more of the major life activities'; or, '(C) being regarded as having such impairment' (s. 12102(2)). One approach that courts have taken to (C) is to require the claimant to specify the particular condition that the employer regarded him or her as having (a so-called **de re** reading).

This is as opposed to simply showing that the employer regarded the employee as having an impairment in general (**de dicto**) (see Anderson, 2008: 1026ff.). The same ambiguity arises in relation to the category *major life activity*. Does the claim have to specify that the employer regarded the disability as impairing a specific major life activity? As an antidote to artificially restrictive interpretations found in decided cases, Anderson argues that judges should read the legal text 'like a layperson (drawing on our natural linguistic intuitions) or like a linguist (with the expertise to describe those intuitions)' (2008: 1026).

One possible counter-argument to the linguist's position is that there is no guarantee that the linguist's analysis will line up with that of a real, as opposed to a fictional, ordinary speaker. The principle that the adverb 'modifies the entire predicate consisting of the verbs and their direct object' (Ernst et al., 2008: 2) runs into the practical problem of defining the language, the register and the speakers for which this is true. Statutes are set out in sections and subsections; there is no conceivable unitary 'native speaker' intuition that bears on the reading of such highly specialized texts. In addition, *knowingly* is arguably not a word of ordinary English at all. It is a legal or legalistic term, as a search of any large corpus immediately reveals (e.g. the Corpus of Contemporary American English, see <corpus.byu.edu/coca>). If there is an ordinary English expression in this domain, it is *on purpose*.

The linguistic thought experiment

In appealing to ordinary meaning, judges frequently follow an intuitive sense of how a word or phrase would be understood 'in general', or how an object or phenomenon would ordinarily be classified. In Wittgenstein's terms, judges frequently 'look for the use'. This technique can be described as a **linguistic thought experiment**, where a particular phrasing is tested for its plausibility and compatibility with ordinary usage. In *People v Blood* (1924) (at 212–23), the key term was *to transport*: 'If, for example, a person goes on a journey, his trunk may properly be said to be transported; but it would be unnatural to say that he was transporting his penknife or other personal articles which he had in his clothes.' This kind of issue often arises with verbs like *to possess* and *to carry*. If a law applies to the *carrying* of illegal firearms, does that include the transporting of a weapon in the trunk (boot) of a car? Applying the same technique, the difference between *advertising* and a *sales pitch* would be that advertising is 'a form of promotion to anonymous recipients', so that in normal usage, promotional material 'read by millions (or even thousands in a trade magazine) is advertising', whereas 'a person-to-person pitch by an account executive' would not be (*First Health Group Corporation v BCE Emergis Corporation* (2001) at 803–04).

The case reports are full of such linguistic thought experiments. For example in *US v Gole* (1998), the court remarked: 'The use of the word "salary" (under any normal usage) would seem to rule out consideration of overtime pay' (at 169). Similarly, in *Maine State Board of Education v Cavazos* (1992), the question was whether the Maine Board of Education could claim reimbursement from the Department of Education for administrative expenses related to a federal loan scheme, in the course of which fees were paid to a private agency (rather than a state guaranty agency). The question was in part who had actually incurred the expenses in question: 'Suppose a householder agrees to pay a gardener $10 to mow his lawn, and the gardener spends $2 for lawnmower oil. One would normally say the householder "incurs" an expense of $10, and the gardener "incurs" an expense of $2. One does not ordinarily think of the $2 as an expense "incurred" by the householder' (at 308).

In the case of *Perrin v Morgan* (1943) mentioned above, in considering whether the phrase *all monies* in a will should be understood narrowly as 'cash' or broadly to include 'all personal property', Viscount Simon tried out various phrases and quoted particular uses of the word. The phrase 'What has he done with his money?' could be used to ask about the contents of a rich man's will; the phrase 'It's her money he's after', when used of a fortune hunter, was not restricted to a particular kind of asset, and '[w]hen St Paul wrote to Timothy that the love of money is the root of all evil, he was not warning him of the risks attaching to one particular kind of wealth' (at 407). The House of Lords found in favour of the broad meaning.

The case of *McAllister v California Coastal Commission* (2009) concerned the meaning of *to minimize* in relation to zoning regulations. The court accepted that zoning policies in the coastal area required that 'visibility and visual impacts be minimized', and agreed with the plaintiff (McAllister) that 'to minimize means to reduce something to the least number, size, amount, extent, or degree of it possible'. McAllister argued that logically this impact should be reduced to zero if possible. The court disagreed, relying the ordinary meaning of *to minimize* (at 955). The meaning could not be extended 'to the total elimination of something if feasible'. Rather 'the plain meaning and ordinary understanding' of the word was 'to reduce, not eliminate': 'Thus, when one says that something has been "minimized," people do not ordinarily understand that the thing has been completely eliminated but expect to find some residue or remainder'; by the same logic, 'if something has been completely eliminated, one would not usually say that it had been minimized.'

In a much discussed case, *Smith v US* (1993), Justice Scalia rejected the idea that trading a firearm for drugs, rather than using it as a weapon, constituted *using a firearm*. To use a tool ('instrumentality') ordinarily meant 'to use it for its intended purpose'. So if someone asks 'Do you use a cane?', the question was not 'whether you have your grandfather's silver-handled walking stick on display in the hall'. It was 'whether you walk with a cane'. In the same way, to speak of *using a firearm* was 'to speak of using it for its distinctive purpose, i.e., as a weapon'. While one could *use* a firearm in a number of ways, 'including as an article of exchange', just as one could *use* a cane to decorate the hall, that was not the 'ordinary meaning' of *using* in either case (at 42). However, the majority decided that the act of trading the gun for illegal drugs was captured by the statutory phrase.

In *Rowland v California Men's Colony* (1993), the court had to decide whether an association of prisoners could be considered a *person*, and therefore whether it could bring proceedings as a pauper (*in forma pauperis*). Could such an association, which had no assets, be a *poor person*? Citing phrases from

Webster's *New International Dictionary* (2nd edn, 1942), the majority argued that one would not naturally talk of such collectivities as being *poor*. An association or corporation could not be said to 'lack the comforts of life', and it made no sense to ask whether it could provide itself, let alone its dependants, with life's 'necessities'. An artificial entity might be insolvent, but could not be 'well spoken of' as *poor*. While it was not impossible to use the phrase *poor* of an association or a corporation, it was not natural or normal. 'Eccentric' usage of this kind should not be lightly attributed to Congress. Poverty was an attribute of natural persons, a 'human condition' (at 203).

However, the dissent cast doubt on this intuition. While poverty might be primarily a human condition, 'using the word in connection with an artificial entity' did not seem to depart 'in any significant way from settled principles of English usage'. There were plenty of examples of the use of 'poor' in connection with 'nonhuman entities' (at 218–19). These included entities mentioned in the law, such as corporations. Justice Holmes had used the term 'poor' in discussing the assets of corporations (*Towne v Eisner* (1918) at 426). Even Congress itself had provisions in the US Code referring to the world's 'poorest countries'. If Congress could use 'poor' to describe a country, then it could use it to describe a 'corporation, partnership, or association' (at 219). While both the majority and the dissent disagreed about the correct result in *Rowland v California Men's Colony*, they used a shared method.

By contrast, a judge may reject the intuitive logic of the linguistic categories. In Hong Kong law a complex set of legal questions arises in relation to the definition of *triad*. Triad societies are regarded in law as criminal conspiracies (*The Queen v Sit Yat Keung* (1985)). Membership of a triad society and all aspects of triad ritual, including triad meetings and initiation ceremonies, are criminalized. But if three known members of triad societies sit down for a meal to discuss business, is that a *triad meeting*? In *R v Wong Sik Ming* (1996), a number of triad members were in a bar discussing triad affairs. They were convicted under the Societies Ordinance (s. 20(2)) of attending a 'meeting of a triad society' (參加三合會社團的集會). On appeal, the judge stated that 'whether something is a meeting or not is a question of fact' (para. 9). A police expert had testified that this constituted a triad meeting, as it was convened 'to settle a dispute that happened earlier on. The purpose was to show the power of their triad society'. However, the judge argued that something more was required: 'as far as the facts of this particular case is concerned, I am of the view that this clearly was a meeting of triads to discuss triad matters, but I have considerable doubt as to whether it was a meeting of a triad society' (para. 9). If a group of solicitors met together to discuss legal problems, that would not constitute a meeting of The Law Society (para. 10): 'I do not think triads require the same formality as a professional body would, but in my judgment, I think there is a doubt in this case as to whether this was capable of being a meeting of a triad society'. The appeal on that charge was allowed. Not every meeting of triads was a *triad meeting*.

In *Park v Appeal Board of Mich. Employment Sec. Commission* (1959), the word at issue was *establishment*. Employees at the Michigan plant had been laid off due to a strike in Ohio. Under state law, they would not be entitled to compensation for loss of earnings if the Michigan and Ohio plants were deemed a single establishment. They could claim only if these plants constituted separate establishments. The Ford Company argued that the 'functional integration and synchronization' between the plants meant that they should be treated as one, their geographical separation across a state boundary notwithstanding. Justice Edwards summed up the case as follows. It was a case 'of great financial importance to the litigants' in which 'over 1,600 printed pages of records and briefs' had been reviewed. But in the end it came down to 'a relatively simple legal question', namely, whether the term *establishment* encompassed 'both Ford plants in the vicinity of Detroit, Michigan, and the Ford forge plant at Canton, Ohio', given that 'the former cannot operate long without the latter' (at 107). There was no definition of *establishment* in the statute. The judge quoted the definition from Webster's *New International Dictionary* (2nd edn):

> The place where one is permanently fixed for residence or business; residence, including grounds, furniture, equipage, retinue, etc., with which one is fitted out; also, an institution or place of business, with its fixtures and organized staff as, large *establishment*; a manufacturing *establishment*.

While it was true that judges and lawyers often did 'astonishing things' with words, '[n]o layman would venture to suggest that the single word "establishment", used in the paragraph above, could in normal usage be applied to both the Ford Rouge plant in Dearborn, Michigan, and the Ford forge plant in Canton, Ohio' (at 116). The judge rejected Ford's argument about the word *establishment*: 'no layman, without a specific motive in mind, would read the statutory provisions quoted above and come to the conclusion that the legislature had any such inclusiveness in its intended use of the word'.

Relations on the bench were clearly far from harmonious. The Chief Justice and one colleague dissented, citing a precedent case, *Chrysler Corporation v Smith* (1941), where the opposite conclusion had been reached. There had been further legislation in this area since 1941 that had left the principle in *Chrysler* undisturbed. It followed that the *Chrysler* decision had been in effect ratified by legislation. The rules of precedent meant that the court was still bound to follow *Chrysler*. However, Justice Black, writing for the majority, called the *Chrysler* decision 'tragic', a 'now conceded blunder' and an 'irreparable injustice', and rejected the appeal to precedent as an 'extreme and wholly discredited form of judicial self-stultification' (at 142). The argument from legislative acquiescence was being applied selectively – 'only when the decision to overrule results in a more liberal interpretation of the once-interpreted statute' (at 149).

Yet one could imagine someone who owned a bakery and a cake shop making this kind of statement: 'The bakery and the shop are a mile apart but I run them as a single establishment.' Justice Edwards, however, implied that such statements would generally have a 'specific motive'. The dictionary definition, from this point of view, would be motiveless. Whether the dictionary definition cited in the case (see above) really did unambiguously rule out a split-site or multi-site establishment is also open to question.

One could read *Park* simply as a case where the ordinary meaning was applied. But that interpretative strategy was itself the outcome of technical legal argument. Further, there was an important socio-economic dimension to the analysis of employment and union structures. The court was split along political lines, and the judges seemed divided much more by their differing levels of sympathy for workers who had lost wages than by their interpretation of the word *establishment*.

There is little discussion in legal theory of the linguistic thought experiment as a method. One exception is Weinstein (2004). In rejecting the use of dictionaries as 'sham formalism', Weinstein argues for what he terms **analogical reasoning** as a methodological alternative. This would be 'definition by analogy', in effect a formalization of the linguistic thought experiment method. It would involve using example phrases or quotations to see which meaning best fits the statutory context: 'A judge should look to the context of the statutory phrase to determine from among multiple usages, which is *most likely* within the given phrase' (Weinstein, 2004: 675).

Ordinary language and public perception

Ordinary language issues play an important role in how legal decisions are received in the media and by the public. Cynicism about the linguistic culture of law is widespread in modern societies, and this is often expressed in the view that lawyers exploit the gap between ordinary language and legal language in an opportunistic manner. In the Hong Kong case of *Fully Profit Asia (Ltd) v The Secretary for Justice* (2013), the word at issue was *house*. In 1952, the Hong Kong Government had granted a lease for five plots of land. Under the terms of the lease each plot came with a restriction or covenant. The owner was not to 'erect or allow to be erected more than one house' on each plot of land. The houses built at that time had five stories. Leave was sought by a developer for permission to build a single 26-storey building in the form of an apartment complex (block of flats) covering all five plots.

The question for the court was whether this proposed structure constituted 'more than one house'. The Court of First Instance (*Fully Profit (Asia) Ltd v The Secretary for Justice* (2011)) ruled that 'the erection of such a structure will clearly exceed those pertaining to a "house" as such term is generally understood to connote' (para. 46). The structure 'intended to be erected on each lot is and can fairly be described as "more than one house"' (para. 47). However, the Court of Appeal (*Fully Profit* (2012)) determined that 'whether "house" included a block of flats would depend on the context' (para. 20). The Court rejected the idea that the test was that of ordinary language: 'I do not believe it was intended that the meaning to be attributed to the word "house" should depend on whether in common parlance the structure would be called a house or a block of flats' (per Tang VP). The word *house* was to be treated in this context as synonymous with *building* (para. 30). The Court of First Instance decision was reversed.

However, in the Court of Final Appeal the original decision was restored. The meaning of the word *house* in the lease 'must have reference to those characteristics of the houses which were actually standing at the time the Government Leases were entered into'. There was an important difference in this context between *house* and *building*: 'It is significant that the word "house" should be used, rather than the word "building"' (para. 17). The application to build the 26-storey building was denied.

A Hong Kong newspaper columnist interpreted the case in terms of a clash between ordinary people and greedy developers. After being obliged for decades to pay inflated prices for shoebox-size apartments, 'we at least shouldn't have to put up with [the developers'] assaults on common language and the meanings of simple words' (Lo, 2013: A2). While this is an emotionally appealing analysis, the case involved detailed discussion of case law and of the intention behind the original restriction (covenant) in the lease. There was also no mention of the Chinese terms for *house, building, apartment block*, etc. used in Hong Kong. 'Ordinary language' and 'ordinary meaning', it might be argued, are constructs of the legal analysis, rather than the direct reflection of popular justice or of usage in Hong Kong. Nonetheless, the fact that both legal professionals and ordinary citizens can bring to bear their intuitions about meanings onto the facts of a particular case, in combination with their sense of what is right or wrong, is a fundamental feature of the linguistic culture of law.

Ordinary language in legal philosophy

Given that the category of ordinary language is central to legal interpretation, it is no surprise that the most influential theory of law, that of H.L.A. Hart (1907–92), also has this category at its centre. Hart stressed that legal rules are formulated in terms of general (decontextual) categories of ordinary language such as *animal, game, building*: 'The law must predominantly [...] refer to classes of person, and to classes of acts, things, and circumstances'. For law to operate successfully 'over vast areas of social life' it needed to depend on 'a widely diffused capacity to recognize particular acts, things, and circumstances as instances of the general classifications which the law makes' (Hart, [1961] 1994: 124). To illustrate this, Hart analyzed a hypothetical rule of law: 'No vehicles in the park.' In its generality, Hart argues, law anticipates certain events or incidents and needs to be able to recognize those acts 'as instances of general classifications'. What law in action confronts, therefore, are particularities or episodes (individual events, happenings, utterances, objects, ...) that are bound in time and space (Veitch et al., 2012: 132).

For Hart, the categories of language could not be regarded as fully closed in relation to particular facts: 'Natural languages like English are when so used irreducibly open textured' (Hart, [1961] 1994: 128). There was inevitably 'uncertainty at the borderline' where general classifying terms were used. **Open texture** emerged when general classifying terms were confronted with particular facts. It was true of 'all fields of experience' that 'there is a limit, inherent in the nature of language, to the guidance which general language can provide' (Hart, [1961] 1994: 126). In the case of legal rules employing terms such as *vehicle*, there were many 'plain cases constantly recurring in similar contexts to which general expressions are clearly applicable'. For example, a motor car was clearly a *vehicle*. But: 'Does "vehicle" used here include bicycles, airplanes, roller skates?' (Hart, [1961] 1994: 126). These were 'fact-situations' where some of the features of the plain cases were present but not others. Like legal rules, 'canons of interpretation' (that is legal maxims) used general terms and could not 'provide for their own interpretation'.

In plain cases, 'the general terms seem to need no interpretation' and 'the recognition of instances' appears 'unproblematic' or 'automatic'. But these cases were 'only the familiar ones, constantly recurring in similar contexts, where there is a general agreement in judgments as to the applicability of the classifying terms' (Hart, [1961] 1994: 126). However there was a **penumbra of uncertainty** surrounding all legal rules, so that it was impossible to conclude that judges simply followed 'logical deduction' or 'deductive reasoning' (Hart, 1958: 607–08; Henly, 1987). Hart pointed out that facts and phenomena were unable to speak, that they were 'dumb' (Hart, 1958: 607):

> The toy automobile cannot speak up and say, 'I am a vehicle for the purpose of this legal rule', nor can the roller skates chorus, 'We are not a vehicle'. Fact situations do not await us neatly labeled, creased, and folded, nor is their legal classification written on them to be simply read off by the judge.

When Hart talks about the category *vehicle* he seems to imply that this is simply an ordinary word dropped into a legal rule. In one sense, this is obviously the case. After all, what else could it be? Easy cases are those where the object in question is clearly a *vehicle*, or clearly not a *vehicle*, according to ordinary usage. Hard cases are those where the object in question is on the borderline. For Hart, there might be some doubt about whether we would call a pair of roller skates a *vehicle*, whereas the plain cases of the application of the legal rule coincide with the unproblematic application of *vehicle* in ordinary usage. Hart implies that the paradigm problem of legal classification arises because of the fuzzy edges of general terms. This dovetails with the understanding of word meaning put forward in prototype theory: 'work in linguistics and cognitive psychology shows that we form concepts, at least in part, by absorbing prototypes, and that concepts become indeterminate at the margins' (Solan 1995: 1073).

Alternatively, one might argue that *vehicle*, by its inclusion in a legal rule, takes on a specific, legal meaning. Deciding the scope of a legal rule is not simply a question of judging how far an ordinary general term applies to the facts of the case. The problem does not lie in the fact that a toy automobile cannot speak up and say whether it is a vehicle. For in any case the toy could not say whether or nor it was a vehicle *for the purpose of the legal rule*. To achieve that, it would have to be trained like a judge. Toys cannot speak, but people can. But even where people speak up and claim membership of a category, law frequently does not recognize their claims (see discussion of *W v Registrar of Marriages*, Chapter 13). Fuller writes of Hart: 'The most obvious defect of his theory lies in its assumption that problems of interpretation typically turn on the meaning of individual words' (Fuller, 1957: 662).

Hart's argument is that law makes demands of ordinary language that take it beyond its traditional habits and the collective distinctions that it has evolved. Similarly, for the philosopher J.L. Austin (1911–60) the inherited linguistic habits of a community represent an accumulation of wisdom and acumen created over many generations (Austin, 1956: 8): 'Our common stock of words embodies all the distinctions men have found worth drawing, and the connexions they have found worth marketing, in the lifetimes of many generations'. These distinctions were the product of an evolutionary process: 'they have stood up to the long test of the survival of the fittest'. Philosophical analysis should proceed by paying attention to distinctions which work well 'for practical purposes in ordinary life', and the fact that language could characterize most situations was 'no mean feat, for even ordinary life is full of hard cases' (Austin, 1956: 11). By contrast, the law produces hard cases which even this subtle and discerning instrument has trouble characterizing. It gives rise to 'a constant stream of actual cases, more novel and more tortuous than the mere imagination could contrive'. In order to solve these cases, it is necessary 'first to be careful with, but also to be brutal with, to torture, to fake and to override, ordinary language' (Austin, 1956: 12).

The ordinary language approach of philosophers such as Hart and Austin was sharply criticized by the philosopher Ernst Gellner (1925–99). Gellner rejected the 'mystique of ordinary language or common sense', seeing it as making a bogus claim to represent the everyday. The appeal to ordinary language was 'a set of high-powered, high-brow, doubly-sophisticated devices for inculcating an alleged common sense or ordinary view' (Gellner, 1959: 113). Gellner is surely correct in saying that there is a mystique around the notion of ordinary language, but whether this represents a fatal objection to law's interpretative practices is open to debate. If a decision can be made with reference to ordinary language, this, so the argument goes, makes law appear more democratic, in that ordinary people are being judged as far as possible according to the categories that they themselves use and recognize. If the vast majority of decisions follow the boundaries of ordinary language categories, then evidence about the nature of those categories is potentially of importance to law. Hart's rule can be understood as a case for the application of hyponymy: the law applies to the hyponyms of *vehicle*. For critics of the linguistic culture of law this reliance on ordinary language is misleading. If we actually set out to determine rigorously what constitutes ordinary meaning and where the boundaries of ordinary language categories lie, we enter a thicket of practical and theoretical problems.

Conclusion

The idea that ordinary language exists as a stable set of categories with which (and against which) law operates is a very powerful one. It underwrites the use of intuitions by judges and other legal professionals, and offers reassurance that the legal system is embedded to the greatest extent practicable in the shared public meanings of the linguistic community under its jurisdiction. However, the appeal to ordinary language always emerges out of an analysis of the case's constellation of contextual meanings and legal principles. It is the judge who decides whether the ordinary or the legal meaning is most relevant, how that meaning may be determined, the kind of authority to be appealed to, or who may conclude that there is no legally significant difference. It is the judge who determines whether the word or phrase at issue should be treated as having a specialized meaning, in that it is employed in a particular sub-culture or trade; whether it is a legal term of art, in that its interpretation involves a consideration of legal doctrine (words like *negligence* or *malice*), and so on. If the court has decided that the word is to be understood in its normal, non-technical meaning, then it may use whatever method it deems suitable, including a mix of intuition, dictionary definitions and linguistic thought experiments.

The notion that the meaning of an ordinary English word is not a question of law is therefore potentially misleading, if taken as a policy statement about legal interpretation. It says no more than it is up to the judge to determine whether a word is used in its ordinary sense or not. It also draws on the highly technical distinction between law and fact. In practice the meaning of an ordinary word is in this sense *always* a question of law, since it is the judge who decides where the boundary lies between ordinary and legal usage, just as a judge decides what is a question of law and what is a question of fact (Flanagan, 2010). Ordinary language is a legal category to which judges appeal, rather than a well-defined social category which can be applied to solve problems of legal interpretation. Further, what is ordinary to one speaker is quite unusual for another. In these two senses, ordinary language is, arguably, a legal fiction.

Summary points

- Words are interpreted according to their ordinary meanings, unless the context indicates otherwise.
- Statutory definitions take priority over ordinary language meanings.
- The boundary between legal language and ordinary language is problematic in legal interpretation; judges frequently use linguistic thought experiments to test their intuitions as to word usage and word categories.
- It is the judge who determines the boundary between legal and ordinary usage, and its significance within a given case.
- Dictionaries are frequently consulted in legal proceedings, but this practice is controversial in legal theory.
- Ordinary language plays a key role in Hart's jurisprudence, where general terms are described as having a core and a penumbra.
- It is often argued is that if ordinary language is used as far as possible in legal adjudication, this increases the transparency, accountability and predictability of law.

- There are a number of potential practical and theoretical problems with the appeal to ordinary language.
- Ordinary language and ordinary meaning should, arguably, be seen as legal fictions.

Overview figures: the linguistic culture of law

The figures below set out some of the basic categories recognized in the linguistic culture of law. Figure 3.1 shows the basic breakdown between specifically legal and non-legal varieties. Figure 3.2 indicates the available sources of authority for a judge who wishes to ascertain the ordinary meaning of a word. Figure 3.3 makes the (controversial) suggestion that ordinary language should be seen as a legal category and that it functions as a legal fiction in relation to 'facts' of ordinary linguistic usage.

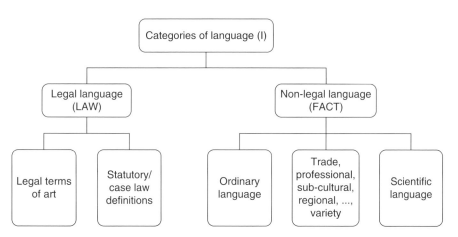

Figure 3.1   Categories of language recognized in the interpretative culture of law (I)

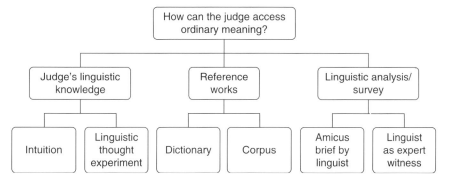

Figure 3.2   Sources of authority available to the judge in determining ordinary meaning

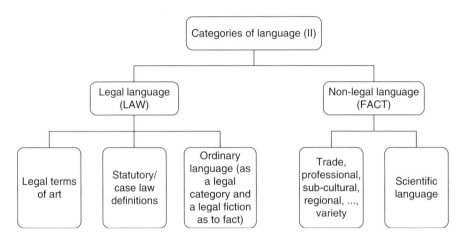

Figure 3.3   Categories of language (II): ordinary language as a legal category and legal fiction

PART II
Case Studies

Part II offers analytical summaries of a selection of cases, chosen to illustrate a range of category types and legal questions. While several cases featured here have been the subject of extensive academic debate, others are relatively obscure. A table that sets out the basic facts of the decision precedes each case:

Case name (Date)	Term at issue	Legal category	Legislation	Holding

The primary aim of Part II is to make the cases comprehensible for the student and general reader, and to encourage further analysis, not only in terms of legal theory, but also in relation to theories of language and interpretation, anthropology, social history and so on. Each decision is summarized in terms of key points, and each chapter concludes with a 'Points for further consideration' section which relates back to issues raised in Part I.

CHAPTER 4

Classification and Legislative Intent

Is a racing pigeon a *pigeon*?

Hong Kong Racing Pigeon Association v Attorney-General (1995)	Racing pigeon	Pigeon	'No person [...] shall keep livestock in or on any premises in a livestock waste prohibition area'; 'livestock' means pigs or poultry; 'poultry' means chickens, geese, pigeons and quail (Waste Disposal Ordinance, Cap. 354, ss. 15, 2)	Racing pigeons were pigeons

Hong Kong Racing Pigeon Association v AG (1994) (High Court)

The statute forbade the keeping of *livestock* in urban areas. *Livestock* was defined as 'pigs or poultry'. *Poultry* in turn was defined as 'chickens, geese, pigeons and quail'. The question arose as to whether the legal rule applied to *racing pigeons*. The judge (Sears J) noted that the law had been originally enacted 'to restrict the large farming operations taking place in the urban areas' that were for providing food. While eating pigeon was common in Hong Kong, racing or homing pigeons were generally smaller than domestic pigeons raised for consumption. These were very valuable birds and would not normally be eaten. There was a House of Lords decision that turned on the word *poultry* in the Fertilisers and Feeding Stuffs Act 1926 (*Hardwick Game Farm v SAPPA* (1969)). In that case their Lordships took the view that 'pheasants, which have never been in captivity, are not poultry': *poultry* referred to birds kept for meat or eggs. However, the word was not defined in the judgment (at 311).

The Hong Kong Racing Pigeon Association (HKRPA) argued that racing birds were kept for sport, not for eating, whereas *poultry*, in the sense of *livestock*, was always intended to end up as food: 'the word "pigeon" does not include racing pigeons, because a racing pigeon is not poultry' (at 310). In urging flexibility, counsel quoted Lord Denning from *Seaford Court Estates v Asher* (1949). There, Lord Denning set out the approach that should be taken where the statute had failed to provide for the facts before the court. Rather than passively following 'the supposed rule that he must look to the language and nothing else', the judge should embark on the 'constructive task of finding the intention of Parliament'. This required consideration not only of the language of the statute, but also of 'the social conditions' that gave rise to the Act and the 'mischief that it was passed to remedy'. He should 'supplement the written word so as to give "force and life" to the intention of the legislature' (at 311).

The judge noted that there were 306 species within the family called *Columbidae* of which the pigeon was a member. There were domestic pigeons, ornamental pigeons, and homing or racing pigeons (at 310). The definitions found in the Public Health (Animals and Birds) Ordinance (Cap. 139) were not favourable to the Racing Pigeon Association. There *birds* were defined as 'poultry and all other birds', and *poultry* included 'domestic fowls, turkeys, ducks, pigeons and geese'. So while *poultry* was defined differently, it did include *pigeon*. Given the common context between the two statutes of public health and restrictions on the keeping and movement of birds, the judge concluded that he would follow the definition of *poultry* given in the Waste Disposal Ordinance.

Overall, the judge saw no reason to exclude racing pigeons from the category of *poultry*. The hardship to the affected parties had been recently alleviated by the raising of the permitted exempt number, from 10 racing pigeons to 20. It had emerged, however, that the Urban Council, a branch of the (colonial) Hong Kong Government, had been keeping ornamental pigeons in its parks, in technical contravention of the law. The Governor had issued a quasi-legislative order (known as an **Order in Council**) exempting the Urban Council. While the judge was sympathetic to the Association, and noted that other birds such as parrots could be kept without violating the law, he ended by concluded that 'racing pigeons are pigeons within the meaning of the Waste Disposal Ordinance' (at 312).

Key points in the judgment

■ The Waste Disposal Ordinance was for the control of *livestock* which included *poultry* which was defined to include *pigeons*.

■ The Public Health (Animals and Birds) Ordinance defined *poultry* differently but it also included pigeons.

■ Racing pigeons were pigeons, and *pigeon* was a sub-category of *poultry* as defined in the Ordinance.

■ There was no reason to exclude racing pigeons from the category of *pigeon*, given that both Ordinances were concerned with public health and hygiene.

Hong Kong Racing Pigeon Association v AG (1995) (Court of Appeal)

The HKRPA appealed but the decision was upheld. Nazareth VP wrote the lead judgment (paras 1–4), stating that the 'ordinary and natural meaning of "pigeons" was clear and it extended to all pigeons, be they table birds, fancy or show birds or even racing pigeons'. The definition in the Public Health Ordinance was not relevant, however, as it did not concern the same matter or subject (that is, it was not *in pari materia*): 'A definition in another Ordinance (particularly one that did not have the same objectives) could not be of assistance, save perhaps in the most residual and attenuated way'. There was 'no ambiguity or obscurity in the definition', and the result of applying the law was not absurd. There was no need to look for background evidence of the intention of the legislature, under the rule in *Pepper v Hart* (1992), or to look for any other external assistance. In any case the legislative history would not have helped the plaintiff. The intent of the law was to address the 'primary mischief' of pollution caused by livestock, especially pig waste, but this did not mean that other forms of livestock waste should be removed from its scope. Liu JA added that the statute concerned 'the keeping of pigeons and the disposal of the waste they made'. Given this, the purpose for which the pigeons were kept 'could not be relevant to the disposal of their waste' (para. 5).

Key points in the judgment

■ Racing pigeons were *pigeons* according to the ordinary and natural meaning of the word.

■ The Public Health (Animals and Birds) Ordinance was not materially relevant.

■ There was no obscurity in the legislation; no absurd result would follow from following the ordinary meaning, and so there was no reason to seek external guidance, for example by looking at the legislative history.

■ The primary mischief was a concern about animal waste and its disposal in the urban areas.

■ The purpose for which the pigeons were kept was not relevant to how the keeping of pigeons and the disposal of their waste were regulated.

Discussion: The 'Russian doll' (*matreshka*) approach to categories

A racing pigeon was clearly a kind of *pigeon*, so from one point of view a definitional automaton or 'language machine' could have processed this decision: *racing pigeon* was a sub-category (hyponym) of *pigeon* which was a sub-category of *poultry* which was a sub-category of *livestock*. These relationships of inclusion can be represented as shown in Table 4.1.

Table 4.1   Relationships of inclusion in the *pigeon* case

livestock			
poultry			pigs
pigeon		chicken, goose, quail	
racing pigeon	domestic pigeon		

An alternative view of the categories involved is represented in Table 4.2. While racing pigeons might be *pigeons*, they were arguably not *poultry*, and certainly not *livestock*, since racing pigeons were not bred for food.

Table 4.2 Distinguishing *racing pigeons* from *pigeons bred for food*

sporting animals, pets, &c.	livestock		
	poultry		pigs
pigeon		chicken, goose, quail	
racing pigeon	domestic pigeon		

This might seem a rather banal case. It took two senior court decisions to decide that a racing pigeon was a *pigeon*, and the Court of Appeal did not waste many words on it. Yet in just a few pages the case exhibits in microcosm many of the key techniques and strategies in common law interpretation. An important feature of common law adjudication is what might be called the 'check-list approach'. Judges tend to run through a list of possible approaches and arguments, and feel most secure when each approach yields the same answer or at least does not disturb the overall cohesion. One might call this facetiously 'arguing your cake and eating it too'. The check-list approach is not a formal model of legal reasoning, given that lawyers are accustomed to arguing 'in the alternative'. This is where arguments take the following form: There is no cause to apply *Pepper v Hart* and consult the debates in the legislature; but, in the alternative, applying *Pepper v Hart* would not in any case have affected the outcome of the case.

The Court of Appeal found that the definition of *poultry* given in the Public Health (Animals and Birds) Ordinance was not relevant. This removed one of the secondary pillars holding up the High Court judgment, but had no impact on the decision. Dictionaries were not consulted (or at least not cited), presumably because of the presence of statutory definitions. In addition, the uncertainty (to the extent that there was any) was understood to arise not from the question of whether racing pigeons were *pigeons*, but rather from a doubt about the intent and scope of the law.

In this case we have a number of sources of authority and interpretative strategies which yield YES, NO, NEUTRAL or UNCERTAIN in relation to the verdict:

- Statutory definition: *pigeon* is a sub-category of *poultry* which is a sub-category of *livestock* = YES.
- Ordinary and natural meaning (literal rule): a racing pigeon is a *pigeon* = YES.
- Definition from another statute: *poultry* includes *pigeon* = YES.
- Other jurisdictions, especially England and Wales: no complete and authoritative definition of *poultry* found which might be a contrary authority = NEUTRAL.
- Science: racing pigeons like domestic pigeons fell under the category of *Columbidae* = YES.
- The 'golden rule' or the 'absurd result' test: in categorizing racing pigeons as *poultry* no bizarre, immoral or absurd result is produced = YES.

- The 'mischief rule': the law was concerned the regulation of the keeping of certain animals and with the problem of animal waste = YES.
- External aids in the form of history: the background to the enactment in the regulation of agricultural activity in urban areas = NEUTRAL.
- External aids under *Pepper v Hart* (discussions in the legislature): these were not relevant as the case was not problematic, but in any case these would not have served the plaintiff's case = NEUTRAL/YES.
- Social consequences, hardship to the affected party: the raising of the limit to 20 alleviated the consequences somewhat = NEUTRAL but it made the decision more palatable.

The following points were not explicitly explored:

- (Strong, Denning-style) purposive approach = UNCERTAIN.
- Ordinary and natural meaning: is a racing pigeon *poultry*? = UNCERTAIN/ NO.
- Ordinary and natural meaning: is a racing pigeon *livestock*? = NO.

The statute creates its own relationships between (the meanings of) words, in particular when it includes definitions or illustrations of categories. This interpretative approach assumes categories that are like the Russian doll: each larger doll fully encloses or contains the smaller; a category [A] is defined by its sub-categories [A = a, b, c, …] which are in turn defined by further sub-sub-categories [a = i, ii, ii, iii]. Thus [iii] falls under [a] which is under [A]. On the logic of this model it makes no sense to say that [i] belongs to category [a] but falls outside [A]. But in 'ordinary and natural' speech we would not generally say that racing pigeons are *poultry*, still less that they are a form of *livestock*. How is it possible that in ordinary speech racing pigeons are *pigeons*, pigeons are *poultry*, and poultry is *livestock*, but racing pigeons are not *livestock*? Linguistic categories arguably do not function in this neat and tidy 'Russian doll' way, though it is of course open to law to stipulate that they do.

Points for further consideration

This case concerns relations of inclusion between categories in a hierarchy (hyponymy). One way to read this decision is that the legal categories were preferred over the functional distinction between animals *bred for food* and those *bred for sport*. But this still leaves the question of what it is that makes a racing pigeon a kind of *pigeon*. Is it the ordinary language category *pigeon*, or the scientific classification or both? Let us imagine that there was no term *racing pigeon* in English, but just *homer* ('homing pigeon'). The Hong Kong Homer Association would have been the plaintiff in this case. Would the court then have needed to argue more directly about the intention behind the statute, or the status of the scientific classification *Columbidae*, rather than following the apparent logic of the linguistic categories?

CHAPTER 5

Characterizing an Event

Were two deaths in the same incident *coinciding*?

Re Rowland (1963)	Husband and wife were on a ship that sank	coinciding	'preceding or coinciding with my own decease'	The deaths were not coinciding

Re Rowland (1963) (Court of Appeal)

In 1956, by a will made on a printed form, Dr Rowland left all his estate to his wife; but in the event of her death 'preceding or coinciding with my own decease', his estate was to be given to his brother and to his infant nephew. The husband and wife left England, as Dr Rowland had an appointment in the South Pacific Health Service. On 9 July 1958 they were passengers on a small ship that sank while travelling between the British Solomon Islands. There were no survivors. Some wreckage and one body were found, but the exact circumstances and date of the accident were unknown. A commission of inquiry into the sinking noted that 'the only body that was recovered had died, not from drowning, but from some other cause, such as death through loss of blood from being eaten by fish'. Nonetheless, the conclusion of the commission was that the ship sank suddenly, since no other body was recovered, very little wreckage was from below decks and various pieces of equipment had been subject to strong pressure.

At issue was who was to inherit under Dr Rowland's will. There were two possibilities: the estate of the wife, or Dr Rowland's closest relatives, a brother and nephew. The Court of Appeal concluded that the deaths of the husband and wife did not coincide. Dr Rowland's estate passed to his wife's estate, with the consequence that the wife's niece became entitled to it. Section 184 of the Law of Property Act 1925 required that in cases of doubt the assumption (or legal fiction) would be applied, namely, that the wife, being the younger, had survived her husband. The husband's brother and nephew appealed.

This case staged a classic confrontation between the advocate of purposive adjudication, Lord Denning (the Master of the Rolls), and Russell LJ, who defended a strict literalist reading of the text of the will. The onus (the burden of proof 'on the balance of the probabilities') was on the appellants (the relatives of Dr Rowland) to show that the deaths were coincident. Otherwise the provision of the Law of Property Act would take effect. Lord Denning engaged in an act of imaginative reconstruction, putting himself in the testator's position. Russell LJ rejected this approach, saying that the court should respect the language of the will and not read into it any special circumstances or background assumptions about what the testator might or might not have had in mind.

Lord Denning (at 8–11) contrasted two possible approaches to the case. The first was to begin with the 'ordinary and grammatical meaning' of *coincide*. The answer would be plain that it meant 'coincident in point of time', which would be equivalent to 'simultaneous' or 'at the same point of time'. From considering the meaning of the word *coincide* one would turn to the word 'simultaneous', 'and at that point you come upon a difficulty because, strictly speaking, no two people ever die at exactly the same point of time'. This meant that giving *coincide* its 'ordinary and grammatical meaning' would give rise to an 'absurdity'. To those who invoked this argument in the name of the 'ordinary man', Lord Denning retorted that the ordinary man would 'be amazed to find such a view attributed to him'. To argue this way was to start 'from the wrong place', that is, with assumption that, in construing a will, the question was 'not what the testator meant' but 'the meaning of his words'. This led to judges interpreting the will according to the words the testator had used, even if they believed that the result was 'contrary to the true intention of the testator'.

For Lord Denning the task of the judge, in a case where there was uncertainty about the meaning of words, was to find the testator's intended meaning, 'not the meaning which a philologist would put upon them'. There was no guidance to be found in a dictionary, even supposing that the testator consulted the same one as the judge: 'What you should do is to place yourself as far as possible in his position, taking note of the facts and circumstances known to him at the time: and then say what he meant by his words.' The question was not what the words might mean to a 'grammarian', but rather 'What did Dr Rowland and his wife mean by the word "coincide" in their wills?' In Lord Denning's view, the lower court's judgment was mistaken, and the deaths had indeed coincided.

Lord Denning's judgment (at 10) conjured up the 'ghosts of dissatisfied testators' who 'wait on the other bank of the Styx to receive the judicial personages who have misconstrued their wills'. He was citing Lord Atkin in *Perrin v Morgan* ((1943) at 406), who in turn referred to an unnamed 'late Chancery judge'. At issue in *Perrin* was whether the phrase *all monies* referred to the whole of the estate or just a specific part (see Chapter 3).

Russell LJ (at 15–19) took the context, given that the word *preceding* was used in the key phrase in the will, to be one referring to time. The meaning in question was 'coinciding in point of time', not any other kind of coincidence, such as 'the type and cause of death'. The moment of death was the 'matter of a moment'. In its 'normal and natural meaning', 'coinciding' involved 'some broad conception of overlapping or of occurring within a particular period'. It meant 'simultaneous', as in *Re Pringle* (1946). The suggestion had been made that the testator meant something wider than the natural meaning, that is, 'on the same occasion and by the same cause'. It had been argued that the will had been drawn up in contemplation of the move to the Pacific and this kind of episode would have been in the mind of the testator. But none of this was persuasive. The phrase meant the same regardless of

> whether the testator and his wife travel daily between Sussex and London by the same train or car or coach, or sail at Cowes together, or are doctors in a fever-ridden area, or missionaries among cannibals, or live on the slopes of Mount Etna, or simply live quietly under the shadow of nuclear warfare. (at 18)

The Court of Appeal upheld the decision of the lower court, and Dr Rowland's estate went to his wife's relatives.

Key points in Russell LJ's judgment

- The legally relevant meaning was 'coinciding in point of time', not death through the same cause or in the same incident.
- This was shown by the use of another temporal phrase, *preceding*, in the will.
- The normal and natural meaning of *coinciding* concerned a relationship in time.
- The will and its key phrase should be read in the same manner, regardless of the place of residence, lifestyle or level of risk of the testator.
- In the absence of certain evidence to the effect that the deaths coincided, s. 184 of the Law of Property Act 1925 applied.

Discussion: public outrage

The decision generated a good deal of public controversy. A series of letters to *The Times* give the flavour of the discussions. A letter dated 30 May, 1962 noted that Lord Denning had declared that the ordinary man would be amazed at the view attributed to him. The letter writer (a Mr I.S. Grant) added: 'He certainly is'. The judgment was symptomatic of the gap between ordinary common sense and legalistic quibbling: 'It is alarming to find a legalistic quibble of this nature having weight in the Court of Appeal.' This bought a repost (A.T. MacMillan, 2 June) which pointed out that it was Parliament that had passed the provision of the Law of Property Act that the court had invoked: 'Mr Grant's letter shows the danger of laymen rushing in – a danger which all who have practised law, as professionals, constantly meet'. A second letter published on the same day was from a self-described 'ordinary woman', who expressed her amazement at the judgment. On 11 June, a further letter reported the views of a number of people, including lawyers, to the effect that the judgment was 'against all common sense': 'The average layman believes that law is made for lawyers, and this belief will be confirmed by the arrogance of Mr A.T. MacMillan's letter'.

Academic commentary has also been divided, with Albery (1963: 362) concluding that 'the decision in *Re Rowland*, despite the storm of popular protest, appears to have been plainly right in law'. However, a more recent commentator took it as self-evident that Lord Denning was right: 'Few now could disagree with [the] dissenting judgment in *Re Rowland*' (Gage, 1980: 195). The legal dilemma this case represents is set out and analyzed in Greenawalt (2010: 232–38).

The case involved a conflict between literal and purposive approaches to interpretation, but was also framed, as the letters to *The Times* show, as a battle between common sense and legal sophistry. Behind this case is a clash between two jurisprudential positions. The first argues that law needs to be grounded as far as possible in the society in which law is embedded, and that if it diverges too radically from widespread intuitions about what words mean and popular notions of justice, its legitimacy is undermined. The second takes law as an autonomous, rigorously consistent arbitration system that is external to mainstream society. On this view, the alienation of law from everyday categories and commonsense justice is precisely what underwrites law's foundational role in society. The unyielding, literal-minded face of law as it confronts social conflicts ensures that law is not simply a party to those conflicts, or is not drawn into taking positions on the basis of what is popular or expedient. While the first view might be seen as democratic in its instincts, it verges on populism, with its threat of the tyranny of the majority, the enemy of the rule of law as classically understood. The main objection to the second position is that law cannot in practice remove itself convincingly from social conflicts by entering a neutral space of adjudication.

Points for further consideration

One might understand the difference between Lord Denning and Russell LJ as follows: Lord Denning makes a retrospective reconstruction of the testator's intention, taking into account what actually happened; Russell LJ refuses to imagine the testator's view when faced with the actual circumstances of the death. The weakness of Lord Denning's position is that intention must always be inferred. Once we are confronted with a particular set of circumstances, that inference is inevitably shaped by the contingent facts of what has actually happened. Watkins (2012: 62) sees this decision as a silencing of the testator's voice by the 'imposition of legal doctrine'. Greenawalt (2012: 238) picks up Baron's (1992: 632) argument that the focus on word meaning in the interpretation of wills is misplaced and that they 'ought to be, but are not, understood as stories'. It is not clear how legal storytelling might work in practice (see Farber and Sherry, 1994). In terms of storytelling, one might see Lord Denning giving voice to the testator, and Russell LJ as giving voice to the stringency of law. But Lord Denning's act of imaginative reconstruction might, in another set of circumstances, seem like an inauthentic appropriation.

CHAPTER 6

The Classification of Mundane Objects I: Food Items in United Kingdom Tax Law

Is a Jaffa Cake a *biscuit*?

United Biscuits (UK) Ltd v Commissioners of Customs and Excise (1991)	Jaffa Cake	Biscuit	'biscuits covered with chocolate or chocolate substitute' (Value Added Tax Act 1983, s. 15, Sch. 5, Group 1)	Jaffa Cakes were cakes

United Biscuits (UK) Ltd v Commissioners of Customs and Excise (1991) (UK Tax Tribunal)

This case generated a great deal of public comment and media excitement in the United Kingdom, not least because the Jaffa Cake is a familiar companion to the national cup of tea. It was described in the judgment as having three elements (para. 5ii):

a small round of sponge cake, soft when fresh; on that is a small dab of sweet orange jam; the whole covered by a thin layer of dark, brittle chocolate; in volume the greater part is sponge cake; the taste is mainly of jam and chocolate.

The tax authorities determined that Jaffa Cakes, previously zero-rated, were a sub-class of *confectionary*, namely 'biscuits covered with chocolate or chocolate substitute', and as such were liable to the standard rate of tax (value added tax or VAT; see Table 6.1 below). If they were not biscuits, they were

Table 6.1 Summary of VAT ratings of food

Food	Zero-rated
Food of a kind used for human consumption	Zero-rated
Except: Confectionary (defined as chocolates, sweets and biscuits; drained glacé of crystallized fruits; and any item of sweetened prepared food which is normally eaten with the fingers)	Standard-rated
Cakes or biscuits	Zero-rated
Except: Biscuits wholly or partly covered with chocolate or with some product similar in taste and appearance	Standard-rated

in any case *confectionary* and did not fall into the exempt category *cake*. It was agreed between the parties that Jaffa Cakes were *confectionary*, so the dispute came down to 'cake or non-cake'. If they were *cake* they would be zero-rated. Since Jaffa Cakes were evidently 'wholly or partly' covered in chocolate, a finding that they were biscuits would lead to a 'standard-rated' status (para. 5ii).

The judge (Mr D.C. Potter, QC) saw the task as two-fold: (i) 'to consider the true construction of the statutory provisions'; and (ii) to determine 'as a question of fact and degree' whether Jaffa Cakes fell 'within the statutory wording, especially the word "cakes"' (para. 5ii). The classification of Jaffa Cakes for the purposes of import tariffs or purchase tax was not relevant. He rejected the use of 'purposive interpretation', citing from *John Pimblett and Sons Limited v Customs and Excise Commissioners* (1988): 'It is a first principle of revenue law that the subject should only be taxed by clear words, and it is impermissible to look at the substance or to imply or read in anything' (at 361). It was for the party claiming exemption to show that its case 'fell clearly into the words of the statute' (*Maughan v The Free Church of Scotland* (1893) at 210). The Tribunal should give the word *cake* its 'ordinary meaning'; assistance might be drawn from 'statistical evidence as to the views of ordinary shoppers, evidence as to the method of manufacture of cakes and of other confectionary such as biscuits, and the opinions of experts'. The standard was that of the ordinary person who had acquired some reasonable understanding of the 'manufacture, ingredients and other features' that went beyond the impression of the 'casual purchaser'. The judge discounted the results of market research and expert evidence which, 'although skilled', went 'beyond the capacity of the ordinary purchaser'. A video that showed how Jaffa Cakes were advertised on television was not accorded any weight. The judge stated that he had 'gained no help from dictionaries', and he could perceive 'no clear demarcation' in 'common language' between *cake* and *biscuit*: 'The same product could be capable of being both cake and biscuit, in my view'. The wording imposed 'no clear dividing line between cake and biscuit' and 'a product which is a biscuit (whether or not covered in chocolate) is capable of being also a cake'.

The final section of the judgment set out the relevant facts and considerations (para. 5ii, 1–11). Table 6.2 contains an interpretative analysis of the decision; it should be noted that not all the terms in the table are those used by the judge. The third column represents the likely opinion of the judge, based on the factor identified. Where '(CAKE)' is shown in the third column, it means that this factor weakly favours the category *cake*.

If this were decided by a vote, then of the 11 factors identified by the judge, five seem to favour *biscuit*, four favour *cake*. The two minor or incidental factors, the name and the nature of the batter, both favoured *cake*. However, the judge did not follow this approach, concluding that 'Jaffa Cakes have characteristics of cakes, and also characteristics of biscuits or non-cakes'. Without further analysis it was determined that Jaffa Cakes had 'sufficient characteristics of cakes to qualify as cakes'; Jaffa Cakes were also not biscuits.

Table 6.2 A break-down of the *Jaffa cake* decision

	Factor	Comment	CAKE-like or BISCUIT-like?
1.	Name	No serious relevance	NEUTRAL (CAKE)
2.	Ingredients	Cake types vary; the sponge in the Jaffa Cake had very similar ingredients to sponge cake	CAKE
3.	Physical texture	Cakes are mainly soft or friable [easily crumbled], not able to be snapped, not crisp	CAKE
4.	Size	Jaffa Cakes are smaller than the average cake, the size of a typical biscuit	BISCUIT
5.	Packaging	Jaffa Cakes are sold in cylindrical packages within cardboard boxes – 'un-cake-like'	BISCUIT
6.	Marketing	Generally sold with biscuits in supermarkets	BISCUIT
7.	Make-up of sponge part	Cake has thin batter containing egg, flour and sugar, which can be moulded, whereas biscuits made from a rather thicker mixture, which is cut ('not an important factor')	NEUTRAL (CAKE)
8.	Aging process	Jaffa Cakes begin moist and end up stale, then hard; biscuits when stale become soft	CAKE
9.	Presentation	As snacks, ordinarily eaten with the fingers; cake normally eaten from a plate, sometimes with a knife or pastry fork	BISCUIT
10.	Appeal	Especially to children, who consume them in one or two mouthfuls, more like a biscuit or sweet	BISCUIT
11.	Composition in terms of cake	The sponge cake part is not merely a base, it is 'a substantial part of the product, not in flavour, but in bulk and texture when eaten'	CAKE

Key points in the judgment

- The case involved the ordinary meaning of *cake* from the ordinary person's point of view.
- The party seeking exemption had to show that the product fell clearly within the definition in the statute.
- The standard was that of the ordinary person who had acquired some acquaintance with the facts beyond that of a casual shopper.
- External evidence might be relevant, but not that of market research or skilled experts, nor evidence of how the product was advertised.
- In a list of factors, Jaffa Cakes shared some features with cakes and others with biscuits.
- Jaffa Cakes were sufficiently cake-like to qualify as cakes and were not biscuits.

Discussion

Put in the simplest terms, the judgment involved a choice between the essential 'cake-likeness' of Jaffa Cakes, their being made primarily of sponge-cake material, and their more 'biscuit-like' social profile, in terms of packaging, size and appearance, and consumption patterns. This set the materiality of the object in question, its physical being, against the multifaceted and open-ended nature of its profile, its social being. In deciding that Jaffa Cakes were biscuit-like cakes, rather than cake-like biscuits, the judge seems to have given priority to the solidity and apparent objectivity of physical being as opposed to the less tangible social being. The decision was applied in *Asda Stores Ltd v Commissioners for Her Majesty's Revenue and Customs* (2009).

Are (Regular) Pringles similar to *potato crisps*?

Commissioners for Her Majesty's Revenue & Customs v Procter & Gamble UK (2009)	(Regular) Pringles	Potato crisps (US = 'potato chips')	'similar to potato crisps and made from the potato' (Value Added Tax Act 1994, Sch. 8, Group 1, Item 5)	Pringles are similar to potato crisps and made from potato

Proctor & Gamble (UK) v Commissioners for HMRC (2007) (Tribunal)

Pringles are a well-known snack food, somewhat like *potato crisps* (or *potato chips* in the US). Potato crisps and similar products are subject to value added tax (VAT) in the United Kingdom, whereas, in general, other food products are not. Under Sch. 8, Group 1 (item 5), the following were *not* exempt 'when packaged for human consumption without further preparation':

> potato crisps, potato sticks, potato puffs and similar products made from the potato, or from potato flour, or from potato starch […]

The tax authorities determined that Pringles were of the same class as potato crisps; this decision was upheld after an internal review. The manufacturer, Proctor & Gamble, challenged this decision before the Tax Tribunal, arguing that Pringles were not similar to the *potato crisp* and therefore should be zero-rated.

The Tax Tribunal (VAT and Duties) made a number of findings of fact. Regular Pringles were made of 'potato flour, corn flour, wheat starch and rice flour together with fat and emulsifier, salt and seasoning' (para. 5(2)). Potato flour made up approximately 42%, with other flours at around 15%; the fat content was 33%. The manufacturing process of Pringles was different from that of crisps, since oil entered the spaces in the texture of the product, thereby 'replacing the water content removed during the frying'. This gave the 'mouth-melt' feel. With potato crisps, by contrast, 'most of the fat stays on the surface' (para. 5(4)).

In terms of shape and appearance, Pringles were manufactured to have 'a regular shape in the form of a saddle', and had 'a uniform pale yellow colour, which is paler than a potato crisp' and 'a crisp texture' (para. 5(5)). They were 'normally eaten in the evening, for example in front of the television or with

drinks with friends and not as part of a meal'. They were 'not normally pur-
chased primarily for nutrition' (para. 5(10)).

Proctor & Gamble (para. 6(1–6)) argued that Regular Pringles were not
similar to potato crisps. Pringles differed 'on the grounds of regularity of
shape, having a shape not found in nature, uniform colouring, texture, taste
particularly "mouth-melt"'. Unlike Pringles, potato crisps did not contain
other non-potato kinds of flour and were not normally packaged in tubes.
None of the ingredients of Regular Pringles made up over 50%; customers did
not see Regular Pringles as potato crisps. The Tribunal in the Pringle Dippers
case (*Proctor & Gamble (UK)* (2003)), which had found that Pringle Dippers
were not 'made from potato', had taken the correct approach. The World
Customs Organization categorized Regular Pringles 'with other savoury
snacks and separately from potato crisps'.

Counsel for the tax authorities (para. 7(1–4)) rejected the Pringle
Dippers decision and its conclusion that the product, to be taxed at the
standard rate, should be wholly or substantially made from potato (para.
10). No potato product could be made entirely out of potato, so there had
been no need for Parliament to use the term 'partly made', and nothing
could be inferred from the fact that this phrase had not been used. There
were strong parallels in terms of shape, texture and consumption patterns
between Pringles and potato crisps. The Tribunal reviewed the history of
the legislation, noting that Parliament had intended to tax food not normally consumed for 'nutrition' but rather eaten as a snack. The legislation
imposed a double test: *mischief*

(a) whether the product was similar to potato crisps, potato sticks or potato
    puffs; and
(b) whether it was made from potato, or from potato flour or potato starch.

The correct approach was that laid out in *Customs and Excise Commissioners v
Quaker Oats Ltd* (1987), namely, to adopt the view of 'the ordinary reasonable
man in the street'. This meant taking into account 'appearance, taste, ingredients, process of manufacture, marketing and packaging' (para. 11). In the
Pringle Dippers case, a differently constituted Tribunal had taken 'the ingredients as the most important, the size of packaging, marketing for dipping,
manufacture, appearance and taste apparently in that order (or at least taking
the first three as the most important in that order)' (at 14).

However, the present Tribunal declined to list factors in order of importance. The 'reasonable man' approach involved applying 'the test as a whole
without applying an order'. It did, however, conclude that the shape was not
of especial importance, given the wide range of products available, nor was the
packaging (para. 14):

> While potato crisps may primarily be sold in smaller packs, they are often
> sold in larger packs, and occasionally in tubes, and a smaller proportion of
> Regular Pringles are sold in smaller packs.

The potato content of potato crisps was about 70%, as against approximately 42% in the case of Pringles. However, the reasonable man 'may not be aware of the fact' as this was not stated on the packaging. The decision was summed up as follows (para. 15):

> Standing back and taking all the factors of appearance, taste, ingredients, process of manufacture, marketing and packaging together (other than the ones we have stated above that we should ignore) and applying the reasonable man test in test (a), we consider that while in many respects Regular Pringles are different from potato crisps and so they are near the borderline, they are sufficiently similar to satisfy that test.

On the question of the potato content of Regular Pringles, the Tribunal offered this analysis (at 17):

> Here the potato flour content is over 40 per cent; it is the largest single ingredient by about 9 percentage points; and it is nearly three times larger than the other flours in the ingredients taken together. We have to give a yes or no answer to the question 'are Regular Pringles [partly] made from the potato, from potato flour or from potato starch' and we are bound to say yes. There are other ingredients but it is made from potato flour in the sense that one cannot say that it is not made from potato flour, and the proportion of potato flour is significant being over 40 per cent. The fact that it is also made from other things does not affect this.

The Tribunal ruled that Regular Pringles snacks were not exempt foods and therefore were subject to standard rates of VAT.

Commissioners for HMRC v Procter & Gamble UK (2008) (High Court)

The decision of the Tribunal was appealed. The High Court understood the Tribunal to have imposed a two-part test, that is, as having decided that the product had to satisfy both parts ('limbs') of the regulation. These were: (limb 1) 'potato crisps, potato sticks, potato puffs and similar products made from the potato'; and (limb 2) 'or from potato flour, or from potato starch'. The Tribunal had determined that Pringles were similar products to potato crisps (limb 1), and in being 'partly' constituted of potato flour were deemed to be 'made from the potato' (limb 2). However, the High Court argued that while each limb informed the other, the test should be construed as a whole. The word *potato* was used in both limbs of the rule and the meaning of 'made from' was a question of law, that is, the meaning of that phrase could not be inferred from its ordinary meaning. The question was 'whether the product was wholly or substantially made from potato, potato flour, or potato starch'. Products such as potato crisps, potato sticks and potato puffs were made primarily of potato and nothing else of relevance:

> The use of the word potato in both limbs of Item 5 reflected the need for the similar products in the second limb to be comprised of potato in a way

that corresponded to the way the potato was comprised in the three products in the first limb.

If this approach was applied, Regular Pringles were not 'made from' potato. They were not 'wholly or substantially' made from potato, as this would be understood in the context of the examples provided in the statute. The only alternative approach would be to ask first whether the product was 'wholly or substantially made from potato, potato flour, or potato starch'. If the answer was yes, other factors would then be used to assess similarity. Those factors

> might include the ingredients, marketing, manufacture, packaging and appearance, but would not include the quantity of potato in the product, as that factor would have been exhausted when considering whether it was wholly or partly made from potato […]

The Tribunal's decision was reversed.

Commissioners for HMRC v Procter & Gamble UK (2009) (Court of Appeal)

The tax authorities appealed. The Court of Appeal (lead judgment by Jacob LJ) stressed that the Tribunal was the original finder of fact and able to survey the question in all its nuances. The original decision should not be overturned, unless there had been a clear legal error, in particular as the Tribunal was a specialist one (paras 7, 11). The question was not one for high theory. As a matter of classification it did not call for 'over-elaborate, almost mind-numbing legal analysis', rather it was 'a short practical question calling for a short practical answer' (para. 14). The Court of Appeal saw nothing to criticize in the reasoning of the Tribunal. Rejecting the position taken in the High Court, the judgment argued that the use of overall impression was fully justified. It was not required that the Tribunal identify and weigh each factor as if 'using a real scientist's balance' (para. 19). Following *Customs and Excise Commissioners v Quaker Oats Ltd* (1987) and *Customs and Excise Commissioners v Ferrero* (1997), the use of the reasonable man approach implied adopting 'what view would be taken by the ordinary man in the street who had been informed as we have been informed', and the 'uninformed view of the man in the street is deliberately not being invoked'. In the end this amounted simply to adopting 'the reasonable view on the basis of all the facts' (paras 20, 21). The question was one of degree and 'multifactorial assessment' – the potato content should be included in any discussion of similarity (para. 24).

As to the scope of *made from*, Proctor & Gamble had argued that Parliament could have used language such as 'wholly or partly', had there been the intention to include Pringles along with potato crisps. This, it was argued, would have made the matter clear, as with the wording: 'cakes or biscuits other than biscuits wholly or partly covered with chocolate' (Sch. 8, Pt 2, item 2). The Court found this argument to be without merit (para. 26). The point about *wholly or partly* would imply that a marmalade made using both oranges and grapefruit would be made of neither (para. 27). Proctor & Gamble had argued that if a product had 'a number of significant ingredients', it 'cannot be said to be "made from" one of them' (cited para. 78). None of the foods in question was 100% potato, so it was 'improbable that Parliament intended that a product, to be similar' should be 100% potato (para. 28). Further, Parliament might just as well have said 'wholly' – it was unreasonable to expect an elaborate consistency between Schedules.

Counsel had urged the Court to define a lower limit to *potatoness*. But there was no particular limit or threshold percentage to determine this. The 'Aristotelian question' of whether the product was in its essence *potato* was an 'elusive test' without clear criteria, and this could not have been intended by Parliament. In this context, Justice Holmes had written the following (para. 32):

> When he has discovered that a difference is difference of degree, that distinguished extremes have between them a penumbra in which one gradually shades into the other, a tyro [beginner, novice] thinks to puzzle you by asking you where you are going to draw the line and an advocate of more experience will show the arbitrariness of the line proposed by putting cases very near it on one side or the other. (Holmes, [1899] 1920: 232–33)

This could be reduced to 'you do not have to know where the precise line is to decide whether something is one side or the other' (para. 32). The Court of Appeal rejected the idea that an elaborate test or complex analysis was required. At issue was the kind of question one could put to a jury, that is, 'is it similar to a potato crisp etc. and made of potato?' (para. 35)

Toulson LJ concurred. The Tribunal had applied 'a fair and natural meaning' (para. 58). Mummery LJ noted that 'similar to' and 'made from' were 'loose textured concepts for the classification of the goods'. The legal argument about *wholly* or *substantially* had drifted from the statutory language that did not include these terms (para. 73). The Tribunal had not been asked to settle 'a scientific or technical question about the composition of Regular Pringles' or respond to a 'request for a recipe'. It was required to decide whether the goods were entitled to a zero rating (at 79):

> On this point the VAT legislation uses everyday English words, which ought to be interpreted in a sensible way according to their ordinary and natural meaning. The 'made from' question would probably be answered in a more relevant and sensible way by a child consumer of crisps than by a food scientist or a culinary pedant. On another aspect of party food I think that most children, if asked whether jellies with raspberries in them were 'made from' jelly, would have the good sense to say 'Yes', despite the raspberries.

The original decision of the Tribunal was restored.

Table 6.3 Summary of decisions in the *Pringles* case

Decision-making body	Were Regular Pringles liable for tax (VAT) in that they were similar to potato crisps?
Assessor of Her Majesty's Revenue and Customs (HMRC)	Yes
Internal review by HMRC	Yes
Tax Tribunal (VAT)	Yes
High Court	No
Court of Appeal	Yes

Key points of the Court of Appeal judgment

- The findings of the specialist Tribunal as to a question of fact should not be disturbed unless there had been a clear error in law.
- The decision in the Pringles Dippers case was not binding on the Tribunal, which was entitled to take a multifactorial approach.
- The Tribunal had taken a reasonable approach when it determined that the potato content of regular Pringles was substantial, and had concluded overall that the products showed sufficient similarity.
- There was no requirement that the food product be close to 100% potato.
- This was not a technical question for abstruse legal, culinary or scientific analysis, rather one for the informed reasonable man, based on all the facts and with the words of the legislation understood in their ordinary and natural meaning.
- A child consumer of crisps would be in the best position to give a relevant and sensible answer, and such a child would likely say that raspberry jellies were 'made from' jelly, the presence of raspberry notwithstanding.

Discussion

The Court of Appeal firmly rejected the use of complex strategies of interpretation and refused to be drawn on the exact percentage of potato that would be required for a product to be characterized as essentially potato or possessing the quality of *potatoness*. It rejected both an approach based on Aristotelian essences and one that sought to draw analogies in wording between one Schedule and another. When counsel for Proctor & Gamble pointed out that Parliament could have used the phrase 'wholly or partly' if it wished to include Pringles, as it had elsewhere, this was dismissed as an 'advocate-type point' (para. 26). The cases contain considerable discussion of how the two limbs of the rule ('the potato crisps, potato sticks, potato puffs and similar products made from the potato, or from potato flour, or from potato starch') should be read. The insistence on adopting a non-technical commonsense point of view reaches its logical conclusion when the reasonable person, who knows what the Tribunal knows, is replaced by the (reasonable?) child consumer at a party who could answer this question in a more relevant way than a 'food scientist' or a 'culinary pedant'. The decision was applied in *United Biscuits (UK) Ltd v Commissioners for Her Majesty's Revenue and Customs* (2011).

Points for further consideration

In the Jaffa Cake case, the decision gave priority to the intrinsic qualities, the essential 'cake-like' make-up of the Jaffa Cake, over its more 'biscuit-like' patterns of consumption and social profile, including its shape and size. In the Pringles case, given that the product contained potato as a major although not majority ingredient, it seems that patterns of consumption and social profile, including the size (the shape was a more ambiguous issue), were the decisive factors. Both decisions laid stress on the ordinary consumer's point of view, though this was particularly evident in the Pringles decision; neither was much concerned with the ordinary meaning or dictionary definitions of the terms *cake, biscuit, crisps.* The Court of Appeal judgment raised implicitly the question of why it took five levels of determination, three of them by judicial bodies, to decide that Pringles were similar to potato crisps. If the question is simply the one that would be put to a jury, then is a lay panel not the logical source of factual authority in tax classification cases such as these?

CHAPTER 7

The Classification of Mundane Objects II: Cases from the United States

Is a tomato a *vegetable* or a *fruit*?

Nix v Hedden (1893)	Tomato	Vegetable	The Tariff Act of March 3, 1886, imposed a duty on the import of 'vegetables in their natural state, or in salt or brine, not specially enumerated or provided for in this act' (c. 121, Sch. G. Provisions)	Tomatoes are vegetables

Nix v Hedden (1893) (US Supreme Court)

The Nix family's import business paid duty on tomatoes brought into the port of New York from the West Indies. Tomatoes were classified as *vegetables* rather than as *fruit*, and *fruit* was exempt under the Tariff Act (1886). The Nixes sought a declaration that tomatoes were *fruit* not *vegetables*. The case report makes somewhat unusual reading, as the original trial seems to have consisted primarily in counsel firing dictionary definitions back and forth across the courtroom floor. Counsel for the Nix family read out definitions of *fruit*, *vegetable* and *tomato*. Witnesses from the fruit and vegetable trade were asked if the words had 'any special meaning in trade or commerce, different from those read'. For the authorities, counsel presented *pea*, *egg plant*, *cucumber*, *squash*, and *pepper*. These were countered with *potato*, *turnip*, *parsnip*, *cauliflower*, *cabbage*, *carrot* and *bean*. The dictionaries mentioned in the case report were Webster's, Worcester's, and the *Imperial Dictionary*. Witnesses basically affirmed that the words *fruit* and *vegetable* had no special meaning in the trade, that the definitions given in dictionaries were correct as far as they went, and that the terms *fruit* and *vegetables* had not changed their meaning since 1 March 1883 when the Act was passed (at 305–07).

In the Supreme Court, Justice Gray noted that the dictionary passages defined *fruit* as 'the seed of plants, or that part of plants which contains the seed, and especially the juicy, pulpy products of certain plants covering and containing the seed'. These definitions did not support the idea that tomatoes were *fruit* in 'common speech' or within the meaning of Act. In the absence of evidence of a special meaning within the trade or commercial sector, words 'must receive their ordinary meaning' (at 306). Dictionaries were not the final authority (at 306–07):

> Of that [ordinary] meaning the court is bound to take judicial notice, as it does in regard to all words in our own tongue, and upon such a question dictionaries are admitted not as evidence, but only as aids to the memory and understanding of the court.

In terms of botany, tomatoes were 'the fruit of the vine', as were cucumbers, squashes, beans, and peas. But 'in the common language of the people', vegetables were produce 'grown in kitchen gardens'. Whether consumed cooked or raw, they were akin to

> potatoes, carrots, parsnips, turnips, beets, cauliflower, cabbage, celery, and lettuce, usually served at dinner in, with, or after the soup, fish, or meats which constitute the principal part of the repast, and not, like fruits generally, as dessert. (at 307)

The Judge observed that the same argument had been proposed in the case of *Robertson v Salomon* (1889), a case about whether beans were *seeds*. It had been held that the classification used in the relevant trade or in everyday speech ('common parlance') should be followed, rather than that of botany or natural history:

> We do not see why they [beans] should be classified as seeds any more than walnuts should be so classified. Both are seeds, in the language of botany or natural history, but not in commerce nor in common parlance. On the other hand, in speaking generally of provisions, beans may well be included under the term 'vegetables.' As an article of food on our tables, whether baked or boiled, or forming the basis of soup, they are used as a vegetable, as well when ripe as when green. This is the principal use to which they are put. Beyond the common knowledge which we have on this subject, very little evidence is necessary or can be produced. (*Robertson v Salomon* (1889) at 414, cited at 307)

The Supreme Court held unanimously that tomatoes were *vegetables* for the purposes of the Tariff Act.

Key points in the judgment

- Trade usage and popular usage did not materially differ as to the meanings of words like *tomato, vegetable, fruit.*
- Dictionary definitions did not support the idea that tomatoes were *fruit*; such definitions were not in any case evidence, but rather aids to memory and understanding.
- In terms of ordinary meaning, tomatoes were *vegetables.*

- The pattern of consumption of tomatoes showed that they were *vegetables*, even though botanical classification was at odds with this.
- Given that trade usage did not differ from common usage, the words in the Act should be given their ordinary meaning.

Discussion

The key point was that there was no special meaning attached to *fruit* or *vegetable* within the trade. It is not clear whether, had importers categorized tomatoes as *fruit* in their negotiations and discussions, this would have been decisive. The decision is read as an assertion of the primacy of everyday or popular categories over the classification of botany. Aprill (1998: 313) notes that the decision does not equate ordinary and dictionary meaning: 'quite to the contrary, the two are in direct opposition, with the dictionary using a technical rather than a common meaning'.

One commentator, looking at this and similar cases, came to this conclusion about the general mode of proceeding ([CJR] 1927: 25–26):

> The rule seems to be this: whenever a word is capable of being given two or more interpretations, that interpretation will always govern which, from the evidence introduced, would seem to be generally accepted by persons of the same occupation, interests, or education of the litigants. If the popular usage of a word be opposed to the scientific definition the former will nevertheless obtain whenever the word was employed with reference to people who generally follow the popular usage.

A slightly different formulation is as follows:

> But in the case of tariff laws it has been held that in imposing duties the Legislature must be understood as describing the articles upon which the duty is imposed according to the commercial understanding, in the markets of the country, of the terms used in the statute. ([Occasional notes] 1904: 5)

The case is further understood as sanctioning the use of dictionaries 'as an aid to the memory and understanding of the court in determining the usual and ordinary meaning of words in tariff laws' (*US v Downing* (1905) at 356). Where the language was 'plain and unambiguous', the court should enforce it, and not 'change it by adopting a different construction, based upon some supposed policy of Congress' (at 356). This becomes: 'This court has sanctioned the use of dictionary definitions in determining the meaning of words in tariff laws' (*Anheuser-Busch Association v US* (1908) at 556–57).

There seems to be a further form of reasoning at work in *Nix v Hedden*. This draws on social norms and behavioural habits involving food production, preparation and consumption. It is not the definition that determines the classification of the object, but rather its embedding in the world of social practices, with its rhythms and classificatory logic. Tomatoes are not served with dessert or at the end of the meal, so they are not *fruit*. This comes close to the principle stated in *US v Downing* that in tax or tariff cases 'use is made the test of classification' (at 354).

This is a frequently discussed case (see Eskridge et al., 2001: 821–22) and is cited in support of a number of legal principles. In the decision it is not explicitly explained why we should prefer the categories of common speech to the classifications of botanists. But the Act was directed at informing traders (and officials) which items or categories are subject to import duty, and it could not be presumed that knowledge of botanic classifications was widely distributed among such classes of people. This was a question of the audience to which the statute was directed, rather than a question of definition in the abstract (Solan, 2005a: 2060). Fortunately for the Court, there was no discernible difference between trade usage and general popular usage.

One problem with this logic of the case is that *vegetable* is not a well-defined botanical term. *Fruit* and *vegetable* are therefore not directly comparable, and the assumption that there are two sets of parallel meanings at issue, namely popular versus scientific, is misleading. But in any case it is not entirely clear that this was the basis of the decision. The case report was muddled. It includes, for example, a rather incoherent witness statement, the legal relevance of which is unstated. There was no detailed analysis of linguistic categories, dictionary definitions, or botanical classification in the reported judgment, nor any account of the workings and policy intentions of the Act. There was no discussion at all about why the distinction between *fruit* and *vegetables* was made. The 1883 Act, which both raised some duties and lowered others, and was passed in a period of controversy between supporters of free trade and protectionism, left agricultural duties largely unchanged (Taussig, 1891: 327).

It appears that the information about botanical classification was derived solely from dictionaries. In any case, it is far from evident as a social fact that tomatoes are classified in ordinary usage as vegetables for all non-scientific purposes. This simply seems to have been assumed by the Court. The question of how far knowledge of botanical categories was distributed among the general population was not raised, and the assumption was that there are two discrete and non-interacting systems, the categories of everyday life and the classifications of botany. Botanical science is taken as a given, even though its classifications are simply taxonomies set up for particular purposes. They do not have the stability of God-given divisions in the order of nature. The social order, its associated food culture and implicit categories, as invoked by the Court, is then assumed to be universal and stable within the jurisdiction.

Is a species of bacteria a *plant*?

In re Arzberger (1940)	Bacteria	Plant	The law protected the rights of those who had 'invented or discovered and asexually reproduced any distinct and new variety of plant other than a tuber-propagated plant' (Plant Patent Law, R.S. 4886, USC title 35, s. 31)	A species of bacteria was not a plant

In re Arzberger (1940) (US Court of Customs and Patent Appeals)

The appellant, Cornelius F. Arzberger, was seeking a patent for a species of bacteria. The bacteria had been developed to facilitate the production of industrial solvents (butyl alcohol, ethyl alcohol and acetone). To succeed in the claim, it was necessary to show both that the species of bacteria was a variety of *plant* and that it was an invention. The claim was rejected by the Patent Examiner on both counts. A species of bacteria was not a plant, and there was 'lack of invention'. The Board of Appeals upheld this decision, which was appealed by Mr Arzberger.

Mr Arzberger had submitted a large number of references from botanical authorities stating that bacteria were classed as *plants*. The Patent Examiner, however, viewed the scientific classification of bacteria as being 'in doubt' (cited at 835–36):

> It is not intended to take issue with these authorities. Notwithstanding, however, it is pointed out that a distinction is drawn between this authoritative classification and the fact that bacteria are midway between plants and animals, i.e., possessing both plant and animal characteristics. This classification is *optional* and based upon the observations that bacteria have a preponderance of plant characteristics.

Thus while scientists classified bacteria as *plants*, this was not the unambiguous outcome of applying classificatory criteria. Rather bacteria showed a 'preponderance' of plant characteristics, but also some animal characteristics. Botanists had opted for the plant classification, rather than being impelled to it by the evidence. To fall within the statute, the classification should be beyond doubt. But even if bacteria were plants in a scientific sense, 'it was obviously not intended by Congress to include them as plants'. The term *plant* was used by Congress in 'the ordinary and accepted sense'; reports of the Senate and House Committees did not mention *bacteria*. The intention of Congress was to protect innovations by plant breeders by offering them 'economic equality' with inventors in industry. This would ultimately benefit farmers and the general public who bought plants. Methods of plant propagation (i.e. 'asexual reproduction' such as 'grafting, budding, cutting, layering, division') did not apply to bacteria. 'Chance finds' were excluded from protection, and this showed that the statute dealt with entities visible to the naked eye. There was no sense in which one could discover bacteria by chance (Patent Examiner, cited and summarized at 836).

The Court accepted that bacteria were uniformly classified as plants by scientists. Webster's *New International Dictionary* included bacteria under its scientifically oriented third sub-entry. However, the first sub-entry reflected the meaning found 'in the common language of the people': 'A young tree, shrub, or herb, planted or ready to plant; a slip, cutting, or sapling' (at 837). To resolve any doubt about whether Congress intended to include 'all organic matter which may be scientifically classified as plants', the Court cited from congressional reports of the Committees on Patents (of both the House of Representatives and Senate). This was the conclusion (at 837):

> It is well known that bacteria occur in the human body, in plants, in air, in soil, and in water, and although they are scientifically classified as plants we think that if Congress had intended that they should be included in the term 'plant' as used in the bill there would be some indication to that effect, either in the bill or in the reports of the Committees. A drop of water may contain thousands of bacteria, but outside of scientific circles a drop of water would not be regarded as containing thousands of plants.

Nix v Hedden had shown that 'the scientific meaning of a word is not always controlling in the interpretation of statute' (at 838). It was therefore not necessary to review the second ground. The decision of the Board of Appeals was affirmed.

Key points of the judgment

- The scientific classification of *bacteria*, which as a question of strict fact had both plant and animal characteristics, was in doubt. Plant characteristics predominated and botanists had chosen to classify bacteria as plants
- Congress used the word *plant* in its ordinary everyday sense and this did not include bacteria.
- Congressional materials confirmed that this statute was concerned with protecting and rewarding innovation in the breeding of plants understood in their horticultural or agricultural sense.

Is a comic action figure a *doll*?

Toy Biz, Inc. v US (2003)	Comic book action figures	Dolls	'Dolls representing only human beings and parts and accessories thereof', sub-heading 9502.10.40 of the Harmonized Tariff Schedule of the United States (HTSUS) (1994)	Comic book action figures were not dolls but other toys

Toy Biz, Inc. v US (2003) (US Court of International Trade)

The question at issue was whether action figures from the Marvel Comic series (*X-Men* or *X-Force*, the *Fantastic Four*, the *Spiderman* series) were classifiable as *dolls* or whether, as the importer claimed, they belonged to the category *other toys*. *Other toys* attracted lower rates of tax than *dolls*. Customs classified the figures as *dolls*, under this definition: 'Dolls representing only human beings and parts and accessories thereof [...]'. Toy Biz argued that they were *other toys*, that is, 'Toys representing animals or other non-human creatures (for example, robots and monsters) [...]'. The basic characteristic of a doll was that it must 'clearly represent a human figure'.

The court affirmed that the tariff provisions were subject to normal rules of statutory interpretation. The court could in addition construe terms 'according to their common and commercial meaning', if this was in keeping with legislative intent (at 1242), consult 'lexicographic and scientific authorities, dictionaries, and other reliable information', as well as referring to Explanatory Notes under the tariff sub-headings. These were intended to clarify the scope of the section (at 1243). There were no specific customs rules governing the interpretation of the tariff, which would create grounds for the court to give the agency's interpretation priority (so-called '*Chevron* deference' or 'administrative deference', after *Chevron, USA, Inc. v Natural Resources Defense Council, Inc.* (1984)) (at 1241, fn. 11).

Toy Biz argued that to be a *doll* the figure must represent 'only' a human being, in the sense of 'exclusively'. The figures at issue had 'tentacles, claws, wings or other nonhuman features', and they clearly represented 'creatures other than humans', with 'features characteristic of nonhumans' (at 1243). They were therefore classifiable as *other toys*. According to an Explanatory Note (95.03(A)(1)), that classification included figures representing 'animals or non-human creatures even if possessing predominantly human physical characteristics (e.g. angels, robots, devils, monsters)'. The Note thus expanded the list of types of figure that should be considered non-human by adding *angels* and *devils*. Therefore even figures 'predominantly human in physical appearance' would be classified as non-human, if they were not actually representations of human beings. The issue was 'not whether the character has some human features, or even whether the character resembles a human being', but 'whether the figure *represents* only a human being' (at 1243).

Customs replied that the heading *dolls* was a so-called *eo nomine* ('by that name') provision. Such provisions involve commodities known by a name used within trade and commerce, and are held to cover all 'all forms of the article'. Other types of provision are those that identify items by: general description; component material; actual or principal use (Hinkelman and Putzi, 2005: 92). Unless there was a legislative statement to the contrary, an *eo nomine* provision covered 'all forms of dolls which represent human beings'. Customs relied on previous case law that had incorporated dictionary definitions. In *Hasbro Industries v US* (1988, 1989), *G.I. Joe* soldier action figures had been classified as *dolls*, in spite of Hasbro's contention that they were the modern equivalent of toy soldiers (classified under *toys*). The term *doll* had 'a common meaning which is broad enough to cover all those distinctive representatives of human figures with which humans play'. Dictionaries, which were the 'most disinterested source for determining the common meaning of a tariff term', defined *doll* as the representation of a human being played with by children. This was 'in itself, virtually decisive' (*Hasbro* (1988) at 945).

Under the previous classification regime (Tariff Schedules of the United States – 'TSUS'), *doll* had been interpreted very widely to include: 'dolls for display or advertising purposes', 'dolls sold as gag items', 'bar gadgets', 'adult novelties', as well as 'small woven rush figures made in Mexico, consisting of a horse and rider', 'a figure of a woman made of straw', etc., and the action figure *G.I. Joe* (see *Russ Berrie & Co. v US* (1976) at 1039). Although these classification decisions were not binding under the new system, Customs argued that they could be instructive where the cases were analogous.

The court noted that the previous TSUS classification read: 'Dolls, and parts of dolls including doll clothing'; the current HTSUS by contrast read: 'Dolls representing only human beings and accessories thereof'. This was a definite change by Congress, which according to accepted rules of statutory interpretation merited close attention. Previous case law could not direct the interpretation of the category *doll* under the new regulatory regime (at 1245). The basic question was the meaning the words *representing* and *only* were intended to carry.

The court accepted Toy Biz's assertion that *only* had as one of its primary meanings 'exclusively', and cited the *Oxford English Dictionary* (*OED*) (2nd edn, 1989). The *OED* also showed that *only* could limit the following word, with the implication 'as opposed to any *other*'. Thus 'Dolls representing only human beings' could be read as 'Dolls representing human beings, as opposed to any *other* beings'. That is to say, *only* modified *human*, and created a contrast with non-human beings. The court had more trouble with the word *representing*, but accepted Toy Biz's assertion that it meant more than simply 'resemble'. This was one of the meanings listed in the *OED*, but other listed meanings were more pertinent: 'to show, exhibit, or display to the eye'; 'to portray, depict, delineate'; 'to symbolize, to serve as a visible or concrete embodiment of'; 'to stand for or in place of'; 'to be the figure or image of'; 'to take or fill the place of'; 'to serve as a specimen or example of'.

One could not read the provision as meaning exclusively 'dolls *resembling* human beings', since the Explanatory Note to the *other toys* provision noted that this included toys 'representing animals or non-human creatures even if possessing predominantly human physical characteristics'. An item could not be classified under both provisions. To be classified as a *doll*, the figure needed to be the 'embodiment' or 'example' of a human being. This was 'more restrictive than merely to resemble a human being', and this was further limited by *only*, with the effect that the provision 'will not allow the representation of any being other than a human being to be classified as a "doll"' (at 1247).

The court then reviewed the *X-Men* action figures, concluding that they had both human and non-human characteristics (at 1249):

> [F]or example, one of the more popular figures of the series 'Wolverine' has long, sharp-looking claws grafted onto his hands that come out from under his skin along with wolf-like hair and ears.

The argument from Customs that claws, robotic eyes and such features did not transform the figures into 'something other than human beings' was not to the point: 'the issue is whether the figure as a whole and in a wider context represents a human being', and the presence of one non-human feature would be decisive (at 1249).

The Marvel characters were *mutants*: 'These fabulous characters use their extraordinary and unnatural physical and psychic powers on the side of either good or evil' (at 1250). The category *mutant* was analogous to *robot* or *monster* under the *other toys* heading. The first definition in the *OED* for *mutation* was 'action or process of changing; alteration or change in form or qualities' (at 1251):

> Thus, a 'mutant' is someone (possibly originally belonging to human species) who has undergone change and become something other than human.

The case of the *Fantastic Four* was more difficult. These characters were not referred to as *mutants* either in their marketing or within popular culture, yet they had superhuman abilities. Mr Fantastic, for example, could 'stretch himself into almost any shape' (at 1252). Given this, the *Fantastic Four* were also not classifiable as *dolls*. The Mole Man, a stout, troll-like humanoid creature, was a 'close call', as he was described as being human, though with 'extraordinary intelligence, cunning and fighting prowess with his staff', and the master of 'a legion of giant monsters'. The *Spiderman* series of action figures, Hobgoblin, Dr Octopus, Kingpin and Kraven, posed similar problems. Hobgoblin had 'blood red eyes with no pupils and features fangs and yellow skin', and Dr Octopus had 'four tentacles coming from its back'. These were clear cases. However, Kingpin and Kraven, although not specifically designated as superhuman, were legendary and freakish figures rather than ordinary human beings (at 1253).

The action figures were therefore classified as *other toys* rather than *dolls*. Toy Biz would pay a lower tariff on their import and could recoup duty already paid.

Key points in the judgment

- Comic action figures were to be classified either as *dolls* or *other toys*; the key phrase under the heading *dolls* was 'representing only human beings'; for *other toys* the phrase was 'representing animals or other non-human creatures'.

- The previous case law (under TSUS), which had adopted an expansive definition of *doll*, was no longer of direct relevance.

- The Explanatory Note to the heading *other toys* explained that it included 'animals or non-human creatures even if possessing predominantly human physical characteristics (e.g. angels, robots, devils, monsters)'.

- Comic action figures potentially fell under both the *doll* and *other toys* headings, but this was not a possible outcome.

- The word *only* should be read so as to mean 'exclusively'.

- The word 'representing' implied more than mere resemblance; rather, it implied that the depicted entity must be an actual human being.

- The question at issue was not the balance between human and non-human characteristics, but rather whether the figures embodied or exemplified human beings.

- Some of the figures were marketed as *mutants* and their mutant status was recognized in popular culture; *mutant* was a category akin to *robot* or *monster* under the *other toys* heading; more difficult were cases where the figures were more human-like.

- The comic action figures all were superhuman or sufficiently fantastical so as to be endowed with legendary or mythical status.

- The comic action figures did not represent human beings, and belonged under the *other toys* heading.

Discussion

The judgment used dictionary definitions as a reference point, characterizing them as the most 'disinterested' authority on word meaning. The judgment also took very seriously popular cultural narratives of the action figures. This is particularly striking in the case of the *mutant* character of the *X-Men* figures, which the judge understood as indicating human beings in the process of transformation into another species. The question of hybridity is at the heart of the judgment, with the action figures understood as representing imaginary human-like beings with special non-human, generally superhuman, characteristics. To be a *doll*, a figure must be the representation of an ordinary human being, either a recognizable individual or a type.

Courts make classification decisions based on the language of the statute. Law is also anchored in and responding to everyday realities. These two aspects of law's interaction with categories and classifications can be illustrated with reference to the reception of these *doll* decisions. The courts in the two *Hasbro* decisions both alluded to the implicit feminization that would accompany the classification of the *G.I. Joe* figure as a *doll* (Anon, 1989). In the mid-1960s, Hasbro created the *G.I. Joe* as part of a strategy to reduplicate the success of *Barbie*, but as *G.I. Joe* was marketed at boys, Hasbro used the term *action figure* rather than *doll* (Wagner-Ott, 2002). The court ended its judgment with these words:

> [F]or what it is worth, the Court notes that this classification [as a *doll*] does not in any way detract from the respect which these figures deserve as representations of the human participants in the never-ending struggle between good and evil. Henceforth, each and every one of these figures must accept the fact that, for tariff purposes and by judicial decision, they must face the world as 'real American dolls'. Hopefully, they will meet this decision as to their tariff classification with courage and pride. (*Hasbro* (1988) at 946)

The Court of Appeals judgment ended on a similar note:

> Even though G.I. Joe has lost this battle, hopefully he will not lose his courage for combat, despite being officially designated by the United States Customs Service as a 'doll'. (*Hasbro* (1989) at 946)

In a sense, the court was simply reasserting the essential *doll-like* nature of figures like *G.I. Joe*, removing the euphemism *action figure* and reaffirming that this was a 'doll for boys'. This perhaps explains the odd mixture of apologetics, irony and martial spirit that characterizes the remarks above.

Following the Toy Biz decision, some fans reacted with shock to the notion that *X-Men* were not human, in particular given that one of themes in the narratives of the mutant *X-Men* was their struggle to prove their humanity. King (2003) quotes the editor of an on-line *X-Men* fan site:

> This is almost unthinkable. Marvel's super heroes are supposed to be as human as you or I. They live in New York. They have families and go to work. And now they're no longer human?

The author of Marvel's *Uncanny X-Men* comic-book series, Chuck Austen, likewise emphasized the *X-Men*'s humanity: 'they're just another strand in the evolutionary chain' (King, 2003).

Is a burrito a *sandwich*?

White City Shopping Center, LP v PR Restaurants, LLC dba Bread Panera (2006)	Burrito	Sandwich	Landlord 'agrees not to enter into a lease [...] for a bakery or restaurant reasonably expected to have annual sales of sandwiches greater than 10% of its total sales'	A burrito was not a sandwich

Lexical example

White City Shopping Center, LP v PR Restaurants, LLC dba Bread Panera (2006) (Superior Court of Massachusetts)

The owners of a shopping mall entered into a 10-year lease with a 'Panera restaurant' (run by PR Restaurants – 'PR'). The lease included a non-competition or exclusivity clause. This would prevent the mall from offering any further leases to businesses that sold sandwiches. There was no definition in the lease, nor any discussion of the scope of the term *sandwich*. PR subsequently learned that the mall was negotiating with a company, Chair 5, that was planning to open a Qdoba Mexican Grill restaurant. This would serve Mexica-style wraps and filled tortillas (thin flatbread), in the form of tacos, burritos and quesadillas. The question was whether this violated the lease agreement on the grounds that these foods were in effect *sandwiches*.

The court emphasized that in the jurisdiction of Massachusetts the interpretation of a contract was 'a question of law for the court'. The interpretation should give 'reasonable effect to each of its provisions', so as to be 'consistent with its language, background and purpose', starting with 'the actual words chosen by the parties' (at 3). Where the language was 'plain and free from ambiguity', it was to be interpreted according to the 'ordinary and usual sense'. The word *sandwich* was not ambiguous, and therefore the court applied 'the ordinary meaning of the word' (at 3). In *The New Webster Third International Dictionary* (2002), a sandwich was defined as 'two thin pieces of bread, usually buttered, with a thin layer (as of meat, cheese, or savory mixture) spread between them'. This led the judge to the following conclusion (at 3):

> Under this definition and as dictated by common sense, this court finds that the term 'sandwich' is not commonly understood to include burritos, tacos, and quesadillas, which are typically made with a single tortilla and stuffed with a choice filling of meat, rice, and beans.

PR had not offered any evidence that the parties intended the term *sandwich* to include these foods, even though it was known that there were Mexican-style restaurants near the Center. PR had attempted to support its position with reference to the tariff case *Sabritas* (1998). *Sabritas* held that *fried taco shells* fell within the category of *bread*. But that case had applied the 'commercial meaning' rather than the 'ordinary meaning' of bread. In the case at hand, 'the commercial meaning of "bread" is inapposite where it is the ordinary meaning that is relevant when interpreting an unambiguous contractual term such as "sandwiches"' (fn. 4). In conclusion, the court reaffirmed that there was no remedy for PR (at 4):

> Even though PR vigorously argues for a broad definition of 'sandwiches' [...] to include food products sold by Qdoba, this argument does not change the fact that burritos, quesadillas, and tacos are not commonly understood to mean 'sandwiches'. Because PR failed to use more specific language or definitions for 'sandwiches' in the Lease, it is bound to the language and the common meaning attributable to 'sandwiches' that the parties agreed upon when the Lease was drafted.

Key points in the judgment

- The contract should be construed so as to give reasonable effect to its provisions, beginning with the words used by the parties.
- The word *sandwich* as used in the lease was not ambiguous and the court therefore should apply the ordinary meaning.
- The tariff case of *Sabritas* involved the commercial not the ordinary meaning of *bread*.
- The ordinary meaning of *sandwich* did not include Mexican foods such as burritos, tacos, and quesadillas.

Discussion

The judgment rested on the commonsense, ordinary meaning of the word *sandwich*, as illustrated in the cited dictionary definition. For the judge, this gave a straightforward answer to the contractual dispute. The broad and inclusive meaning urged by PR Restaurants did not accord with the straightforward 'common sense' applied by the judge. The judgment did not cite any definitions of *burrito*, *taco* and *quesadilla*, nor explore any similarities or potential analogies, in terms of function, construction, ingredients, between Mexican wraps of various kinds and sandwiches. The *Sabritas* case actually talks of the 'common and commercial meaning' as determining the outcome in the absence of clear guidance from statute or case law. To determine this 'common meaning' for a tariff term, 'the Court may utilize standard dictionaries and scientific authorities, as well as its own understanding of the term' (at 1127). The court in *Sabritas* began its analysis 'by noting that tortillas are unquestionably commonly and commercially accepted as bread in the United States' (at 1128). There is a wealth of historical and definitional discussion in the judgment. The *White City Shopping Center* judgment does not go beyond the boundaries of its own intuitive response to the question, that boundary having being set by the initial assertion that the term *sandwich* was not ambiguous. There was no market analysis in the judgment, of types of consumers or patterns of consumption, even though the contract was essentially an agreement designed to protect one party from competition in its market niche.

According to an analysis of this case in terms of race, class and culture (Florestal, 2008: 9), the decision was met 'with what I term the "Duh!" response; there was an overwhelming chorus of agreement that of course a burrito is not a sandwich' (Florestal, 2008: 9). Florestal suggests that this intuitive response can be traced to attitudes to race, class and culture, and criticizes the judgment for displaying the formalism rejected by Judge Benjamin Cardozo in the early twentieth century. This saw the 'precise word' as the 'sovereign talisman' and 'every slip' as 'fatal' (*Wood v Lucy* (1917) at 214). Florestal argues that the sandwich was in fact a highly varied form of food that been transformed over time. The court's use of a single definition combined with intuition was problematic: 'Words are slippery entities upon which human beings struggle to place concrete meaning'. The resort to the dictionary often 'merely compounds the problem'. The dictionary definition cited by the judge actually had a second section, 'namely food consisting of a filling placed upon one slice or between two or more slices of a variety of bread', which brought *sandwich* much closer to *burrito* (Florestal, 2008: 12). Given that the case was heard in what was explicitly a 'plain meaning' jurisdiction, the fact that the judge found no ambiguity meant that the interpretation of the contract was a matter of law for the judge. No external inquiry of a factual nature was necessary. But even the dictionary offered two contrasting definitions (Florestal, 2008: 16). In the *Frigaliment v BNS* (1960) case, the judge had had no problem in determining that *chicken* was ambiguous (see Schane, 2006: 12ff.).

An affidavit from a culinary expert stated that sandwiches were 'of European roots', whereas the burrito was 'specific to Mexico'. This illustrates for Florestal how the food items were perceived through the prism of race. Sandwiches were seen as 'white', as opposed to the 'Mexican' *burrito*. Further, given their association with English nobility (the eponymous Earl of Sandwich), 'sandwiches are generally perceived as "higher class" than burritos'. The sandwich to a degree crosses class boundaries, whereas the burrito, with its origins in a culture of sweat and toil, 'is consigned exclusively to the low class realm' (Florestal, 2008: 47). This is what lay behind the instinctive response to the classification question.

The Hoagie, invented by Italian dockworkers in Philadelphia ('an overwhelming meat-cheese-lettuce-tomatoes-and-onions laden concoction that is topped off with a dash of oregano-vinegar dressing and served on an Italian roll') could co-exist in the same category with the 'quintessentially English cucumber sandwich', whereas the 'burrito meets resistance not just because of its class but also because of its race – and the way the two play off each other' (Florestal, 2008: 50). Florestal concludes that the burrito has been in part assimilated into American food culture, especially when it is termed a *wrap*, but that it remains marked by its origins and the ambivalent racial status of Mexicans within American society. The case was not necessarily wrongly decided, but 'common sense or a shared understanding of the term' was no substitute for the 'rigorous application of contract interpretation doctrine' (Florestal, 2008: 59).

Points for further consideration

The decision in *Nix v Hedden* is often seen as exemplifying the preference for ordinary or popular meaning over botanical classification. But it can also be understood as giving preference to the socio-cultural profile of the tomato and its function within US food culture over its intrinsic qualities. The case is also cited as authority for the use of dictionaries 'as aids to the memory and understanding of the court', but the definitions cited apparently tended to favour the botanical classification. In *Arzberger* the decision was followed, but the purpose or policy behind the statute was also considered. Why is the legislative intent apparently not relevant in *Nix v Hedden*, but relevant in *Arzberger*?

One commentator has used *Nix v Hedden* to make a general point about statutory interpretation:

> The question for decision in a statutory interpretation case is not really the 'meaning' of the individual statutory words in the abstract. It is whether the particular fact pattern of the case fits inside or outside the classes, categories, or prototypes represented by the statutory words. In statutory interpretation, the complications and uncertainties are such that a tomato may be a vegetable, or it may be a fruit, depending on the case and context. (Mullins, 2003: 45)

But is not this also the case for so-called 'ordinary' communication? Are not always a particular context and a contextually defined set of relationships at stake in our everyday acts of interpretation?

Given the common criticism of the *Barbie* doll that it is a fantasy caricature of the proportions of a woman's body, should not the reasoning in *Toy Biz* imply that *Barbie* falls under *other toys*? In a postmodern twist, Pellisser (2012) reports that a Ukrainian woman has apparently 're-designed her physical form to resemble Barbie, the plastic Mattel toy'.

CHAPTER 8

Technological Change and Legal Categories

Is an airplane a *vehicle*?

McBoyle v US (1931)	Airplane	Motor vehicle	The term 'motor vehicle' shall include an automobile, automobile truck, automobile wagon, motor cycle, or any other self-propelled vehicle not designed for running on rails (National Motor Vehicle Theft Act, 1919, s. 408, title 18, US Code)	An airplane was not a vehicle

McBoyle v US (1930) (Circuit Court of Appeals for the Tenth Circuit)

McBoyle was convicted in the District Court (Western District of Oklahoma) under the National Motor Vehicle Theft Act. The offence was that of transporting a stolen vehicle across a state line. The vehicle in question was a Waco airplane stolen from the US Aircraft Corporation in Illinois and flown to Guymon, Oklahoma. McBoyle appealed, arguing that (para. 15)

> the word 'vehicle' includes only conveyances that travel on the ground; that an airplane is not a vehicle but a ship; and that, under the doctrine of ejusdem generis, the phrase 'any other self propelled vehicle' cannot be construed to include an airplane.

The judgment quoted a definition from the *Century Dictionary*, which glossed the original Latin as 'conveyance, carriage, ship', and the meaning as: 'Any receptacle, or means of transport, in which something is carried or conveyed, or travels'. The court noted that the Latin term *vehiculum* meant 'a ship as well as a carriage' (para. 7). Webster had the following definitions:

> (1) That in or on which any person or thing is or may be carried, esp. on land, as a coach, wagon, car, bicycle, etc.; a means of conveyance; (2) That which is used as the instrument of conveyance or communication.

The comprehensive legal encyclopedia, the *Corpus Juris* (vol. 42, p. 609, s. 1) offered this definition of *motor vehicle*:

> a vehicle operated by a power developed within itself and used for the purpose of carrying passengers or materials; and as the term is used in the different statutes regulating such vehicles, it is generally defined as including all vehicles propelled by any power other than muscular power, except traction engines, road rollers, and such motor vehicles as run only upon rails or tracks.

Both 'the derivation and the definition' of *vehicle* was sufficiently broad 'to include any means or device by which persons or things are carried or transported'. It was not limited to land-based vehicles, though that might be the 'limited or special meaning of the word'. But it would not be inaccurate to say that 'a ship or vessel is a vehicle of commerce' (para. 10). In summary, an airplane was a motor vehicle within the meaning of the Act:

> An airplane is self-propelled, by means of a gasoline motor. It is designed to carry passengers and freight from place to place. It runs partly on the ground but principally in the air. It furnishes a rapid means for transportation of persons and comparatively light articles of freight and express. It therefore serves the same general purpose as an automobile, automobile truck, or motorcycle. It is of the same general kind or class as the motor vehicles specifically enumerated in the statutory definition and, therefore, construing an airplane to come within the general term, 'any other self propelled vehicle', does not offend against the maxim of *ejusdem generis*. (para. 11)

There was also a need to ascribe a meaning to the phrase 'any other self-propelled vehicle', and the court decided that this included 'an airplane, a motorboat, and any other like means of conveyance or transportation which is self-propelled, and is of the same general class as an automobile and a motorcycle' (para. 13).

The conviction was upheld in a two against one decision. The dissenting opinion by Judge Cotteral cited the rule that penal statutes should be construed strictly (the rule of lenity) and must 'state clearly the persons and acts denounced'. Congress could have inserted the relevant terms: 'The omission to definitely mention airplanes requires a construction that they were not included' (para. 3). The fact that 'vehicles running on rails' were exempted was a clarification; it implied that the statute applied to 'vehicles that run, but not on rails'. It was unreasonable to conclude that airplanes fell within the description of 'self-propelled vehicles that do not run on rails'. Application of *ejusdem generis* implied that the motor vehicle in question should fall within the same class as 'automobile, automobile truck, automobile wagon, or motor cycle'. This was not the case with *airplane*. While proceedings of debates in Congress were not aids to construction, they were revealing as to the background to the enactment. There was widespread concern about the 'public menace' of theft of automobiles, but airplanes were not even mentioned.

McBoyle v US (1931) (US Supreme Court)

Justice Oliver Wendell Holmes wrote the opinion of the (unanimous) Supreme Court. He conceded that the term *vehicle* could and had been used to include aircraft in some legislation: 'No doubt etymologically it is possible to use the word to signify a conveyance working on land, water or air, and sometimes legislation extends the use in that direction'. An example was the Tariff Act (1922, c. 3567, s. 410(b)), but other statutes defined *vehicle* in a sense restricted to 'a means of transportation on land' (Rev. St. s. 4 (1 USCA s. 4)). In the Tariff Act of 1930 (c. 497, s. 401(b)) aircraft were expressly excluded from the meaning of the word *vehicle*. In this statute, however, the word was used with its meaning 'in everyday speech', and this 'calls up the picture of a thing moving on land' (at 26):

> So here, the phrase under discussion calls up the popular picture. For after including automobile truck, automobile wagon and motor cycle, the words 'any other self-propelled vehicle not designed for running on rails' still indicate that a vehicle in the popular sense, that is a vehicle running on land -- is the theme. It is a vehicle that runs, not something, not commonly called a vehicle, that flies.

Congress could have included mention of this category had it been minded to do so. The citation continues (at 26):

> Airplanes were well known in 1919 when this statute was passed, but it is admitted that they were not mentioned in the reports or in the debates in Congress.

The words of the statute carefully enumerated 'the different forms of motor vehicles' and it was not a possible reading to extend this to aircraft ('a term that usage more and more precisely confined to a different class').

On balance, Justice Holmes held that to be fair the law should draw the line clearly, even though 'it is not likely that a criminal will carefully consider the text of the law before he murders and steals'. It was 'reasonable that a fair warning should be given to the world in language that the common world will understand, of what the law intends to do if a certain line is passed' (at 27). The rule was laid down 'in words that evoke in the common mind only the picture of vehicles moving on land'. The Court should not simply extend this to aircraft, 'simply because it may seem to us that a similar policy applies, or upon the speculation that, if the legislature had thought of it, very likely broader words would have been used'. The authority cited at the end of the judgment was *US v Bhagat Singh Thind* (1923), the case in which *white person* was given its ordinary, popular meaning (see Chapter 12). The judgment was reversed.

Key points in the Supreme Court judgment

- The term *vehicle* could be used to refer to conveyances travelling on land, water and air.
- The statutory definition, if applied strictly, included *aircraft*.
- In other legislation where *vehicle* included *aircraft* this was done by explicit wording.
- The case concerned the popular picture called up by the word *vehicle*.
- The common theme of the vehicles enumerated was that they 'ran on land', and this was an essential property of the class in this context.
- Aircraft were well known when the statute was passed, and Congress could have included explicit reference to them.
- It was right that fair warning should be given in clear language to the world at large, and the benefit of the doubt should go to the accused.
- It was not proper to speculate on what Congress would have enacted had it considered facts such as these.

Discussion

This is a famous decision by a famous judge. For all its brevity, it has a special place in the history of debates about legal interpretation, given the lack of consensus among legal scholars as to its correctness and the case's importance as background to the famous discussion by H.L.A. Hart of the rule 'no vehicles in the park' (Solan, 1998: 81). Holmes based his decision on the principle that in criminal matters, the world at large was entitled to be warned of the content of the offence in language that it understood. This was true even if it was entirely fictional, even comic (a commentator speaks of Holmes's 'dry wit' – Dumbauld, 1944: 1039) to think of the legal text being consulted in advance by a criminal in a case such as this. Brown (1931: 449) summed up the principle behind the decision as reflecting 'the common sense doctrine' that, as was stated in *US v Bhagat Singh Thind* (1923), the words of a statute should be 'interpreted in accordance with the understanding of the common man from whose vocabulary they were taken'.

The Court might conceivably have framed this decision in a less populist manner, and omitted the assertion of a communality between the language of law and the 'vocabulary of the common man'. It would have involved focusing more directly on the scope of the language, using the argument that if there was a doubt about the set of objects picked out by the term *vehicle* or *motor vehicle*, the defendant was entitled to the benefit of that doubt. However, the judgment acknowledged that in a strict etymological or literal sense, an airplane was unambiguously a *vehicle*. The statute was therefore not strictly ambiguous (so the rule of lenity would not apply), in that the definition and criteria supplied covered the category *airplane*. Hence it was necessary to make an appeal to the popular mind and the idea that there was a universal picture called up in the mind on hearing the word *vehicle*. The judgment can be understood as a sharp reminder to Congress that drafting needed to be precise, especially where there was a tension between the categorical language of the statute and everyday or popular conceptions, and that it should not rely on judges to second-guess its intentions.

It is perhaps puzzling that there was no discussion in the Supreme Court judgment of the primary mischief at which the statute was directed, namely, taking stolen vehicles across state lines. It remains strikingly aloof from policy discussion, in effect ignoring, or refusing to speculate about, legislative intent (Solan, 2005b: 474). The category *vehicle* is treated as an independent socio-psychological entity, existing as a given, and considered outside the facts of the case. The statute is in this sense treated 'as autonomous text' (Tiersma, 2001: 474). One argument is that, in such cases, terms 'should be restricted to their "core" or prototypical meaning, because this is the meaning that members of the speech community are most likely to share' (Tiersma, 2001: 474). But it has been argued that the reasoning in this judgment is not convincing, as 'ordinary speech' has sufficient flexibility to include airplane under the 'broad definition' of *motor vehicle*, in the category 'any other self-propelled vehicle not designed for running on rails' (Kelley, 2001: 127). Further, appeals to the rule of lenity in understanding this decision are, arguably, misjudged: 'every sane person knows that it is wrong to steal' (Wisotsky, 2009: 323–24). There was no requirement that a reasonable person should know that a specifically *federal* offence was being committed (see also Hall, 1935: 758–59). Solan argues that Holmes should have taken the time of the court decision (1931) as his reference point, rather than the time of enactment, i.e. 1919 (Solan, 1998: 82): 'had the enacting Congress been sitting when he made his ruling, it would have had no trouble incorporating airplanes into its "picture" of a vehicle'.

Is a bicycle a *carriage*?

Corkery v Carpenter (1950)	Bicycle	Carriage	'drunk while in charge on any highway [...] of any carriage, horse, cattle, or steam engine' (Licensing Act 1872, s. 12)	A bicycle was a carriage

Corkery v Carpenter (1950) (High Court)

One afternoon, in the town of Ilfracombe in Devon, south-west England, the defendant, Shane Corkery, was observed 'drunk and creating a disturbance and incapable of having proper control over his bicycle'. He was not riding the bicycle, however, but pushing it. Nonetheless, Mr Corkery was arrested by a police officer for being drunk in charge of a bicycle on the highway. Mr Corkery resisted arrest, and subsequently damaged his cell. He was then further charged with maliciously causing damage and convicted on both counts. One argument put forward on appeal was that a bicycle was not a carriage and therefore the arrest without warrant was unlawful. It followed that Mr Corkery had been justified in seeking 'to break out of such unlawful confinement' (at 103).

Counsel for Mr Corkery argued that a 'cardinal principle of interpretation is that in statutes concerning matters relating to the general public words are presumed to be used in their popular meaning' and that the popular meaning of *carriage* did not include a bicycle (at 103). The words of the music hall song 'Daisy Bell' (composed by Harry Dacre, 1892) were called in evidence of this:

It won't be a stylish marriage,
I can't afford a carriage,
But you'll look sweet upon the seat
Of a bicycle made for two.

Webster's Dictionary of 1920 stated that *carriage* was archaic, 'except in the case of wheeled vehicles or railway carriages'. There were a number of tollgate cases and an opinion in *Stone's Justices Manual* that suggested that a bicycle might be a *carriage*. But there was no consistency in the case law, and these cases were not directly relevant as none was on s. 12 of the Licensing Act. This was a 'penal section' which allowed for arrest without warrant, and therefore the court should put 'a narrow construction' on it: 'The test is whether s. 12 conveys to the mind of the reader that it was Parliament's intention to include a bicycle'. It was contended that it would require doing 'violence' to the language of the Act to bring *bicycle* within its scope.

One problem for the defence was the decision in *Taylor v Goodwin* (1879), where a speeding cyclist was convicted of 'furiously driving a carriage' (Highway Act 1835, s. 78). Counsel for Mr Corkery argued that the legislature had lacked confidence in that decision and therefore passed s. 85 of the Local Government Act 1888, by which 'bicycles, tricycles, velocipedes, and other similar machines are hereby declared to be carriages within the meaning of the Highway Act'. A further case, *R v Parker* (1895), which involved an offence of causing bodily harm by 'furious driving' of a 'carriage or vehicle' (Offences Against the Person Act 1861, s. 35), had not made the particular determination that a bicycle was a carriage (though it was a 'carriage or vehicle'). The common denominator of the categories in s. 12 of the Licensing Act ('carriage, horse, cattle, or steam engine') was a force or 'motive power' external to the individual's muscular power. The Act referred to the person being 'in charge', rather than 'in possession' which was used in the firearms sections (at 104).

Lord Goddard CJ stressed that it was necessary as a first step to examine the purpose behind the section. It was clearly 'for the protection of the public and the preservation of public order'. It was evident that the term *carriage* was wide enough to include *bicycle* (though this might not be true for every Act) and any vehicle capable of carrying a person or goods. *Taylor v Goodwin* (1879) was an authority on this point, even though it was decided under a different statute. For Lord Goddard, the matter was straightforward: 'It is a carriage in my opinion because it carries' (at 106). In *Taylor v Goodwin*, the court had said:

The expressions used are as wide as possible. It may be that bicycles were unknown at the time when the Act was passed, but the legislature clearly desired to prohibit the use of any sort of carriage in a manner dangerous to the life or limb of any passenger. (at 229)

Applying that case, 'nothing can be more dangerous than a drunken man with a bicycle on a highway', and this was true even if he were pushing it.

The decisions in the tollgate cases were very much determined by the particular wording. In *Cannan v Earl of Abingdon* (1900), the Act allowed for a toll on coaches and carriages:

The bicycle or tricycle is a thing which carries. It may carry a man, as a horse does, or a carriage does; it may carry luggage or goods as we know that tradesmen's tricycles do. It is, therefore, in my opinion, a carriage, and, being a carriage, it is made by the terms of the Act of Parliament liable to pay the toll. (at 71)

In other cases, it was held that bicycles were not liable for toll charges because of the wording. In *Williams v Ellis* (1880), the Turnpike Act imposed a toll on 'every horse, mule, or other beast drawing any coach, sociable, chariot, berlin, landau, vis-à-vis, phaeton, curricle', and in addition 'every carriage of whatever description, and for whatever purpose, which shall be drawn or impelled, or set or kept in motion by steam or other power or agency'. The same was true for *Simpson v Teignmouth and Shaldon Bridge Co* (1903), where a list of various coaches ended with 'for every other carriage hung on "springs"'.

A bicycle was a *carriage* within the meaning of the Act and therefore the defendant had been lawfully arrested and properly convicted (at 107).

Key points in the judgment

- The Act was primarily concerned with public safety and public order.
- A bicycle was a carriage because it literally carried people or things.
- *Taylor v Goodwin* (1879) was authority for the view that a bicycle was a carriage where public safety and public order were at stake.
- Case law on whether bicycles were subject to tolls depended on the particular wording of the Act in question, and there were decisions that included *bicycle* within *carriage* and others that did not.
- The term *carriage* was wide enough to include a vehicle such as a bicycle, even though this may not have been in contemplation at the time of the Act.

Discussion

The defence argued that this was a statute directed at the general population and that therefore the words used were to be understood in their popular meaning. Counsel for the defence sought to show that the word *carriage*, in ordinary usage, did not include *bicycle*, illustrating this intuitive point by citing a popular song in which *carriage* and *bicycle* were shown to be mutually exclusive terms, and by referring to a dictionary. As this was a criminal statute and there was doubt about the applicability of the statutory language, it followed that the defendant should be given the benefit of that doubt (the rule of lenity). The classification question should therefore be answered using narrow construction.

Lord Goddard started from the mischief against which the statute was directed, namely, public order and safety. The classification question therefore was framed by the wider intention ascribed to Parliament. There was no neutral answer to this question valid for all legal contexts, but there was a case as authority on a closely related statute. In some essential sense a bicycle was in any case a carriage 'because it carries'. Similar reasoning was cited from *Cannan v Earl of Abingdon*: 'The bicycle or tricycle is a thing which carries. […] It is therefore in my opinion a carriage'. But it is not quite clear what the basis is for this form of reasoning. One possibility is that this is a kind of syllogism:

> All carriages carry
> A bicycle carries
> A bicycle is a carriage

But this is not a persuasive form of reasoning:

> All birds are mortal
> Socrates is mortal
> Socrates is a bird

The fact that one generic category and one specific category share a common feature is not sufficient to conclude that the specific category is a sub-set of the generic one.

Another way of understanding this reasoning is as follows. The basic determining feature of carriages is shown by the word *carriage* itself, which includes, or is derived from or somehow etymologically related to, the verb *to carry*. The common origin or relationship between *to carry* and *carriage* leads to the identification of a meaningful tautology ('carriages carry') which identifies the essential attribute of the category. It is then argued that bicycles also share this key attribute, in that the way in which carriages carry things or people finds an analogy in the way that bicycles carry things or people. The fact that in the case of the bicycle the propulsion comes from the person 'carried' is not material.

Points for further consideration

In *McBoyle*, the court declined to update the language of the statute. In *Corkery v Carpenter*, the court preferred to identify a general mischief which the law was seeking to prevent, so as to bring the facts within the purview of the statute. Would it be possible in principle to find a further rule (a meta-rule) to distinguish between these two ways of reaching a decision?

Commenting on *Corkery v Carpenter*, Harris (1981: 192–93) talks of the availability of 'last resort' questions in everyday communication, such as 'What did you say?' and 'What did you mean?'. He comments: 'It is no coincidence that law, which is itself a last resort where ordinary communication between individuals has broken down, should exhibit public and formal versions of the mechanisms which individuals employ privately and informally in pursuing their communicational aims'. What does this suggest about the relation of everyday communicational practice to legal strategies in law for ascertaining interpretative meaning?

If there was an English word *joltup* which meant exactly the same as *carriage* and had the same distribution as the word *carriage* in the relevant Acts and cases (and there was no word *carriage*), how would this have affected the reasoning in *Corkery v Carpenter*?

CHAPTER 9

Lawful and Unlawful Searches

In this chapter the question of technological change, as well as the definition of *vehicle*, is considered in relation to the Fourth Amendment of the US Constitution. The text runs as follows:

> The right of the people to be secure in their persons, houses, papers, and effects, against unreasonable searches and seizures shall not be violated; and no Warrant shall issue except where is probable cause, supported by Oath or affirmation and particularly describing the place to be searched and the persons or things to be seized.

Police officers cannot normally enter a building without a warrant, and a warrant requires reasonable grounds for the belief that a crime has been committed. This requirement is known as **probable cause**. If a warrantless search is to be carried out, there must be **exigent circumstances** which justify immediate action, such as an urgent need to act on the spot to save life, to prevent evidence being destroyed, to detain suspects who show evidence of preparing to flee, etc. If a search is ruled unreasonable, then normally evidence gathered during the search cannot be used as evidence in court.

The Fourth Amendment has been understood historically as protecting primarily property rights and privacy rights that arise out of property. However in *Katz v US* (1967) the Supreme Court widened the scope of protection. *Katz* concerned the police recording of a conversation in a public telephone booth. Rather than define the booth as a 'constitutionally protected space', the court asserted that 'the Fourth Amendment protects people, not places' (at 351). What is protected is 'the reasonable expectation of privacy' (REOP) (*Katz v US* (1967) at 360). This made protection under the Fourth Amendment a personal right, in Justice Brandeis's words, 'the right to be let alone' (see Warren and Brandeis, 1890: 195, citing Cooley, 1888: 29 and Richardson et al., 2012: fn. 57).

Is a wire-tap a *search*?

Olmstead v US (1928)	Search	Wire-tap	'unreasonable searches and seizures', Fourth Amendment, US Constitution	A wire-tap was not a search

Olmstead v US (1928) (US Supreme Court)

The petitioners had been convicted of a range of offences under the National Prohibition Act (1919) and the Eighteenth Amendment. These made unlawful the manufacture, transport, storage and sale of alcoholic drinks ('intoxicating beverages'). Olmstead was the manager (or 'leading conspirator') of a large-scale 'bootlegging' business. The evidence against him had been obtained by the tapping of his phone and those of other conspirators by federal officers. No warrant had been obtained for the wire-tap, but neither had there been a trespass onto Olmstead's property. The interception had been done remotely, from the basement of an office building, and directly from the street-lines. If it was determined that the wire-tap was a *search* within the meaning of the Fourth Amendment, then the absence of a warrant (or 'exigent circumstances') would have meant that it was an *unreasonable search* and therefore illegal. The evidence thus obtained could have been excluded.

The majority judgment (written by Chief Justice Taft) discussed case law relevant to both the Fourth and the Fifth Amendments. The Fifth Amendment provides that no one 'shall be compelled in any criminal case to be a witness against himself'. In *Weeks v US* (1914), evidence from seized papers, which had led to a conviction for using the postal system to run a lottery, was excluded on appeal. This had led to the 'striking outcome' that evidence obtained by the Government in violation of the Fourth Amendment must be excluded from trial, since in effect the defendant was being forced into self-incrimination forbidden under the Fifth Amendment. (There was substantial discussion of this point in the judgments, but this topic is not pursued further here.)

If the Fourth Amendment did not render the search in *Olmstead* unconstitutional then the self-incrimination was irrelevant, since, Taft CJ pointed out, no one had obliged the defendants to talk about their crimes over the telephone. Chief Justice Taft was emphatic that the Fourth Amendment showed that 'the search is to be of material things – the person, the house, his papers, or his effects'. The warrant had to 'specify the place to be searched and the person or things to be seized' (at 464). Chief Justice Taft rejected any analogy between a phone conversation and the content of a sealed letter. Letters had a particular legal status protected by law. Furthermore, it was 'plainly within the words of the amendment to say that the unlawful rifling by a government agent of a sealed letter is a search and seizure of the sender's papers or effects' (at 464). There was no equivalent protection owed to 'telegraph or telephone messages' (at 464–65):

> The amendment does not forbid what was done here. There was no searching. There was no seizure. The evidence was secured by the use of the sense of hearing and that only. There was no entry of the houses or offices of the defendants.

The extension of the Amendment to cover the telephone would stretch its meaning far beyond what was reasonable (at 465):

> By the invention of the telephone 50 years ago, and its application for the purpose of extending communications, one can talk with another at a far distant place. The language of the amendment cannot be extended and expanded to include telephone wires, reaching to the whole world from the defendant's house or office. The intervening wires are not part of his house or office, any more than are the highways along which they are stretched.

The court had laid down in *Carroll v US* (1925, at 149) that the Fourth Amendment should be interpreted 'in the light of what was deemed an unreasonable search and seizure when it was adopted', but also 'in a manner which will conserve public interests, as well as the interest and rights of individual citizens'. The defence of liberty could not 'justify enlargement of the language employed beyond the possible practical meaning of houses, persons, papers, and effects'; it could not apply the words 'search and seizure' so as to forbid the use of 'hearing or sight' (at 465). While it was open to Congress to pass legislation that would require a warrant in such cases, it was not for the courts to pre-empt this (at 466):

> The reasonable view is that one who installs in his house a telephone instrument with connecting wires intends to project his voice to those quite outside, and that the wires beyond his house, and messages while passing over them, are not within the protection of the Fourth Amendment. Here those who intercepted the projected voices were not in the house of either party to the conversation.

Dissenting, Justice Brandeis argued that the 'general language' of legislation should be interpreted so as to deal with more than the original 'evil' at which it was directed: 'a principle to be vital must be capable of wider application than the mischief which gave it birth'. This was 'peculiarly true of Constitutions' which were 'not ephemeral enactments, designed to meet passing occasions' (at 472–73). As Justice Marshall had declared, constitutions were 'designed to approach immortality as nearly as human institutions can approach it'. Without the ability to change, the general principles of the Constitution would lose their value and 'be converted by precedent into impotent and lifeless formulas. Rights declared in words might be lost in reality' (at 473). The Constitution needed to keep pace with the way the world was changing, in that 'subtler and more far-reaching means of invading privacy have become available to the government'. This was unlikely to end with wire-tapping (at 473–74):

> Ways may some day be developed by which the government, without removing papers from secret drawers, can reproduce them in court, and by which it will be enabled to expose to a jury the most intimate occurrences of the home. Advances in the psychic and related sciences may bring means of exploring unexpressed beliefs, thoughts and emotions.

In *Goldman v US* (1942), the Supreme Court applied the *Olmstead* precedent, though with varying degrees of enthusiasm. Evidence had been obtained by the use of a 'detectaphone', a device which, when applied to the wall of an office from the outside, allowed the agents to follow what was being said. Justice Murphy, in the lone dissent, conceded that if 'the language of the Amendment were given only a literal construction, it might not fit the case now presented for review' (at 138), but it was the court's duty to keep pace with social and technological changes. While he disagreed with *Olmstead*, Justice Murphy argued that in any case it did not apply to the facts before the court. In *Olmstead* the petitioners intended to project their voices beyond the walls of the building by means of the telephone, whereas 'it can hardly be doubted that the application of a detectaphone to the walls of a home or a private office constitutes a direct invasion of the privacy of the occupant, and a search of his private quarters' (at 141).

Key points in the Supreme Court majority judgment

- Following *Weeks v US* (1914), evidence would be excluded if it had been improperly obtained.
- In this case, the issue of self-incrimination did not arise, as the phone calls were not made under any compulsion.
- The only question was whether the search was lawful.
- *Search* implied access to material things, such as a person's papers or home.
- There was no analogy between a letter and a phone call.
- There was no entry and nothing had been seized.
- Telephone wires were not part of the house and carried the voice far beyond it.
- In protecting the public interest, the defence of individual rights did not justify widening the language of the Amendment so drastically so as to exclude the use of hearing and sight.

Key points in the dissenting opinion

- Constitutional language should be interpreted broadly, so as to keep pace with social and technological change, otherwise it would lose its relevance.
- The speed of technological change made it conceivable that the Government could obtain private documents or information in ways previously unimaginable.
- The speed of development in disciplines like psychology made it conceivable that advanced methods for accessing private thoughts and feelings might be developed.

Is a mobile motor home a *motor vehicle*?

California v Carney (1985)	Motor home	Motor vehicle	'The right of the people to be secure in their persons, houses, papers and effects against unreasonable searches and seizures shall not be violated, and no warrants shall issue but upon probable cause', Fourth Amendment, US Constitution	The motor home was not a home, it was a motor vehicle

Background: The motor vehicle exception

There exists a well-established rule in relation to searches in US constitutional law, known as the **motor vehicle exception**. In general, the police do not require a warrant to search a private motor vehicle, so long as there is probable cause for the search (*Carroll v US* (1925)). The seizure in *Carroll* was of contraband goods being moved by road. The goods in question were 'intoxicating liquors', whisky and gin, prohibited under the Eighteenth Amendment which was in force from 1920 to 1933. The fact that a motor vehicle could be 'quickly moved' was central to the decision. The police had to 'act upon a belief, reasonably arising out of circumstances known to the seizing officer' (*Carroll v US*, at 284). While there were privacy interests in an automobile, it was the court's view in *Carroll* that the mobility of a vehicle created a key difference from a dwelling or other permanent building. The Fourth Amendment had been consistently understood as recognizing

> a necessary difference between a search of a store, dwelling house, or other structure in respect of which a proper official warrant readily may be obtained and a search of a ship, motor boat, wagon, or automobile for contraband goods, where it is not practicable to secure a warrant, because the vehicle can be quickly moved out of the locality or jurisdiction in which the warrant must be sought. (at 285)

The reasoning in *Carroll* was tied to a very specific factual scenario. Yet the exception has at times appeared close to being a decontextual rule about the constitutional status of the automobile. In its purest form, the exception would imply that any automobile in any location and in any condition could be searched without a warrant, provided that there existed probable cause. This trend led the Supreme Court in *Coolidge v New Hampshire* (1971) to protest that the word had acquired a magical effect: 'The word "automobile" is not a talisman in whose presence the Fourth Amendment fades away and disappears' (at 461). However, the Supreme Court in *US v Knotts* (1983, at 281) held that someone 'traveling in an automobile on public thoroughfares has no reasonable expectation of privacy in his movements from one place to another'. In *Pennsylvania v Labron* (1996), it was held that once probable cause had been found, there was no need for a warrant to search the vehicle, even if there was ample time available to obtain one and there were no 'exigent circumstances' (at 939). In *Chambers v Maroney* (1970) and *US v Johns* (1985), the vehicle was already held at the police station at the time of the warrantless search. *Automobile* as an abstract category, its 'ready mobility' as an abstract quality, as well as the 'pervasive regulation' that the automobile was subject to, came largely to define the legal basis of the search (Katz, 1986).

If there is an abstract rule that applies globally to all automobiles, then once there is probable cause, all that is required is identification of the place as an *automobile*. The label serves as the magic word or category ('talisman'). On this model, a private home and an automobile are at opposite ends of the continuum in terms of constitutional protection from unreasonable searches. If, however, each factual scenario must be analyzed on its own merits, the police must consider a set of potentially open-ended factors in the particular situation at issue, i.e. a purely contextual rule.

Table 9.1   The abstract rule versus the contextual rule in *Carney*

ABSTRACT RULE		
	Private home	Automobile
Privacy expectation	Highest degree	Lowest degree
Conditions for search	Probable cause + warrant	Probable cause only
Exception for warrant requirement	Exigent circumstances	Automobile exception (= exigent circumstances)
Effect once probable cause shown	'Magic word' guarantees high degree of protection (presumption that warrantless search unreasonable)	'Magic word' offers police high degree of access (presumption that warrantless search reasonable)
CONTEXTUAL RULE		
	Private home	Automobile
Privacy expectation	Contextual evaluation by law enforcement	Contextual evaluation by law enforcement
Warrant requirement	Required unless there is probable cause + exigent circumstances	Required unless there is probable cause + exigent circumstances
Effect	Need for full analysis of actual situation by police officers	Need for full analysis of actual situation by police officers

In practice, the legal situation has been a mixture of the two approaches, with a strong tendency towards the use of 'magic categories'. However, the courts have dealt with all kinds of different places and have also applied both abstract and contextual reasoning (see below). What is important for this discussion is that the motor home (a motorized residence) falls as an abstract category simultaneously into the most protected category (the private home) and the least (the automobile).

Summary of the facts

Mr Carney and his vehicle had come to the attention of agents of the Drug Enforcement Agency (DEA). The vehicle was parked in an off-street lot near the centre of San Diego in the afternoon. A youth was observed to enter the motor home, and the curtains were drawn shut. On leaving after an hour or so, the youth was questioned. He told the agents that Mr Carney was trading marijuana for sex. The officers asked the boy to knock on the door of the motor home, and when Mr Carney stepped out, one of the officers entered and saw marijuana, plastic bags and a scale on the table. The officers then carried out a search without a warrant, and arrested Mr Carney. A subsequent full search of the vehicle at the police station (known technically as an 'inventory search'), also without a warrant, found further stores of marijuana. At trial, a motion to suppress the evidence was rejected, as it was ruled that the motor home fell within the motor vehicle exception. The search was therefore reasonable. The statement by the youth and other unsupported but corroborating information was sufficient for probable cause. Mr Carney was convicted of possessing marijuana for sale. The question on appeal was whether Mr Carney's Dodge Mini motor home fell within the motor vehicle exception.

Three levels of argument

In the judgments discussed below, one can find statements concerning: (I) the abstract motor home as type, its characteristic interior and fittings, the kind of privacy that it allows, the possibility of connecting it to the utilities in a relatively permanent manner, etc.; (II) the actual motor home in the case, its interior and fittings, the use of curtains by the owner, the fact that it was capable of being driven on the highway and licensed to do so, as well as the nature of the location where it was parked, the time of day, etc. The judgments are also marked (III) either by a strong emphasis on the requirements of law enforcement, or, alternatively, on the 'home as castle' motif.

Table 9.2   Three levels of argument: the motor home in *Carney*

	Object of analysis	Examples
Issue I	Properties of motor homes in general	Fittings, fixtures, curtains, typical location, mobility, etc.
Issue II	Properties of the actual motor home parked in San Diego	Fittings, fixtures, curtains, actual location, mobility, time of day, licensed, etc.
Issue III	Jurisprudential framing	Inherent mobility of the automobile; need for clear guidelines for police action; pervasive government regulation of automobile versus sanctity of home; burden of justifying exception

People v Carney (1981) (California Court of Appeal)

The conviction at trial was affirmed in the Court of Appeal by two votes to one. The majority defined the motor home primarily as a motor vehicle (issue I). This is shown by the characterization of the cupboards and refrigerator of the motor home as 'no different from the glove compartment or trunk of the automobile as built-in compartments in the vehicle for storing personal effects' (at 436). As far as the actual vehicle was concerned (issue II), it was mobile and situated in a parking lot, so it was contextually a vehicle rather than a home. In terms of its legal framing or jurisprudence (issue III), the court stressed that the label *motor home* did not undo the 'flexible meaning to be given the term "reasonable" when applied to "automobile" searches'. This was merely an 'additional factor' which required further factual justification (at 436). The basic rationale of the 'automobile exception' applied in this case, and the search was reasonable given the facts.

The dissent argued strongly for the classification of the motor home as a *residence*. It stressed that the motor home in question was equipped as an actual home (issue II). In general, a motor home of this type should be treated as a *home* (issue I):

> Thus the reasonable expectation of privacy as to the cupboards and refrigerator within such a motor home is not to be measured by the degree of protection present in the search of an ordinary passenger compartment of a car or its trunk. Rather a cupboard or refrigerator in such a mobile home possesses all the indicia of a depository of personal effects to which a reasonable expectation of privacy has traditionally attached, and a warrant is required before any delving into such hidden places. (at 437)

People did indeed live in motor homes, whereas they usually did not remain in an automobile 'unless it is going somewhere' (issue I, at 437). There was no doubt that the motor home in question was a dwelling (issue II): 'despite its mobile character by whatever name it is called, this structure is still a species of home, albeit small, albeit on wheels' (at 437). The jurisprudence repeated the term 'sanctuary' several times (issue III), a place 'in which the individual may seek freedom to escape from the intrusion of society'. The conclusion was that 'such sanctuaries are held inviolate from warrantless search except in emergencies of overriding magnitude' (at 437). There were no such facts to support the idea of an emergency, and nothing resembling the exigent circumstances in *US v Williams* (1980). In that case a motor home was held to be analogous to a residence (issue I), though it was held on the facts that there were 'exigent circumstances' due to the presence of dangerous chemicals (issue II).

People v Carney (1983) (Supreme Court of California)

The Supreme Court of California reversed (six to one) the decision of the Court of Appeal, holding that the motor vehicle exception did not apply. The judgment emphasized the nature of the abstract category (issue I). The case law was divided about whether the exception applied to all automobiles regardless of situation. As a result, the mobility of the vehicle, its capacity to be 'quickly moved', was no longer the prime justification for the automobile exception. Rather the 'diminished expectation of privacy' associated with the automobile, given its configuration, and in particular the extensive government regulation, underlay the exception (at 605–06).

In the case of a motor home, the expectations were much more like those associated with a dwelling than an automobile (issue I). The 'hybrid' motor home had the 'mobility attribute of an automobile combined with most of the privacy characteristics of a house' (at 606). Its primary function was not transportation but 'to provide the occupant with living quarters, whether on a temporary or a permanent basis' (at 607). There was official support for this classification: 'Both Vehicle Code [...] and Health and Safety Code [...] refer to a mobile home not as a vehicle but as a transportable "structure"' (at 606).

The court then shifted to look at the actual motor home (issue II). It was equipped

> with at least a bed, a refrigerator, a table, chairs, curtains and storage cabinets. Thus the contents of the motor home created a setting that could accommodate most private activities normally conducted in a fixed home. The configuration of the furnishings, together with the use of the motor home for all manner of strictly personal purposes, strongly suggests that the structure at issue is more properly treated as a residence than a mere automobile. (at 606–07)

In a footnote, the court regretted that the record did not give more details about the other fittings, including whether the motor home had 'bathing and toilet facilities' (at 607, fn. 4).

The court then wove discussion of issues (I) and (III) into a narrative. The protection of the home as a 'place of refuge' was the central focus of the Fourth Amendment: 'The fact that a motor home is not affixed to real property does not demean its protected status as a house' (at 607). The court elaborated on the constitutional protection of the home, which enjoyed 'maximum protection' from searches (issue III). It included quotations from case law on the theme of 'a man's home is his castle' (*US v Nelson* (1972) at 885). The 'poorest man may in his cottage bid defiance to all the force of the Crown [...] the King of England cannot enter – all his force dares not cross the threshold of the ruined tenement' (William Pitt, quoted in *Miller v US* (1958) at 307).

The structure in question (issue I) had the 'principal function' of providing 'living quarters' rather than serving as a 'means of transportation'. This fact about its function was 'reasonably apparent from the exterior of the motor home' (at 607): 'For these reasons, it is entitled to a degree of protection similar to that accorded an Englishman's cottage or "ruined tenement"' (at 607). Those staying temporarily in hotels or motels were protected from intrusion, and no convincing argument had been offered as to 'why persons who rely on motor homes for such shelter should be penalized by depriving them of similar protections' (at 608).

An automobile was rarely used to store personal belongings, whereas a motor home was (issue I). In this it was analogous to a home, an office or a piece of luggage (at 608). In contrast to an automobile, 'the interior and contents of an ordinary motor home are not generally exposed to the public, nor are the occupants, the furnishings or any personal effects in plain view' (at 608). The windows were designed to provide privacy, and could be covered by blinds or curtains. There was 'an objectively reasonable expectation of privacy' (at 608). There were statements to the effect that a motor home was a dwelling in *US v Williams* (1980). This principle applied equally (issue I) to 'the home resting on wheels' and 'the home resting on a cement foundation' (at 609).

The Fourth Amendment was about the right of an individual 'to retreat into his own home and be free from unreasonable government intrusion' (issue III). In *Silverman v US* (1961), the court had quoted Judge Jerome Frank on the home as 'oasis', 'shelter', 'insulated enclave', an 'inviolate place which is a man's castle' (from *US v On Lee* (1951) at 316). The home on wheels was no less a home than one resting on cement, and in this case the outward appearance would have been enough (issue II). Even if the entry was reasonable, it would cease to be so once it was evident that a home is being searched (at 609, fn. 7). Thus 'a motor home is fully protected by the Fourth Amendment' (issues I and III) (at 610). In the instant case, the search was reasonable, in that it met the required standard for obtaining a warrant. But there was no warrant, and a warrant was required in the absence of exigent circumstances.

The dissent by Justice Richardson argued that the majority judgment was based on a misleading generalization (issue I) and thus failed to give guidance to law enforcement officers. The majority had determined that a motor home was not 'subject to the automobile exception', but had failed to define its terms (issue I):

> What precisely are 'motor homes'? They are almost infinitely variable in size, shape, design, access, and visibility. Some of the smaller ones are the most enclosed. Others are separately attached as trailers, while still others have direct access from the driver's cab. Is a camper or recreational vehicle a 'motor home'? What about a large van or truck? (at 614)

The majority used the term 'as if it were readily understood', whereas 'I find no definition either in statute or dictionary' (at 614). If any motor vehicle serving as a residence was entitled to constitutional protection, how were the police to determine its status in advance of a search? (issue I) (at 614):

> Some people live in the cab of a truck. For others, 'home' may be a sleeping bag thrown in the back of a pickup truck. The interior of many vehicles is obscured by tinted glass or shades or venetian blinds. Does this fact alone establish the vehicle as a 'residence' for Fourth Amendment purposes? [...] If a motor home is a residence, what is the address of the residence?

'Broad generalizations' were not useful (issues I and II). If the facts indicated that the vehicle was being used as residence, for example by being attached to utility services, then the exception would not apply. But if there was no residential use or this use was secondary, then the exception should apply. After all, in the case of motor homes, 'the "residence" can be three states away in a matter of hours' (issue I) (at 615). The dissent therefore cast doubt on the definitional certainty on which the majority seemed to rely, and argued for a contextual approach. There was, however, clearly an emphasis on the general quality of mobility that characterized most motor homes, and a presumption that unless the vehicle showed definite signs of being situated in a permanent or semi-permanent fashion, it was a vehicle.

California v Carney (1985) (US Supreme Court)

The Supreme Court reversed, in a split decision (six to three), upholding the search. Chief Justice Berger wrote for the majority. The judgment noted that the origins of the automobile exception were in police action against contraband goods on the move, where the serving of a warrant was not practicable because the goods could be 'quickly moved' (issues I and II). The mobility of the vehicle created 'circumstances of such exigency' that 'rigorous enforcement of the warrant requirement' was impossible (at 391, citing *South Dakota v Opperman* (1976) at 367). Further, the expectation of privacy was less in an automobile than in a home or an office, even in vehicles that were not immediately mobile (issue I). The configuration of the automobile lowered that expectation, because 'the passenger compartment of a standard automobile is relatively open to plain view' (at 391). But even warrantless searches of closed areas such as a locked trunk (boot) and the closed compartment under the dashboard had been held to be reasonable. The justification for this was not primarily the reduced expectation of privacy. There was a wide range of contexts in which police officers might stop and examine a vehicle amounting to 'pervasive regulation of vehicles capable of traveling on the public highway'. The general public was well aware that there were lower expectations of privacy in automobiles 'because of this compelling governmental need for regulation' (issue I) (at 392).

   If a vehicle capable of being driven on the highway was parked in a location 'not regularly used for residential purposes' (whether temporary or not), then the two factors came into play. The first was whether the vehicle in question was 'readily mobile'; the second was whether it was licensed to be driven on public streets, and therefore there was a reduced expectation of privacy. While the vehicle had 'some if not many of the attributes of a home', it was 'so situated that an objective observer would conclude that it was being used not as a residence, but as a vehicle' (at 393). The fact that the vehicle was capable of functioning as a home did not offer a clear dividing line given that, in an 'increasingly mobile society', many forms of vehicle were being used for shelter, i.e. as a home. It was not proposed to define the vehicle exception simply by reference to the type or size of vehicle or the nature of its fittings (at 393):

> To distinguish between respondent's motor home and an ordinary sedan
> for purposes of the vehicle exception would require that the exception

be applied depending on the size of the vehicle and the quality of its appointments.

It was also necessary to consider that the motor home 'lends itself easily as an instrument of illegal drug traffic and other illegal activity' (issue I) (at 394). The other uses to which a vehicle might be put were not a determining factor. Its ready mobility and a location indicating objectively its use as transportation were decisive (issues I and II). Factors that might indicate that a vehicle was being used as residence would be (issue II)

its location, whether the vehicle is readily mobile or instead, for instance, elevated on blocks, whether the vehicle is licensed, whether it is connected to utilities, and whether it has convenient access to a public road. (at 394, fn. 3)

The dissent argued in essence that the 'hybrid character' of the motor home put it 'at the crossroads' between privacy and law enforcement interests (issue I). There was little need for the Supreme Court to hear this case. An American citizen had not been deprived of a constitutional right; rather, the California Supreme Court had upheld such a right. Whatever tensions or contradictions existed in state law should be left to 'percolate'; this intervention was premature and had 'stunted the natural growth and refinement of alternative principles' (at 395–98). There were no prior cases on point concerning hybrids such as 'motor homes, house trailers, houseboats, or yachts', and the Court was not in a position to grasp 'the diverse lifestyles associated with recreational vehicles and mobile living quarters' (at 399). The Supreme Court had rushed to judgment before the case law had developed a full range of different analyses and approaches.

The need for a warrant was the primary rule (issue III). If the motor home were 'parked in the exact middle of the intersection between the general rule and the exception for automobiles, priority should be given to the rule, rather than the exception' (at 402). The 'inherent mobility' of the motor home was insufficient to justify a presumption of exigency and an exception to the warrant requirement (issue I). Where the motor home was parked away from the public highway, the expectation of privacy was similar to that in a 'fixed dwelling'. The warrantless search was reasonable only if the motor home was travelling on the public highway or there were exigent circumstances (at 402). The motor home was parked in an off-the-street lot in downtown San Diego (issue II). It was only a short distance from the courthouse, 'where dozens of magistrates were available to entertain a warrant application'. There clearly was probable cause to obtain a warrant, but there were no exigent circumstances.

Inherent mobility had been rejected as the determining criterion in case law (issue I). The Supreme Court had rejected a warrantless search of a footlocker ('storage trunk or chest') in *US v Chadwick* (1977). The view that 'the rationale of the automobile exception applied to movable containers in general' had been rejected. There was a greater privacy expectation in private luggage than in an automobile, and this had been reaffirmed in *US v Ross* (1982). It was evident that the interior of a mobile home had a greater expectation of privacy than a footlocker, and therefore the criterion of 'inherent mobility' was insufficient justification (issue I) (at 405–06). The dissent described the motor home in question (issue II) as able to 'accommodate a breadth of ordinary everyday living' and 'a substantial living space inside'. There were 'stuffed chairs around a table, storage cupboards, bunk beds and a refrigerator; curtains and large opaque walls' prevented anyone viewing activities within the vehicle. Summing up, the dissent concluded that the inner configuration showed (issue II) that the 'vehicle's size, shape, and mode of construction should have indicated to the officers that it was a vehicle containing mobile living quarters' (at 406).

To the argument that police officers would have the 'impossible task' of deciding which vehicles were fitted with living quarters, the dissent looked to 'common English usage' (issue I). Definitions cited from *Webster's Ninth Collegiate Dictionary* (1983) distinguished between a *motor home* which was 'equipped as a self-contained traveling home', a *camper*, only equipped for 'casual travel and camping', and an *automobile* which is 'designed for passenger transportation' (at 406). Further, California state law distinguished between ordinary vehicles, in which it was forbidden to open or consume alcoholic drinks, and the living quarters of *housecars* and *campers*, where such was permitted. This indicated that 'descriptive distinctions' of this or a similar kind are 'humanly possible' (issue I) (at 407).

In a final rhetorical blast (issue III), the dissent rejected any class-based analysis of the type of dwelling protected. While a motor home might not be a castle, it was usually 'the functional equivalent of a hotel room, a vacation and retirement home, or a hunting and fishing cabin'. While such dwellings might be 'spartan as a humble cottage' when set against 'the most majestic mansion', nonetheless 'the highest and most legitimate expectations of privacy associated with these temporary abodes should command the respect of this Court' (at 407–08).

Key points in the US Supreme Court majority judgment

- The fact that a motor home could be quickly moved brought it within the motor vehicle exception for warrantless searches.
- There was a reduced expectation of privacy in motor vehicles because of their open design, but primarily because they were subject to heightened government regulation and police scrutiny.
- The motor home in question was not parked in a clearly residential location; it was in a location where an objective observer would conclude that it was being used as a vehicle.
- The motor home in question was readily mobile and licensed for the public roads.
- There was a reduced expectation of privacy in this case, even though the motor home had some of the features of a dwelling.
- Motor homes were particularly suitable for drug dealing and other illegal activities.

■ The fact that a motor vehicle was (for example) elevated on blocks or connected to public utilities would indicate that it was being used as a residence.

Key points in the dissenting opinion

■ The nature of the motor home as a hybrid entity put it at the intersection between privacy concerns and the demands of law enforcement.

■ There was no pressing need for the Supreme Court to hear this case and establish a national rule, thereby disturbing the ongoing development of state law.

■ The requirement for the warrant was the primary rule, and any exceptions needed strong justification.

■ Inherent mobility was insufficient as a criterion for *vehicle*, if the motor home was parked off or away from the highway.

■ There was probable cause but there were no exigent circumstances, and a warrant could conveniently have been obtained.

■ If a search of luggage normally required a warrant, this was even more true of a search of a motor home.

■ The motor home in question was fitted out as a residence, and this would have been clear to the police officers once they entered it.

■ Police officers could and should distinguish between different forms of vehicles in enforcing legal rules, as this was part of normal English usage.

■ The privacy of a humble dwelling was as much protected as that of a large mansion.

Popular culture reference

In the TV drama series *Breaking Bad* (season 3, episode 6, first aired in 2010) a DEA agent attempts to break open a Recreational Vehicle (RV) parked on a car lot. He knows there is a suspect inside (in fact there are two), and he has good reason to believe that the RV has been used to produce methamphetamines. The owner of the lot confronts the agent and asks if he has a warrant, suggesting that the agent is a trespasser. The agent counters that he has no need of one if he has probable cause. The lot owner retorts that probable cause usually relates to vehicles at traffic stops. The agent points to the 'round rubber things, wheels' on the RV: 'This is a vehicle'. It is not a vehicle, comes the reply, it is a 'domicile, a residence and thus protected by the Fourth Amendment from unlawful search and seizure'. The owner asks the agent: 'Did you see this drive in here?' There is further argument about whether bullet holes masked with tape are 'readily apparent' so as to constitute probable cause. Probable cause, in combination with the 'vehicle exception', would allow the agent to enter without a warrant. One of the men inside then shouts out: 'This is my own private domicile and I will not be harassed'. The agent calls in for a warrant, but the suspects trick him into leaving before it arrives. The RV is then destroyed.

The judicial gaze

Table 9.3 shows the correlation between the conclusions each judgment drew about motor homes in general (issue I), about the particular motor home in the case (issue II), and the jurisprudential framework applied (issue III).

Table 9.3 Correlations in the judgments in *Carney*

	Issue I	Issue II	Issue III
Court of Appeal (CA)			
Majority	vehicle	vehicle	Automobile exception and factor of inherent mobility gave greater flexibility in defining a reasonable search
Dissent	residence	residence	A residence was a sanctuary; there were no exigent circumstances
Supreme Court CA			
Majority	residence	residence	A residence was a castle in which there was a high expectation of privacy; there were no exigent circumstances
Dissent	vehicle	vehicle	Police needed practical guidelines and clear definitional guidance; there was a strong presumption that an immediately moveable motor home was a vehicle
Supreme Court US			
Majority	vehicle	vehicle	Inherent mobility of automobile; automobile is accepted as being subject to high levels of scrutiny and regulation; the mobile home is particularly suitable for carrying out illegal activities
Dissent	residence	residence	There is a strong burden to be met in justifying any exception to warrant rule; each and every domicile, however humble, deserves the same level of constitutional protection

Judgments which place great emphasis on the inviolability of the home (issue III) also define the motor home in general (issue I) and the motor home at issue (issue II) as primarily a *home*. Those which find that the search was reasonable and put weight on the operational needs of the police characterize motor homes in general and this particular motor home primarily as a *vehicle*. The series of cases illustrates an important point about categories and classification in law. The activities of category analysis and classification are interwoven with the jurisprudence. There is no clear direction to the reasoning, in that the categories are not established independently of the decision-making process. Different judges looked at the same type of vehicle and the same factual situation against the same case law background and came to opposite conclusions. Raigrodski (2013: 89–90) points out that both the majority and the dissent ignored the sexual and commercial nature of the transactions taking place in the mobile home.

Discussion

Definitional and doctrinal complexity remains. What is the status of a large wooden or cardboard box situated on public land and used as a shelter by a homeless person? Is it akin to garbage bags left in a public space that can be searched (*California v Greenwood* (1988))? Is it a container analogous to *luggage*, a category which gives rise to expectations of privacy? Or is it a home? Do the ready mobility of the box and its owner's squatter status allow police to search the 'cardboard castle' without a warrant (Townsend, 1999)? In *People v Thomas* (1995) it was ruled that a warrantless search of such a *box-home* was constitutional. *Katz* notwithstanding, the legitimate occupation of private property remains fundamental to the Fourth Amendment (see Raigrodski, 2013: 70–71).

Olmstead remains of fundamental relevance today, as the law faces technological changes that redefine established notions of space, jurisdiction, property, ownership, money, identity, speech, privacy, information and so on. *In US v Carey* (1999), the court rejected the analogy between, on the one hand, looking for documents in a file cabinet and in the process finding evidence of a crime in plain view and, on the other, searching files on a seized computer (see Gore, 2003: 417). In *Kyllo v US* (2001), the Supreme Court ruled five to four that use of a thermal imaging device to detect high levels of heat generated by marijuana cultivation constituted a *search* (at 40):

> Where, as here, the Government uses a device that is not in general public use, to explore details of the home that would previously have been unknowable without physical intrusion, the surveillance is a 'search' and is presumptively unreasonable without a warrant.

The dilemma that this technological innovation represented was analogous to that in *Olmstead*, at least as far as the problematic boundary between the private inner space and the public outer space was concerned.

In 2012 the Supreme Court held that the attaching of a GPS tracker to a private car constituted a *search*, and in the absence of a warrant constituted a violation of the Fourth Amendment (*Jones v US* (2012)). In his judgment Justice Scalia emphasized that the word *property* was used in the Fourth Amendment, and found support for his reading in the decision in *Entick v Carrington* (1765, at 817):

> [O]ur law holds the property of every man so sacred, that no man can set his foot upon his neighbour's close without his leave; if he does he is a trespasser, though he does no damage at all; if he will tread upon his neighbour's ground, he must justify it by law.

There have been extensive discussions of how the US Federal Communications Act (1934), in particular s. 606, defines presidential powers in relation to the

Internet in wartime or in the face of a grave threat to national security. It has been argued that the President potentially controls a 'cybersecurity internet kill switch' (Opderbeck, 2013).

In June 2013, former technical analyst Edward Snowden revealed details of massive cybersurveillance programs carried out by the National Security Agency (NSA), as well as other programs of the US, UK and French Governments. This has led to acrimonious debate about the scope and legality of s. 215 of the Patriot Act (2001) and s. 1881a of the Foreign Intelligence Surveillance Amendments Act (2008). Section 215 of the Patriot Act allows a court to order the handing over of *tangible things*, defined as 'books, records, papers, documents, and other items'. There is no requirement of probable cause or even reasonable grounds. Section 1881a of the Foreign Intelligence Surveillance Amendments Act authorizes the acquisition of *foreign intelligence information* from an 'electronic communication service provider', e.g. Facebook, Google, Amazon. Among the many issues raised are questions about what it means to *target* a communication or an individual, the definition of *foreign* in the context of global communication, the status of *meta-data*, i.e. information about who communicates whom, when and for how long, whether a program that scans emails and SMS messages for particular terms or collocations constitutes a *search*, and whether the indiscriminate storing of electronic communications constitutes a *seizure*. One fundamental question in relation to these programs is that of **standing**. Who can bring an action in relation to alleged secret violations of the Fourth Amendment (see *Clapper v Amnesty International USA* (2013); Nash, 2013: 1296–97)?

Points for further consideration

> The common law has always recognized a man's house as his castle, impregnable, often, even to its own officers engaged in the execution of its commands. Shall the courts thus close the front entrance to constituted authority, and open wide the back door to idle or prurient curiosity? (Warren and Brandeis, 1890: 220)

By the 'back door', the authors presumably mean non-physical forms of surveillance and monitoring. Historically, letters and the mail enjoy a high degree of legal protection. In *Goldman v US* (1942), Justice Murphy commented: 'It is strange doctrine that keeps inviolate the most mundane observations entrusted to the permanence of paper, but allows the revelation of thoughts uttered within the sanctity of private quarters' (at 141). While it seems that the law gives greater protection to writings on paper than other forms of communication, are not the communicated spoken word, the text message, the email no less tangible or concrete than a letter? If the 'core meaning' of terms like *search* and *seizure* is a physical intrusion into a space and the taking of physical things, then is not the Fourth Amendment unsuited to the contemporary world of electronic communication? Or can the metaphorical understanding of these terms compensate for this limitation? Can the concept of 'reasonable expectation of privacy' (REOP) from *Katz* (Weaver, 2013), detached from the physical terminology of the Fourth Amendment, provide a better framework?

The judges' understanding of word meaning and their perception of the nature of the motor home under scrutiny in *Carney* were arguably determined primarily by their underlying attitude to the jurisprudential principle at stake. If this is a general characteristic of judicial reasoning, then would this not suggest that adjudication is based neither on shared word meanings nor on shared perceptions of reality?

CHAPTER 10

Colonial Encounters: What is a Sacred Object?

Is a cow a *sacred object*?

Queen-Empress v Imam Ali and Anor (1888)	Cow	Object	'Whoever destroys, damages or defiles any place of worship, or any object held sacred by any class of persons, with the intention of thereby insulting the religion of any class of persons' (Indian Penal Code, s. 295)	A cow is not an object

Queen-Empress v Imam Ali and Anor (1888) (Allahabad High Court, India)

The case of *Queen-Empress v Imam Ali and Anor* (1888) concerns an incident which took place on 30 August 1887, in Tilhar, Shahjahanpur, in the north of India. Queen Victoria had been declared Empress of India in 1876, hence the prosecution was in the name of the 'Queen-Empress'. Two men, Imam Ali and Amiruddin, were convicted and fined by a magistrate for each slaughtering a cow by the roadside. They had been charged under s. 295 of the Indian Penal Code:

> Whoever destroys, damages or defiles any place of worship, or any object held sacred by any class of persons, with the intention of thereby insulting the religion of any class of persons, or with the knowledge that any class of persons are likely to consider such destruction, damage or defilement as an insult to their religion, shall be punished with imprisonment […] and shall also be liable to a fine.

The magistrate convicted, based on the fact that the defendants, who were Muslims (*Mahomedans* or *Muhammadans* in the terminology of the day), would have known that the slaughtering of the cow was an offence to Hindus (sometimes spelled *Hindoos* in texts of that period).

On appeal in the Allahabad High Court, Sir John Edge CJ defined the 'sole question' to be that of whether a cow was an *object* within the meaning of s. 295 (originally s. 275). He noted that if one applied the 'usual principle of construction', the word *object* would be understood as being 'of the same kind' (*ejusdem generis*) of entity as a 'place of worship'. It would be 'some inanimate object such as an idol &c.' (para. 2). The legislature evidently had in mind inanimate objects, otherwise the word *object* would have been defined in the statute. If the law applied to cows, then any slaughter, even in a slaughter house, would be illegal, as the intentional killing of a cow 'would be considered an insult by a strict Hindu'. In the other judgments, the point was made that had the legislature intended the killing of animals, then words other than or additional to 'destroys, damages or defiles' would have been used, such as 'or kills, maims or otherwise injures any animal' (para. 6). The relevant meaning of *object* included 'churches, mosques, temples and marble or stone figures representing gods' (para. 7).

The longest judgment was written by Justice Saiyyid Mahmood (spelled as Mahmud in other sources), a Muslim like the accused, but from an elite northern Indian family. Justice Mahmood began with the statement that in cases of 'doubtful or ambiguous meaning', penal statutes should be interpreted in favour of the accused party. Further, the principle of *ejusdem generis* applied, under which

> the operation of words of a general signification is restrained when they follow closely upon words of a limited meaning, upon words which refer to a particular class of things or persons, or which necessarily exclude such matters as are of higher dignity. In all these cases general words are confined to things and persons ejusdem generis with those enumerated or of inferior quality (para. 10, citing Wilberforce 1881: 179–180).

Justice Mahmood added a further general principle of statutory interpretation, namely, that 'when words importing a popular meaning are employed in a statute, they ought to be construed in such a sense', unless the legislature had offered an alternative definition (para. 10):

> Now the word 'object' no doubt has a technical and extensive meaning in philosophy and would include not only an animal but also a human being, and indeed if we go further, the word would in philosophy include also abstract concepts. But such is not the manner in which the popular mind understands the words, nor can we attach any such meaning to the word in interpreting a penal enactment such as Section 295 of the Indian Penal Code.

If *object* was taken to refer to animate beings such as animals, then there was 'no logical reason why we should not include a human being within the meaning of that word'. The word *object* clearly 'must be understood to be limited to inanimate objects' (para. 10).

If the judgment had ended at this point, one might have concluded that this was a fairly routine case involving the application of well-established and uncontroversial principles of statutory interpretation. However, Justice Mahmood then launched into a discussion of the religious background to the case and the state of Hindu–Muslim relations. Even though this entered territory of intense public interest and controversy, he claimed that was consistent 'with the rule of judicial etiquette which requires that Judges should abstain from taking part in matters of a purely political character' (para. 11). Incidents such as this had been proliferating, and the importance of the issue was shown by the fact that it was not just cows that were held sacred: 'the bovine species is not the only class of animals held sacred by the Hindu population of India, and indeed I may add that even trees, such as the pipal, are included among the objects of worship or veneration by that section of the community' (para. 11). While ancient Hindu sages had enjoined the sacrifice of cows on sacred occasions, there was no doubting that the cow was a sacred animal 'in the present day' – though this would not affect the interpretation of the word *object* in the statute.

Mahmood alluded to the increasing number of similar cases; previously the two communities had not 'recklessly hurt the religious prejudices of each other' to the same extent (para. 12). It was not evident how the law should deal with such matters, where 'in the most offensive manner the slaughter of a cow is accomplished by a Muhammadan before the eyes of a Hindu fellow-subject, or cases in which a Hindu procession is carried with offensive demonstration in front of a Muhammadan mosque' (para. 12). This raised the question of whether the new liberties enjoyed by 'Her Majesty's Subjects' were not 'too much in advance of the stage of civilization' which India had attained. Offering an analysis in terms of the social class of the accused, the judge lamented the lack of consideration and absence of the 'gentlemanly feelings' seen here that one would find among the 'better classes' of Muslims. Cows had been slaughtered 'on the road-side and in a locality which would be visible to any Hindu passer-by' (para. 12). At the beginning of his judgment, Justice Mahmood had said that it was not necessary to say much about the 'exposition of the law', since the case was clear. At the close, he reasserted that the questions was straightforward and 'a pure question of law'.

As Justice Mahmood in particular would have been aware, the ruling was not likely to be well received by Hindu opinion and the Hindu press. His remarks can be read as offering a defence against the charge that he, as a Muslim from a family associated with Muslim political activism and enmeshed with the colonial establishment, was colluding with the British judiciary in denying devout Hindus legal protection for their religious sensibilities.

The Indian Penal Code had been substantially completed by 1837, but was not enacted until 1860. An explanatory commentary by the law commissioners published in 1838 explained that the principle that lay behind the section was that 'every man should be suffered to profess his own religion, and that no man should be suffered to insult the religion of another'. This protection should be extended regardless of 'whether that religion be true or false' ([PCBI] 1838: 87). There was a strong tendency within early British colonialism to view Hinduism as a false superstition. By contrast, Islam was recognizably a monotheistic religion with an organized textual canon of authority, with the Qur'an at its centre. The continuation of 'British Government in India' was potentially under threat from 'religious excitement among the people'. This was not least because Christians were a tiny elite minority in the population, ruling over 'millions of Mahomedans of different sects [...]; and tens of millions of Hindoos, strongly attached to doctrines and rites which Christians and Mahomedans join in reprobating' ([PCBI] 1838: 87). Behind the section lay a fear of disorder and revolt: 'No offence in the whole Code is so likely to lead to tumult, to sanguinary outrage, and even to armed insurrection. The slaughter of a cow in a sacred place at Benares, in 1809, caused violent tumult, attended with considerable loss of life' ([PCBI] 1838: 87). If the purpose of s. 295 was the prevention of religious-based conflicts (termed today 'communal violence'), then the fact that the explanatory notes specifically mentioned civil unrest triggered by the slaughtering of a cow might have weighed in favour of conviction. The notes, however, had no direct legal authority, and the judgments did not allude to the Benares incident. It does not appear from the case report that the slaughter took place in a sacred place or was in any way calculated to inflame Hindu sensibilities, beyond the fact that it was publicly visible. The slaughtering of cows was not *per se* illegal.

Key points in the judgment

- The sole question was whether a cow was an *object* within the meaning of s. 295.
- The application of *ejusdem generis* enabled the determination of the legally relevant meaning of the word *object* which was within the same frame as *place of worship*.
- A place of worship was not an animate being, and what was meant by *object* was an idol or statue, or some other sacred image.
- The meaning of the word *object* in general had a wide range of possible meanings, including philosophical ones (Justice Mahmood); the word was used in a non-technical sense in the statute, and the 'popular meaning' should be applied, which would not include animate beings such as cows.
- If the legislature had meant to include cows within the protected class of objects, it would have used further verbs, in addition to *destroy, damage* or *defile*; it was not normal usage to say: 'it is forbidden to destroy, damage or defile a cow'.

Discussion

The court could be represented as choosing between a broad and a narrow meaning of the word *object*. The broad meaning would include any entity that can be identified, categorized or labelled, whether abstract or concrete, animate or inanimate; the narrow meaning of *object* would refer to physical or concrete or entities, a tangible thing, but not a living being. There is a third meaning of the word *object*, namely, the target or goal of intentional action, which was not mentioned. One can talk of an 'object of desire' and an 'object of worship'. In coming to the conclusion that it did, the court categorically excluded all cows from the legally relevant category (Groves, 2010: 109).

Is a cow that is set loose still *property*?

Romesh Chunder Sannyal v Hiru Mondal (1890)	Cow	Object Property	'Whoever destroys, damages or defiles any place of worship, or any object held sacred by any class of persons, with the intention of thereby insulting the religion of any class of persons' (Indian Penal Code, s. 295)	A cow is not an object; a cow which has been dedicated at a ceremony and set loose is not property

Romesh Chunder Sannyal v Hiru Mondal (1890) (Calcutta High Court, India)

A related case was heard before the Calcutta High Court in 1890. This arose out of an incident in Nattore, in Bengal. A bull had been dedicated and branded during the death ceremony (*adya sradha*) to honour the mother of the local nobleman or Rajbari. It was subsequently killed by two Muslims. The facts were recounted as follows:

> After the dedication and setting at large the Rajbari cowherd tended the bull under the supervision of the Rajbari sirdar [steward]; he gave it a seer of rice a day and used to drive it away if he found it eating any one's crops. The bull was used by the villagers for breeding purposes, and there is some evidence to show that it was not so used without permission having been obtained from the Rajbari. Some eighteen months after the bull had been so dedicated and set at liberty, Hiru Mondal, and Modhu Mondal, both Mahomedans, with others killed it. The killing took place at night in a straw-field some distance from the village, and was not witnessed by any Hindu.

This case differed from the first in two important respects. First, the bull was reported to be one that had taken part in a dedication ceremony; secondly, the killing was not done in a public place. If the original intent of s. 295 had been to protect animals that had some specific sacred context or association, then this case would surely have fallen within it. However, there was no immediate affront to Hindu feeling, as the killing took place in a secluded spot.

Since *Imam Ali* had held that *object* in s. 295 as a matter of definition did not include cows, the accused had been acquitted by the deputy magistrate. The magistrate also considered whether the slaughter fell under the definition of *mischief*, in which case it would have had to be shown that there had been destruction of *property* (ss. 378, 403, 425, Indian Penal Code): 'Now it has been held that a bull so dedicated and set at large is nullius proprietas [no person's property] and it is therefore incapable of being the subject of mischief'. For the same reason one could not speak of 'criminal misappropriation or larceny' (cited, para. 3). While the killing of such a bull was 'simply outrageous to the religious feeling of a Hindu and specially of one who dedicated it', there was no criminal liability.

On behalf of the Government, the Advocate-General (Sir George Paul) sought to reverse the acquittals. However, Justice Norris ruled that 'a bull dedicated and set at liberty' was not in any relevant sense property (*Queen-Empress v Bandhu* (1886)), and, further, that *Imam Ali* had been correctly decided. The *ejusdem generis* rule had been properly applied. The explanatory note concerning the Benares incident was of legitimate relevance in the construction of s. 295, but it did not demonstrate that 'the word "object" should include a cow' (para. 11): 'What caused "the violent tumult at Benares in 1809" was not the slaughter of the cow, but its slaughter in a sacred place'. The defining element was the pollution of the sacred place, not the slaughter of the cow (para. 12).

While there were statements in *Queen-Empress v Nalla* (1888) to the effect that there was a difference between an animal turned completely loose and an animal that was turned loose but which remained dedicated to a specific temple, this was not directly relevant. The fact that the bull was fed daily by the Rajbari cowherd at 'the direction of his employers' was not in any way inconsistent with a 'total surrender' of 'all their rights as proprietors' by those who had set it at liberty.

Key points in the judgment

- The decision in *Imam Ali*, in particular the application of *ejusdem generis*, was correct, and a cow was not an *object* in the legally relevant sense.
- The bull in question was not *property* in the legally relevant sense.
- The explanatory materials published in 1837 were of potential relevance in the interpretation of s. 295; the Benares example, however, showed that the mischief against which the section was directed was the pollution or desecration of a sacred place.

Discussion

The court found no reason to question the definitional or categorical basis of the judgment in *Imam Ali*. The more interesting discussion related to the question of whether the bull was *property*. The court regarded it as settled law that cows or bulls which are set loose are in general not owned in any legally relevant sense, even though in this case the bull was 'dedicated and set at large after being branded on the hind part'. The feeding and care of cows and bulls were sacred duties of any Hindu, and the supervision to which the bull was subject did not constitute ownership. The logic of the court's position was that the bull, not being owned as property in any sense recognizable at common law, was no person's property (*nullius proprietas*). A contemporary decision by the Privy Council made a parallel argument about land (*Cooper v Stuart* (1889)). This described Australia as 'a colony which consisted of a tract of territory practically unoccupied, without settled inhabitants or settled law, at the time when it was peacefully annexed to the British dominions' (at 291). This was the doctrine of *terra nullius* ('land belonging to nobody'). If the bull was *nullius proprietas* it was therefore any person's property, just as Australia was *terra nullius*. Lying behind this argument is the common law's understanding that it is primarily recognizably productive control and use that establishes ownership rights in natural phenomena. In Australia, the consequences of this understanding of property rights for the aboriginal inhabitants were catastrophic.

Analysis of the two cases

The focus on word meaning relegated discussion of the social context to the background. The 'popular meaning' ascribed to *object* was not one identified with any place, or time or group of people; rather, there was an appeal to a generalized but non-specific meaning, a linguistic intuition, that one would not describe a cow as an *object*. There was no discussion of what the sacred status of cows comprised, whether cows are actually 'worshipped' and whether some cows were more sacred than others. There were two social groups identified, namely, Muslims and Hindus, but there was no discussion of any social views about cows and their slaughter, beyond the attribution of sacred status to the cow. The socio-cultural context was taken as read; it was taken for granted that the case involved a clash of two opposing interests, with the court metaphorically positioned in the middle. Nor was there any analysis of 'Hindu' notions of property and ownership, either within or outside the common law frame.

The linguistic categories were taken as supplying an adequate ontology. It was assumed that the legally relevant status of the cow could be read off directly from the language of the statute. This was adequate for representing the relationship between the language of the statute and the range of objects, places and processes that make up ritual behaviour and public peace. What the law protected was a relationship between a place or thing and an identified group of people. But it was not explained why an animate object of worship was marginal to the class of *object*, in the context where we are talking about religious belief.

One way to understand this case is that the resort to linguistic categories and linguistic common sense avoids a consideration of, and any attempt to grasp, the classifications or ontological system of the 'Hindu' themselves. If we take this view then perhaps the cases were wrongly decided: 'Hindu opinion had right to be outraged' (Groves, 2010: 109). But was the case in fact wrongly decided? Groves points out that, except in the case of Justice Saiyyid Mahmood, the judges 'did not think it relevant to their brief to consider whether their decision might have some adverse social or political outcome'. Their focus was 'entirely on the wording of the section', and even 'today courts still grapple with this dilemma – facts versus consequences' (Groves, 2010: 117–18).

The colonial government was anxious for a conviction, but the law had not been changed since the *Imam Ali* case. Section 295 remains unaltered to this day. However, Article 48 of the Constitution of India 1949 requires the state to 'take steps for preserving and improving the breeds, and prohibiting the slaughter, of cows and calves and other milch and draught cattle'.

Points for further consideration

One can see these two decisions as embodying the neutrality of law, in that law does not take sides in the religious disputes of its subjects but simply applies the plain language of the legal text. Within the colonial frame, this claim to neutrality echoes the self-understanding of British colonialism itself. However, can these decisions not also be seen as an example of law's sometime sublime indifference to the conceptual world over which it rules?

CHAPTER 11

Defining Identity I: Job or Profession

Does a Christian minister perform *labor* or *service*?

Church of the Holy Trinity v US (1892)	Labor or service of any kind	Minister	'the importation or migration of any alien or aliens [...] into the United States [...] to perform labor or service of any kind in the US' (Alien Contract Labor Law, Sess. II c. 164; 23 Stat. 332, 1885)	The work of a minister was labor or service but the statute was not intended to apply to Christian ministers

Church of the Holy Trinity v US (1892) (US Supreme Court)

The Church of the Holy Trinity in New York had concluded a contract for employment with an English minister, the Reverend E. Walpole Warren. He was to serve as its new pastor, and had taken up his post in 1887. A federal statute, the Alien Contract Labor Law (1885), made it unlawful for any person to offer, or to facilitate, any contract of employment with a foreign citizen (*alien*) before that person's migration into the United States. The Act was subtitled: 'An act to prohibit the importation and migration of foreigners and aliens under contract or agreement to perform labor in the United States'. The statute covered contracts 'to perform labor or service of any kind'. Section 4 provided for the punishment of a ship-master who knowingly brought into the United States 'any alien laborer, mechanic or artisan'. Section 5 exempted 'professional actors, artists, lecturers, or singers' from the scope of the statute. The minister was a British citizen, previously of Holy Trinity Church, Lambeth, in London, though he had spent some time at the Church in the United States as part of a 'preaching mission' (Chomsky, 2000: 901). There was no dispute that the Reverend Warren was resident in England prior to the contract being agreed.

The Circuit Court for the Southern District of New York (*US v Rector of the Church of the Holy Trinity* (1888)) found the Church liable for breaching the statute and imposed a fine of $1,000. The court recognized that it was the primary aim of the Act to 'prohibit the introduction of assisted immigrants' under a system offering low wages to workers imported on fixed-term contracts requiring that the passage be repaid. This system was undercutting the wages of American workers, although 'there [was] no reason to suppose a contract like the present to be within the evils that the law was designed to suppress' (at 304). However, 'where the terms of a statute are plain, unambiguous, and explicit, the courts are not at liberty to go outside of the language' to search for 'what may be imagined to have been or not to have been the intention of congress' (at 304).

The title (i.e. the explanatory subtitle) of the statute used the words 'to perform labor'. The term *labor* (UK English, *labour*) had as one of its meanings the 'restricted meaning' of 'manual work', rather than 'the work of the skilled artisan, or the professional man'. However, an interpretation of the title could not be used to broaden or narrow the scope of the statute as a whole: 'no rule in the construction of statutes is more familiar than the one to the effect that the title cannot be used to extend or restrain positive provisions in the body of the act' (at 304). The statute had used the phrase 'labor or service of any kind'. These 'comprehensive terms' would cover '[e]very kind of industry and every employment, manual or intellectual'. The exemption for 'professional actors, artists, lecturers, or singers' implied that logically and as a matter of statutory interpretation, the prohibition applied to 'ministers, lawyers, surgeons, architects, and all others who labor in a professional calling' (at 305).

The Church appealed. In a decision that remains controversial to this day, the Supreme Court unanimously reversed. Justice Brewer, in much cited words, conceded that the act of the Church in hiring the minister was 'within the letter of this section', that is, the language of the statute literally applied to the facts, 'for the relation of rector to his church is one of service, and implies labor on the one side with compensation on the other' (at 511). The statute used the general words *labor* and *service*, but went further, as if to guard against 'any narrow interpretation and emphasize a breadth of meaning'. However, while there was 'great force to this reasoning', it could not have been the intention of Congress to forbid this particular employment contract: 'It is a familiar rule that a thing may be within the letter of the statute and yet not within the statute, because not within its spirit nor within the intention of its makers'. Frequently statutes used very general or broad language, but this language did not always literally apply: '[A] consideration of the whole legislation, or of the circumstances surrounding its enactment, or of the absurd results which follow from giving such broad meaning to the words' was capable of clarifying that in some cases the literal result could not be what the legislator had intended.

There was case law authority for the construction of statutes 'quite contrary to the letter'. In *Stradling v Morgan* (1560), it was held that a statute that covered *all things* or *all people* might be interpreted to mean 'some things' or 'some people'. This was permissible if the reading accorded with the 'intent of the legislature', if 'constancy' was maintained 'between different sections of the act', or if there were external reasons ('foreign circumstances') (at 512). Lord Coke had stated the principle as follows (as cited in *Margate Pier Co. v Hannam* (1819) at 280): 'Acts of parliament are to be so construed as no man that is innocent or free from injury or wrong be, by a literal construction, punished or endangered'.

The Court gave a series of examples where the literal application of a statute would have produced an absurd result and the verdict went against 'common sense'. For example, a person authorized to arrest a murder suspect could not be guilty of obstructing the mail, just because the suspect was carrying the mail at the time of arrest (*US v Kirby* (1869) at 486–87):

> All laws should receive a sensible construction. General terms should be so limited in their application as not to lead to injustice, oppression, or an absurd consequence. It will always, therefore, be presumed that the legislature intended exceptions to its language which would avoid results of this character. The reason of the law in such cases should prevail over its letter.

It was true that the statute's title should not be interpreted 'to add to or take from the body of the statute'. However, if there was uncertainty about the scope of the legislation, it might be of help in determining the intent. In *US v Palmer* (1818), Chief Justice Marshall used the title 'An act for the punishment of certain crimes against the US' to limit the effect of the words 'any person or persons' and thereby narrow the scope of the statute. In this case, no one reading the title would think that it applied to professionals: 'the thought expressed in this reaches only to the work of the manual laborer, as distinguished from that of the professional man' (at 513). This was the 'common understanding' of the terms *labor* and *laborers*, and 'it is to be assumed that words and phrases are used in their ordinary meaning' (at 513).

An additional guide to the interpretation was to ascertain the 'evil' against which the statute was directed. It was proper for the courts to look at the background and the events leading to the enactment. A previous judgment had identified the system of 'the shipment of great numbers of an ignorant and servile class of foreign laborers' (*US v Craig* (1886) at 798). It was 'cheap, unskilled labor' that was the target of the legislation. There was no suggestion that the market for 'brain toilers' – and still less for ministers – was 'depressed by foreign competition' (at 514). The Congressional record confirmed this, speaking of this kind of imported labour as 'ignorant of our social condition', 'isolated', 'from the lowest social stratum', eating 'the coarsest food' and living in 'hovels of a character before unknown to American workmen'. They usually did not become citizens and were 'certainly not a desirable acquisition to the body politic' (at 514). The Senate Committee on Education and Labor had considered recommending an amendment excluding professional services, but had concluded that the Act would be understood in any case to refer to manual labourers.

Much of the judgment was devoted to an account of the fundamentally Christian nature of the United States. No legislature in the country ought to be understood to be acting against religion, 'because this is a religious people'. This was a constant of the discovery, conquest and colonial settlement of the Americas. The Declaration of Independence spoke of the 'Creator', the 'Supreme Judge of the world' and 'Divine Providence'. Every state constitution expressed 'profound reverence for religion' and affirmed its centrality. Official oaths ended with 'so help me God'. The First Amendment declared that 'Congress shall make no law respecting an establishment of religion, or prohibiting the free exercise thereof'. There was 'universal language' pervading these statements: 'They affirm and reaffirm that this is a religious nation. These are not individual sayings, declarations of private persons. They are organic utterances. They speak the voice of the entire people' (at 516). The Supreme Court, in *Updegraph v Commonwealth* (1824), had stated that 'Christianity, general Christianity, is, and always has been, a part of the common law of Pennsylvania'. The law enjoined especial respect for Christianity (*People v Ruggles* (1811), at 295):

> Nor are we bound by any expressions in the constitution, as some have strangely supposed, either not to punish at all, or to punish indiscriminately the like attacks upon the religion of Mahomet or of the Grand Lama; and for this plain reason, that the case assumes that we are a Christian people, and the morality of the country is deeply ingrafted upon Christianity, and not upon the doctrines or worship of those impostors. (cited at 516)

American institutional and public life was permeated with religious sentiment and language. In addition to these features of official life, there was 'a volume of unofficial declarations to the mass of organic utterances that this is a Christian nation' (at 516). No Congress would have approved a law which expressly limited the recruitment of eminent Roman Catholic, Episcopal (Anglican), Baptist or Jewish religious leaders. There was 'a definite evil, in view of which the legislature used general terms with the purpose of reaching all phases of that evil'. In the event 'the general language' was 'broad enough to reach cases and acts which the whole history and life of the country affirm could not have been intentionally legislated against'. The act of employing the minister, 'although within the letter, is not within the intention of the legislature' and could not be 'within the statute' (at 516–17).

Key points in the judgment

- The act of offering the contract fell within the literal meaning of the statute ('labor or service of any kind') but not its intention.
- The result of excluding a foreign minister from employment in the United States was absurd.
- When the result went against common sense, case law showed that courts had the authority to set aside the literal application of the statute.
- This did not mean that the Court was substituting its will for that of the legislature.
- The (sub)title could be used for guidance as to the scope of the statute, and *labor* in its ordinary meaning did not refer to professional employment.

- The Congressional record and case law confirmed that the evil or mischief against which the statute was directed was imported manual labourers working for low wages and undercutting the labour market.

- These migrants were in habits and outlook an undesirable acquisition for the body politic.

- The United States was a Christian nation; no legislation could be presumed to act against the Christian religion.

Discussion

The statute featured in this case was one of several legal measures taken against migrant workers in that period, including the Chinese Exclusion Act (1882). This hostility was fuelled by the desire of workers to protect wages, but also exemplified the grip that racial theories had taken on the governing class of the United States. The *New York Times* in its report showed the clear influence of ideas about race and character, describing Mr Warren's 'strong English physique' and 'pleasant open face, which bears the impress of character and positiveness' ([NYT] 1887: 8).

The judgment was grounded in the evocation of the United States as a Christian country. While Christianity was not an established religion, it was the foundation of the social and legal order. No legislation could therefore be understood as intending to undermine that foundation. Given religious freedoms, one could not imagine a law preventing distinguished religious figures from a range of faiths entering the United States. Nor could there have been an intention to exclude professional 'brain toilers' in general.

This case is at the centre of debates about statutory interpretation. In its own terms, the judgment identified a more precise socio-economic 'evil' or mischief than the general language warranted. The use of absurdity as a technique of construction (cf. the so-called 'golden rule') raises notorious difficulties, particularly in cases where a relatively senior court (here, the Appeals Court) has decided that the result was not absurd (Manning, 2003). The complex analyses of the Supreme Court's pioneering use of the Congressional record cannot be summarized here (see Eskridge et al., 2001: 680–82; Vermeule, 1998; Chomsky, 2000). Blatt (2010) has stressed the fact that after the Appeals Court decision, Congress amended the law in 1891 to exempt 'ministers of any denomination'. The amendment is not mentioned in Brewer's judgment (it did not apply to cases already in progress), possibly because he was unaware of it (Blatt, 2010: 654).

For its critics, the judgment's preference for 'spirit' over 'letter', and for context over text, epitomizes ideologically driven, activist decision-making by judges. It offends against three prohibitions that underlie textualist approaches. The judge should not look *behind* the statute at discussions and debates in the legislature and its committees (legislative history), *outward* into society to find a moral, socio-cultural or political standard to apply, or *inward* to moral conscience and private beliefs. For Scalia, the judgment in *Holy Trinity* is a prototypical example of the misuse of 'legislative intent' to override the 'text of the law'. What actually gets expressed is 'judicial intent', that is, the views and beliefs of the judges (Scalia, 1997: 18). The granting of the employment contract 'was within the letter of the statute' and therefore fell under the statute: 'Congress can enact foolish statutes as well as wise ones, and it is not for the courts to decide which is which and rewrite the former' (Scalia, 1997: 20). Using the decision as authority was 'nothing but an invitation to judicial lawmaking'. The decision was wrong because '[t]he text is the law and it is the text that must be observed' (Scalia, 1997: 21, 22).

The Court considered a secondary argument, arguing for a narrow rather than a broad interpretation of *labor*. It used the statute's title to argue that the law targeted manual or unskilled workers. However, this was offered primarily as suggestive of legislative intent. The Court accepted that the words 'labor and service of any kind' were of a high generality and inclusive of all jobs and professions. Both church ministers and waiters might be said to *serve*.

However, Eskridge et al. (2001: 679–82) cast doubt on whether the judgment was really not 'within the letter of the statute'. They cite contemporary dictionary definitions and case law to show that the words *labor* and *service* were primarily used in their narrow meanings. *Webster's* of 1879 and 1886 defined *labor* as 'physical toil or bodily exertion [...] hard muscular effort directed to some useful end, as agriculture, manufactures, and the like'. The second, 'less authoritative' definition was: 'Intellectual exertion, mental effort' (Eskridge et al., 2001: 680).

Judges had interpreted *labor* and *laborer* to imply physical or unskilled work. In the case of *In re Ho King* (1883), which concerned an actor, the *Worcester* definition of *laborer* was cited:

> One who labors; one regularly employed at some hard work; a workman; an operative;—often used of one who gets a livelihood at coarse manual labor, as distinguished from an artisan or professional man.

The Treaty with China of 1880 and the statute of 1882 had used the term in its 'popular meaning', and it did not 'include an actor any more than it does a merchant or teacher' (*In re Ho King* (1883), at 725). Similarly, *service* was defined by *Webster's* to cover subordinate or humble roles:

> The act of serving; the occupation of a servant; the performance of labor for the benefit of another, or at another's command; the attendance of an inferior, or hired helper or slave, etc., on a superior employee, master, and the like. (*In re Ho King* (1883), at 725)

Black's *Law Dictionary* (1891) defined *service* as 'being employed to serve another; duty or labor to be rendered by one person to another' (Eskridge et al., 2001: 680).

The argument might be made the narrow meaning of *labor* also constrained the scope of *service*, or that both *labor* and *service* were to be understood so as to exclude professions such as minister, doctor and lawyer. 'Labor and service of any kind' would then be understood as referring to 'unskilled manual employment, service jobs, of all kinds' or even 'unskilled and skilled manual employment, service jobs, of all kinds'. The excepted categories listed in s. 5 were 'professional artist, lecturers, singers'. As these are the only categories mentioned, it might be argued that all others were forbidden by the statute. This is the principle of *expressio unius est exclusio alterius* ('the mention of one thing implies the exclusion of another'). Further, these were not unskilled or manual professions, which would confirm the generality and global inclusivity of the statute. However, these exempted categories were forms of employment generally subject to short-term contracts. If the mischief against which the statute was directed was the importation of labour on fixed contracts, then the exemptions did not touch on the domain of the liberal professions, that is, ministers, doctors, lawyers, professors, accountants, etc. Section 4, in providing for the punishment of a ship-master who knowingly brought into the United States 'any alien laborer, mechanic or artisan', suggested that the Act targeted skilled and unskilled laborers, a diverse group of workers, but not educated professionals. The section was not mentioned in the judgment, however (Eskridge et al., 2001: 680).

The Court took the rhetorical high ground, rather than working directly with or on the language of the statute. It clearly felt most secure operating primarily at the level of history, socio-politics and organic nationalism in narrowing the scope of the statute, with 'bedrock social values concerning religion' (Manning, 2003: 2403). The Court found in effect that the employment of the minister was undoubtedly a contract for *labor or service of any kind*. It also determined that the law did not apply. The Court further argued that the title of the statute was relevant in determining the intent of Congress, which in effect narrowed the meaning of the statutory phrase 'labor and service of any kind'.

Arguably, it was the Court's extreme literalism that created the problem. The Court took what it defined to be the letter of the law as the only possible interpretative meaning. It was this problem which Justice Brewer went to such rhetorical and methodologically innovative lengths to resolve. The case stages the clash of powerful ideas of class, race, religion and organic nationalism against an equally powerful adherence to literalism. Only an evocation of the entire historical and socio-cultural order of the United States could resolve this conflict. A radical decision was born out of the Court's literalism and its profoundly conservative principles.

Points for further consideration

This case has become the site of a set-piece battle between proponents of purposive interpretation (Driesen, 2013) and proponents of textualism (Scalia, 1997; Scalia and Garner, 2012: 11–13). However, did not the Court ultimately rely on the moral foundation of US law and society, rather than the purpose of the statute, to avoid the literal meaning?

The argument has been made that the Court could have used textualist methods to reach the same decision, focusing on the title of the statute, the phrase *to perform labor or service of any kind*, applying the rule of lenity (Eskridge, 1998: 1535). However, Scalia and Garner retort: 'That is not possible. The text of the statute contains no ambiguity at all: "labor and service of any kind" unambiguously includes not just labor but *service* of any kind' (2012: 222–23). What kind of evidence might one adduce to show that a word or a phrase is or is not ambiguous? Does not the fact that some commentators find ambiguity in the phrase make it at least in one sense ambiguous?

If textualism is correct in its understanding of the role of language in legal interpretation, would not academic linguistics be a better source of authority for word meaning than dictionaries? (See Slocum, 2012.) If 'linguistic analysis can be useful in ascertaining the meaning of a constitutional provision', could such an analysis act as a corrective where a textualist analysis seems to go against its own principles? (See Kaplan, 2012: 428; and discussion of *District of Columbia v Heller* (2008).)

CHAPTER 12

Defining Identity II: Nation, People and Race

Is the Cherokee nation a *foreign state* in relation to the United States?

Cherokee Nation v State of Georgia (1831)	Cherokee Nation	Foreign state	'The judicial Power shall extend to all [...] controversies between a State or the citizens thereof and foreign states, citizens or subjects' (US Constitution, Art, III, s. 2)	The Cherokee Nation is not a foreign state

Cherokee Nation v State of Georgia (1831) (US Supreme Court)

Cherokee residents of the state of Georgia sought the intervention of the Supreme Court in order to prevent further territorial dispossession and expulsion by the Georgia state authorities. In 1819, the Cherokee had resolved not to cede any further territory, and in 1827 had created a constitution that in much of its structure and language mirrored that of the United States. Georgia subsequently passed a series of laws annulling Cherokee constitutional arrangements, contracts and other trappings of legality, and authorizing a land survey and seizure of 'gold, silver, and other mines'. The Cherokee Nation, led by Chief John Ross (1790–1866), was represented before the Court by William Wirt (1772–1834). The state of Georgia went unrepresented, as it did not recognize the Supreme Court's jurisdiction over state laws.

The fundamental question at stake was the status of the Cherokee Nation and its right to take legal action in the Supreme Court under the constitutional category of *foreign state* (Art. II, s. 2). The lead judgment, written by Chief Justice John Marshall (1755–1835), is important for its definition of the relation between the Native Americans and the United States. The complaint sought recognition for 'the Cherokee Nation of Indians, a foreign state, not owing allegiance to the US, nor to any State of this union, nor to any prince, potentate or State, other than their own' (cited at 3). It stressed that the Cherokee had 'abandoned the hunter state and become agriculturists, mechanics, and herdsmen' (at 6).

In finding against the Cherokee, Chief Justice Marshall offered an elegant statement of the principle of judicial self-restraint: 'If Courts were permitted to indulge their sympathies, a case better calculated to excite them can scarcely be imagined' (at 15). He painted a grim picture of the fate of the Cherokee since the European conquest, with a people 'once numerous, powerful, and truly independent, found by our ancestors in the quiet and uncontrolled possession of an ample domain, gradually sinking beneath our superior policy, our arts and our arms'. The Cherokee had yielded territory in a series of treaties, 'each of which contains a solemn guarantee of the residue' but which had each in turn been violated: 'To preserve this remnant, the present application is made'.

In addressing the status of the Cherokee, Chief Justice Marshall accepted that 'the Indians are acknowledged to have an unquestionable, and heretofore unquestioned right to the lands they occupy, until that right shall be extinguished by a voluntary cession to our government' (at 17). But the status of the Cherokee was not equivalent to that of a *foreign nation*. Indian nations were more accurately referred to as *domestic dependent nations*:

> They occupy a territory to which we assert a title independent of their will, which must take effect in point of possession when their right of possession ceases. Meanwhile they are in a state of pupilage. Their relation to the United States resembles that of a ward to his guardian. (at 17)

While it was evident that the Supreme Court had jurisdiction in cases where individual states were parties, it was not clear that the Cherokee belonged to any of the relevant constitutional categories (at 16). The state of Georgia 'may then unquestionably be sued in this Court', but 'Is the Cherokee Nation a foreign state in the sense in which that term is used in the Constitution?' (at 16). The plaintiffs pointed to a long history of treaties concluded with the United States, in particular those of Hopewell (1785) and Holston (1791), and argued that since as individuals the Cherokee were 'aliens', their 'aggregate composing a State must [...] be a foreign state' (as summarized by Chief Justice Marshall, at 16). Chief Justice Marshall ended with these words:

> If it be true that the Cherokee Nation have rights, this is not the tribunal in which those rights are to be asserted. If it be true that wrongs have been inflicted, and that still greater are to be apprehended, this is not the tribunal which can redress the past or prevent the future. (at 20)

One of the central points of contention in the case was the proper reading of the Commerce Clause of the US Constitution, which empowered Congress to 'regulate commerce with foreign nations, and among the several States, and with the Indian tribes' (Art. III, s. 8). Chief Justice Marshall argued that the wording clearly showed that there were 'three distinct classes' being referred to, and that therefore there was no way that the designation *foreign nation* could be applied to the Indian tribes, who had been 'contradistinguished' (at 18), that is, allocated to a category of their own. Otherwise, the clause would have read 'to regulate commerce with foreign nations, including the Indian tribes, and among the several States' (at 19). While it was true that 'the same words have not necessarily the same meaning attached to them when found in different parts of the same instrument' and word meaning was 'controlled by context' (though less so in the case of 'proper names'), there was nothing to support the application of the term *foreign nation* to the Indian tribes. Justice William Johnson (1771–1834) likewise argued that the words *state* and *foreign state* were used 'in contradistinction'. The term *foreign nation* would not be applied to the Cherokee in international law ('the law of nations' required a real state not 'a hunter horde') or in the ordinary speech of the day ('vernacular use'), nor was it so used in the Constitution (at 28).

Henry Baldwin (1780–1844) stressed that the term used to refer to an entity, such *nation, tribe, horde, savages, chiefs, sachems* ('paramount chiefs'), *warriors of the Cherokees, the Cherokee Nation*, did not define its legal substance (at 33–34). Fidelity to the text of the Constitution meant acceptance of the authority of 'the plain meaning of a word or expression'. To proceed otherwise would be 'judicial sacrilege' (at 41). In cases of doubt, the 'practice, usages, and settled principles' of administrations before and after the adoption of the Constitution, and 'the solemn decisions of this Court' would be a guide to the 'true meaning and spirit of plain words' and not 'extrinsic circumstances' (at 41–42) or foreign definitions. 'Mere phraseology' could not make nations out of the Indians, or out of tribes, foreign states (at 44). At Hopewell, the Cherokee had 'contracted in the name of the headmen and warriors of all the Cherokees'. At Holston in 1791, 'in abandoning their last remnant of political right', they had contracted under the title of 'Cherokee Nation'. The less their actual power, the more grand their title, 'thus ascending in title as they descended in power'. The *treaty* was in fact a *contract*, and awareness of the reality behind these labels would 'divest words of their magic' (at 46).

These linguistic arguments were intertwined with issues of rights of discovery, possession of territory, recognition and identity, and sovereignty. Justice Johnson argued that 'no nation on earth' would deal with the Cherokee as a nation (at 24). Was it being suggested that 'every petty kraal of Indians, designating themselves a tribe or nation' should be recognized?

> They have in Europe sovereign and demi-sovereign States, and States of doubtful sovereignty. But this State, if it be a State, is still a grade below them all, for not to be able to alienate without permission of the remainderman or lord places them in a state of feudal dependence. (at 26–27)

(A *remainderman* inherits land once the previous owner's interest, for example a life interest, comes to an end.) The Cherokee were in some sense analogous to 'the old Israelites', who had a form of self-government or autonomy but 'without land that they can call theirs in the sense of property' (at 27). Justice Baldwin argued that the complaint was seeking a 'bow to a jurisdiction hitherto unknown' which would be 'preexistent and paramount over the supreme law of the land' (at 50).

Justice Smith Thompson (1768–1843), dissenting, took issue with both the political and linguistic arguments of the majority. The terms *state* and *nation* were synonyms, implying 'a body of men, united together to procure their mutual safety and advantage by means of their union' (at 52). There was no question but that the Cherokee were a *sovereign state* (at 53). The more contentious question was whether the Cherokee were a *foreign state*, and this needed to be answered by examining 'the practice of our own government and the light in which the Nation has been viewed and treated by it' (at 54). For Justice Smith Thompson, the Cherokee had never lost 'their separate national existence, and the rights of self-government' (at 54). While the Indian Nation could not 'transfer the absolute title to any other than ourselves', and politically lived under a 'qualified subjection', they did enjoy the rights of occupancy over their territory (at 55). The Cherokee were without doubt a *foreign nation*, as the word *foreign* was understood in dictionaries and in the usage of 'approved writers' (at 56). There was no reason to deny the Court jurisdiction (at 59), and it was on this basis that a series of treaties had been concluded with the Cherokee Nation.

On the linguistic arguments, Justice Smith Thompson summarized Chief Justice Marshall as saying that 'if the Indian tribes are foreign nations, they would have been included without being specially named'. This was however 'mere verbal criticism' (at 61). The phrase *Indian tribes* could not be read as being included with the 'several States', as there would have been 'no fitness in immediately thereafter particularizing "the Indian tribes"' (at 62). But the argument was much less straightforward in relation to *foreign states*. The Indians were divided into larger and smaller groupings, so questions about trade might arise with a tribe for which the general term *nation* was not appropriate: 'Congress could not then have regulated the trade with any particular tribe that did not extend to the whole nation' (at 63). Alternatively, the term *tribe* may have been used with the meaning of *nation* so as to avoid repetition, 'and entirely omitting to name the Indian tribes might have afforded some plausible grounds for concluding that this branch of commercial intercourse was not subject to the power of Congress' (at 63). The Constitution was not consistent in the use of such terms. *Nation* and *tribe* were 'frequently used indiscriminately' (at 63) and, for example, one could find *foreign state*, *foreign nation* and *foreign power* (Art. III, ss. 2 and 8; Art. I, s. 10) (at 64).

On the point of sovereignty, Justice Smith Thompson pointed to the anomaly of a party deemed capable of making a treaty or a contract but denied the right to enforce it (at 50). Sovereignty was not extinguished by the Cherokees' act of putting themselves under the protection of the British Crown (at 68): 'Their land is held in common, and every invasion of their possessory right is an injury done to the Nation, and not to any individual' (at 74). Justice Joseph Story (1779–1845) joined Justice Smith Thompson in affirming that the Cherokees composed 'a foreign state within the sense and meaning of the Constitution', and therefore they 'constitute a competent party to maintain a suit against the State of Georgia' (at 80).

Key points in the majority judgment

■ The Indian Nations were *domestic dependent nations*, not *foreign nations*.

- The relation between the United States and the Native Americans was one of *guardian* to *ward*.
- The Commerce Clause showed by its wording that *foreign nations* and *Indian tribes* were distinct categories.
- The use of the term *nation* had no legal validity or effect, and did not reflect the underlying legal substance.
- The use of the term *treaty* had no legal validity or effect, and did not reflect the underlying legal substance which was that of a *contract*.
- Sovereignty over the full territory of the United States was vested in the US Government.
- The Cherokee did not have standing to bring an action against one of the states before the Supreme Court.

Discussion

There was an uneasy (though unstated) parallel here between the position of the United States, formed out of a rebellion against the British Crown, and that of the Cherokee, who had created a constitutional order which mirrored in many key respects that of the United States. This case also implicated the contested relations between the power of the Federal State (and the Supreme Court) and the autonomy of individual states of the Union. Four of the six justices who heard the case were apparently sympathetic to the underlying legal basis of the Cherokee claim. In refusing to hear the substance of the case, the Court sidestepped a constitutional and political hornet's nest (see Burke, 1969; White, 2010: 674ff.). The Cherokee were acknowledged to have taken up settled forms of existence, including farming, and this buttressed a claim to the right of sovereign possession rather than mere right of occupancy. It is a basic principle of law that law will not recognize and act upon any form of classification, including self-classification, unless it accepts the substance of the underlying claim that the category represents. For the majority of judges, the Cherokee calling themselves a *nation* or a *state* did not make them a sovereign nation. They were not a *foreign nation* in any recognized sense. Even if the Cherokee were called a *nation* in the Treaty of Holston (1791), that treaty (or rather, *contract*) represented in substance a further stage in stripping them of sovereignty. The word *nation* was hollow. To attribute substantive meanings to it was a form of 'word magic'. Whatever the Cherokee called themselves, they were not a sovereign nation foreign to the United States. There was an inverse relation between language and reality, as the more the Cherokee were stripped of the trappings of sovereignty, the more they invoked the language of autonomy.

However, how was the substance of the underlying claim to be evaluated? Paradoxically, in evaluating the substance of an underlying claim, the Court at various points made reference to linguistic usage. For example, one point made in this case was that the Cherokee claimed to be a *foreign nation*, yet this was unknown to the usage of international law, everyday speech and the language of the Constitution. Chief Justice Marshall's reasoning with respect to the

Commerce Clause relied on an argument that the clause in effect involves the judicial creation and recognition of categories through language. He attached profound significance to the distinctions made there, even though the Clause merely lists a series of entities that it falls to Congress to regulate. His reading of the Commerce clause itself arguably relied on 'word magic', since the Commerce Clause did not on its face set out to define the precise legal status of the entities enumerated there. As noted, Justice Smith Thompson in his dissent termed this technique 'mere verbal criticism' (at 61). A contemporary academic commentator, however, sees Chief Justice Marshall's analysis as an 'excellent example of relying on congruence among clauses to interpret the text' (Bloom, 2009: 38).

Justice Smith Thompson in dissent pointed out that the Cherokee were recognized as a party to treaties with individual states of the Union. If the Cherokee were competent to conclude a legally binding agreement, even if merely a contract and not an 'international' treaty, then on what grounds could they be denied the right to a hearing in order to enforce it? So much for the legal maxim: 'Equity will not suffer a wrong to be without a remedy.'

Is a high-caste Hindu a *white person*?

US v Bhagat Singh Thind (1923)	High-caste Hindu	White person	The Naturalization Act 'shall apply to aliens being free white persons and to aliens of African nativity and to persons of African descent' (39 Stat. L. 875, s. 3, of 5 February 1917)	A high-caste Hindu is not a white person

US v Bhagat Singh Thind (1923) (US Supreme Court)

Dr Bhagat Singh Thind (1892–1967) was granted US citizenship on 9 December 1918, but it was almost immediately revoked. Dr Thind was described as a 'high-caste Hindu' but he was a Sikh, presumably with a high-caste background, born in the Punjab in northwestern India. *Hindu* and *Sikh* had begun to be seen as mutually exclusive ethnic categories only in the late nineteenth century. In the colonial census of India of 1871–72, Sikhism was treated as a sub-variant of Hinduism, whereas in the 1901 census Hindu and Sikh were distinct categories. It was potentially to Dr Thind's advantage to be seen as a high-caste Hindu. Influential theories of Indian history held that the Hindu high castes were relatively pure-blooded descendants of the ancient Aryan invaders. Dr Thind petitioned for reinstatement of his citizenship.

In the background to this decision was the Supreme Court decision in *Takao Ozawa v US* (1922), which held that a 'person of the Japanese race' was not *white* for the purposes of naturalization. Discussing the criteria by which race might be determined, the Court in *Ozawa* made a series of comments (at 197). First, words such as *white* involved 'a racial and not an individual test'.

This was supported 'by reason and authority'. What this meant was that the individual whose identity was at issue would not be subject to scrutiny as an individual, for example in terms of his or her skin colour:

> Manifestly the test afforded by the mere color of the skin of each individual is impracticable, as that differs greatly among persons of the same race, even among Anglo-Saxons, ranging by imperceptible gradations from the fair blond to the swarthy brunette, the latter being darker than many of the lighter hued persons of the brown or yellow races. Hence to adopt the color test alone would result in a confused overlapping of races and a gradual merging of one into the other, without any practical line of separation. (at 197)

A series of decisions had affirmed that the term *white person* in this context was synonymous with *person of the Caucasian race*. This made the problem simpler, but still left an area of uncertainty at the borderline:

> The effect of the conclusion that the words 'white person' means a Caucasian is not to establish a sharp line of demarcation between those who are entitled and those who are not entitled to naturalization, but rather a zone of more or less debatable ground outside of which, upon the one hand, are those clearly eligible, and outside of which, upon the other hand, are those clearly ineligible for citizenship. Individual cases falling within this zone must be determined as they arise from time to time by what this court has called, in another connection (*Davidson v New Orleans*, 96 US 97, 104), 'the gradual process of judicial inclusion and exclusion'. (at 198)

Denying that any considerations of 'individual unworthiness or racial inferiority' were involved, the Court concluded that Mr Ozawa was 'clearly of a race which is not Caucasian and therefore belongs entirely outside the zone on the negative side'. The Court did not need to look more closely at the categories of *white person* and *Caucasian*.

When it came to a determination of the naturalization status of Dr Bhagat Singh Thind, the Court saw itself as being in this more difficult zone, in the sense that the case was not so immediately disposed of as *Ozawa*. The fundamental problem was that influential nineteenth-century theories had postulated some form of kinship between Indians, especially those of 'high caste', and Europeans, based on affinities between Sanscrit and languages such a Greek, Latin, German, English and Welsh. This so-called 'Aryan hypothesis', originally formulated on the basis of observed linguistic resemblances, raised many questions about a possible blood kinship or racial relationship. One idea was that there was a common racial origin between at least some Indians and Europeans, but that present-day Indians were the result of mixing between ancient invading Aryans and the aboriginal, dark-skinned inhabitants.

The term *Caucasian*, associated in its racial meaning with the comparative anatomist Friedrich Blumenbach (1752–1840), was recognized by what the court in *Ozawa* had termed the 'science of ethnology'. A footnote in *Thind* quoted the *Encyclopaedia Britannica* (11th edn, p. 113) entry, and the judgment referred to various contemporary authorities on race, including Joseph Deniker's *The Races of Man* (1900), August Henry Keane's *Man, Past and Present* (1899), Thomas H. Huxley's *Evidence as to Man's Place in Nature* (1863), and to the *Dictionary of Races or Peoples* ([US Senate] 1911). Both *Aryan* and *Caucasian* were used in some contexts as synonyms for *white*. This motivated the Court's statement to the effect that establishing 'a line of descent from a Caucasian ancestor will not *ipso facto* and necessarily conclude the inquiry' (at 208). The Court was anxious to distance itself from the academic debate with its controversies and disagreements, and to stress that while *Caucasian* and *white* were treated as synonyms for many purposes, they were not identical:

> 'Caucasian' is a conventional word of much flexibility, as a study of the literature dealing with racial questions will disclose, and, while it and the words 'white persons' are treated as synonymous for the purposes of that case, they are not of identical meaning […] (at 208)

The statute had not employed the word *Caucasian*, and this term was unknown to the original framers of the statute in 1790. The term *white person* was from 'common speech', rather than having a 'scientific origin'. *Caucasian* was useful as 'an aid to the ascertainment of the legislative intent', but not as a substitute for the original wording. In past decades it had 'acquired a popular meaning', and while this was not totally 'clearly defined', it was evident that the popular meaning, as distinguished from the scientific one, was of 'appreciably narrower scope'. It was this popular meaning that was relevant to the construction of the statute,

> for it would be obviously illogical to convert words of common speech used in a statute into words of scientific terminology when neither the latter nor the science for whose purposes they were coined was within the contemplation of the framers of the statute or of the people for whom it was framed. (at 209)

The terms *Caucasian* and *white person* could be treated a synonyms in their popular understandings. The scientific meaning of *Caucasian* was too broad, and of uncertain scope. The words of the statute should be interpreted 'in accordance with the understanding of the common man from whose vocabulary they were taken' (at 209).

While there were suggestions in the scientific literature that those of Hindu stock from the Punjab might be classified as *Aryan* or *Caucasian*, the category *Aryan* had been discredited in contemporary ethnology. The relations between the Aryan languages proved nothing about racial origins: 'a common linguistic root buried in remotely ancient soil, is altogether inadequate to prove common racial origin' (at 210). There was no reason to assume that the original Aryan language was spoken by a single race; further, groups of different races could, through historical processes, end up speaking the same language:

> Our own history has witnessed the adoption of the English tongue by millions of negroes, whose descendants can never be classified racially with the descendants of white persons, notwithstanding both may speak a common root language. (at 211)

From the Court's point of view, there could be no question of any racial affinity between those of African and those of European descent. Since both groups spoke the same language, this demonstrated that racial affinity could not be read off from linguistic affinity.

The term *Caucasian* was no less problematic. According to the *Encyclopaedia Britannica* entry cited (fn. 2), for example, the 'ill chosen' name of Caucasian 'brings into one race peoples such as the Arabs and Swedes, although these are scarcely less different than the Americans and Malays, who are set down as two distinct races'. It included far more racial groupings 'than the unscientific mind suspects', including, depending on the authority, Hindu, Polynesians and Hamites (at 211). Thus 'the well informed white American would learn with some degree of astonishment that the race to which he belongs is made up of such heterogeneous elements'. There was no agreement among the various authorities as to the nature and number of the races that made up humanity, and it was in practice widely accepted that 'to arrange them in sharply bounded divisions is an undertaking of such uncertainty that common agreement is practically impossible' (at 212).

Given this uncertainty, it was difficult to assign a group to any particular racial category, and in any case the possibility of racial mixing could not be excluded. This had apparently happened in some parts of India, where the Aryan invader interbred completely with the 'dark-skinned Dravidian' (Hindustan, Berar), whereas in the Punjab and Rajputana, there had been greater success in protecting racial purity. Nonetheless, the rules of caste notwithstanding, 'intermarriages did occur producing an intermingling of the two and destroying to a greater or less degree the purity of the "Aryan" blood' (at 213–14).

Scientific classification could offer no clear guide; rather, it was 'the words of familiar speech' which were intended by the original framers to include 'only the type of man whom they knew as white'. Originally these were from Britain and northwest Europe; more recently 'immigrants from Eastern, Southern and Middle Europe, among them the Slavs and the dark-eyed, swarthy people of Alpine and Mediterranean stock' (at 213). 'Alpine' and 'Mediterranean' were terms of racial classification for southern Europeans.

Free white persons was a phrase of 'common speech', which was equivalent to Caucasian in its popular meaning only. The 'physical group characteristics' of Hindus were different as 'a matter of familiar observation and knowledge'; others of European parentage would quickly mix into the white population, whereas 'the children born in this country of Hindu parents would retain indefinitely the clear evidence of their ancestry'. This was not a matter of racial superiority, rather racial difference. The 'great body of our people' would reject assimilation instinctively, and in 1917 Congress had excluded the whole of Asia for the purposes of immigration (at 214–15).

Key points in the judgment

■ In contrast to the easy case of *Ozawa*, the case of whether a high-caste Hindu was a *white person* required more careful deliberation.

■ The category *white person* was frequently explained with reference to the scientific categories of *Aryan* and *Caucasian*.

■ There was no scientific consensus as to the definition and scope of these categories.

■ *Aryan* referred to an ancient white race which had invaded India; but given substantial intermarriage, *Aryan* was now most reliably used to refer to relations between languages, not races.

■ *Caucasian* was used to refer to one of the racial sub-divisions of mankind, but there was no consensus as to which groups were included in its scope which was much wider than the popular meaning of *white*.

■ In its popular usage, Caucasian had a narrower meaning, and this was synonymous with *white person*.

■ The popular commonly understood meaning of *white person* excluded Indians.

Discussion

In the background to this case was the hostility of Congress to non-white migration to the United States, and a high level of anxiety about racial mixing and assimilation. The judgment reflects those concerns, while denying any racist intent. The problem for the Court was that high-caste individuals from northwest India could potentially claim membership in the category of *Aryan* and thereby racial affinity with Europeans. The category *Caucasian*, which had been embedded in the authoritative case law, was also very wide, and also in some accounts included Hindus. In popular usage, both *Aryan* and *Caucasian* were synonyms for *white*. Thus there was at least the appearance of scholarly authority behind Dr Thind's claim. As a high-caste Indian, he was in some sense an Aryan and therefore *white*. The Court's response was that common usage and popular belief would never describe a native of Punjab as *white*. Congress, in using the term *white persons*, would not have intended otherwise. The extensive discussion of the scientific literature was intended to impress upon the reader the lack of consensus with regard to racial classification, and the potentially excessive inclusivity of both *Aryan* and *Caucasian*. This approach was complemented by the appeal to popular meaning and popular racial understanding. Ultimately the judgment amounted to the blunt statement that Indians were not white because white Americans would never accept that they were.

The self-classification by Dr Thind, at least for purposes of this case, as a high-caste Hindu and therefore as *white* was rejected by the Court. It made this determination on the authority of popular usage and what it saw as com-monsense understandings of race. The Court merged its own point of view with that of the average white citizen, and rejected the relevance or reliability of the scientific approach to race for reaching an understanding of the lan-guage of the statute. Most interesting is the Court's reliance on the distinction between the range of broad scientific meanings attached to *Caucasian* and the narrow popular understanding which was synonymous with *white*. This allowed the Court to insulate the term from its expansive scientific meanings and subsume it under *white*. The everyday usage of Caucasian in the meaning of 'white' remains current to this day in the United States.

In fact, the Court could have without great difficulty constructed a narrative out of the scientific literature, albeit a controversial one, to show that Hindus or Indians were not racially of the same stock as white Americans. But that approach would have handed authority over racial classification to external experts and undermined the authority of the court in future cases. It would have opened judicial decision making to the professional uncertainties of eth-nology. The Court chose instead to base its argument on what it clearly saw as the more solid ground of common usage and popular categories of racial dif-ference, and to treat the phrase *white persons* as non-technical language to be construed in its everyday meaning. What this creates is an inversion, in that the scientific meaning is deemed overly vague, imprecise and inclusive, whereas the popular meaning is presented as narrow and focused.

Even from today's perspective, it might be argued that the decision was technically correct, since Congress presumably did not intend to include Indians from the Punjab or anywhere else on the sub-continent under the label *white persons*. However, the judgment can be read as riddled with anxiety about the evident categorical disorder in the science of race and the possibility that the zone of uncertainty was extremely wide. If Congress was passing laws based on race, it was evidently problematic if no clear guidance as to the crite-ria for racial classification was available. The judgment took refuge in popular meaning (and popular racism), whereas in another ideological context a law raising analogous definitional problems and using the term *white* as a racial category might have been found to be too imprecise to be enforceable, that is, **void for vagueness**.

Are Sikhs a *racial group*?

Mandla v Dowell Lee (1983) (House of Lords)	Sikhs	Racial group	'a group of persons defined by reference to colour, race, nationality or ethnic or national origins' (Race Relations Act 1976, s. 3(1))	Sikhs are a racial group

Mandla v Dowell Lee (1982) (Court of Appeal)

This case concerned school rules governing the appearance of pupils. Lee and Park Grove Private School refused to admit a Sikh pupil, Gurinder Singh

Mandla, unless he was willing to remove his turban and cut his hair. Sikh religious practice mandates that hair should not be cut and a turban be worn. It was alleged that this was unlawful discrimination under the Race Relations Act 1976. While the school rules concerning dress and appearance were the same for all pupils, the argument was that the rule constituted so-called **indirect discrimination**: the burden of the rule would fall disproportionately on Sikhs given their traditions, as the pupil in question would have to choose between honouring his traditions and attending the school. The central issue in the litigation was whether Sikhs were a *racial group* within the meaning of the Act. This term was defined by reference to 'colour, race, nationality or ethnic or national origins'. The County Court answered this in the negative. (Other points of law raised by the case, namely, the meaning of the words *can* in s. 1(1)(b)(i) and *justifiable* in s. 1(1)(b)(ii), are not discussed here.)

In the Court of Appeal, Lord Denning MR laid stress on the fact that the statute did not include 'religion or politics or culture':

> You can discriminate for or against Roman Catholics as much as you like without being in breach of the law. You can discriminate for or against Communists as much as you please, without being in breach of the law. You can discriminate for or against the 'hippies' as much as you like, without being in breach of the law. But you must not discriminate against a man because of his colour or of his race or of his nationality, or of 'his ethnic or national origins'. (at 2)

To the argument that Sikhs were defined by their *ethnic origins*, and that they therefore fell within one of the protected categories, Lord Denning gave his understanding of the history of this term (at 2–3). The word *ethnic* had come in the late nineteenth century to be used in English to denote 'peoples who were not Christian or Jewish'. This was the meaning given in the *Oxford English Dictionary* of 1890, drawing on the Greek meaning of *heathen*. It has been used in a related sense by Jewish translators from Hebrew into Greek of the Bible, with the meaning of *non-Jew* or *Gentile*. But its more modern meaning was given in the *Concise Oxford Dictionary*, as 'pertaining to race, ethnological'. *Ethnological* was further defined as 'corresponding to a division of races'.

For Lord Denning this was the proper way to understand the term: 'That is the meaning which I – acquiring my vocabulary in 1934 – have always myself attached to the word "ethnic". It is, to my mind, the correct meaning'. The second supplement to the *Oxford English Dictionary* (1972) had given the word 'a much wider meaning than that which I am used to' (at 3):

> Also, pertaining to or having common racial, cultural, religious or linguistic characteristics, especially designating a racial or other group within a larger system; hence (U.S. colloquial), foreign, exotic.

One example given in the supplement of the 'non-committal' term *ethnic group* was that of the Jews. For Lord Denning, this merely confirmed that *ethnic* really meant 'racial'. It was 'a racial characteristic' that distinguished Jews from non-Jews. The *Shorter Oxford Dictionary* described Jews as being 'of the Hebrew race'. Case law showed that conditions attached to a will stipulating that a daughter should only marry a Jew, and cutting her off should she marry a non-Jew, would be held void for uncertainty, since 'Jew' could mean 'a dozen different things'. Lord Denning's conclusion was that *ethnic group* meant that 'the group as a whole share a common characteristic which is a racial characteristic. It is that they are descended, however remotely, from a Jewish ancestor'. Drawing on the judgment in *Ealing London Borough Council v Race Relations Board* (1972), Lord Denning argued that *origins* meant 'descent, parentage', and he concluded that this indicated 'a group which has a common racial characteristic' (at 3).

The question naturally arose as to why the word *ethnic* was in the statute at all. Normally there would be an assumption that in a list of qualities or attributes, each word adds a new dimension or quality. If *ethnic* merely meant 'race', then there was a need to explain its inclusion. Lord Denning found the answer in the judgment of Lord Cross in the *Ealing* case (at 4):

> The reason why the words 'ethnic or national origins' were added to the words 'racial grounds' which alone appear in the long title was, I imagine, to prevent argument over the exact meaning of the word 'race'.

Lord Denning glossed this as saying that 'there might be much argument as to whether one group or other was of the same "race" as another: but there was thought to be less as to whether it was a different "ethnic group"' (at 4). In particular, he believed that the term had been introduced to cover the case of the Jews, against the background of their persecution in Nazi Germany. Sikhs, however, were not an ethnic group, since there was no difference in language or blood between them and other groups from the Punjab or from India as a whole. They were distinguished from other groups only by the religion and culture of Sikhism, not by any 'racial characteristic whatever' (at 5).

Oliver LJ (as he then was) likewise focused on the word *ethnic*, which he accepted was of 'uncertain meaning' and had changed from the original Greek term. But he approached it from the point of view that the language of the statute was intended to provide guidance as to conduct in society. Dictionaries could provide only 'the most general assistance':

> The one thing that must surely be clear is that Parliament cannot have intended to create (as it did in this Act) a criminal offence which involves an extensive etymological research before any member of the public can determine whether he is offending or not. The word must, I infer, have been used in its popularly accepted meaning; but, having said that, one is faced with the difficulty of discovering what the popularly accepted meaning is. (at 6–7)

If the broad definition urged by the appellants was applied, namely, 'a state of being united by common features such as language, race, culture, religion, literature and habit of life', then this would be far too inclusive. Even if it was conceded that *ethnic* went beyond a narrow racial meaning, perhaps to include cultural or linguistic communities, 'No one, for instance, in ordinary speech, would describe a member of the Church of England or the Conservative Party as a member of an ethnic group' (at 7). While many Sikhs did share an ethnic origin, it was possible to enter or leave the community, and their ethnic origin was not excusive to Sikhs.

Kerr LJ (as he then was) also picked up the theme of the 'elusive' meaning of the word *race*, noting (at 9) that 'Some scientists and social anthropologists deny that it has any meaning. But it clearly has a meaning for Parliament and ordinary people'. The first and most basic criterion in the statute was 'colour', which referred to a human characteristic which could not be changed at will: 'the definition of "racial group" remains confined to human attributes which, save for changes of nationality, are unalterable'. The case concerned primarily discrimination with regard to religion. The phrase *national origins* did not apply, as the *OED* definition of *nation* showed: 'an extensive aggregate of persons so closely associated with each other by common descent, language or history as to form a distinct race or people, usually organised as a separate political state and occupying a definite territory'.

In Kerr LJ's view, the newer, more general (and non-racial) meanings of *ethnic* had created serious problems for the courts, for which 'Parliament must accept responsibility' (at 11). Thus the additional colloquial meaning included in the 1972 *OED Supplement* of 'foreign or exotic; un-American or plain quaint' meant that Parliament was requiring the courts to interpret a word used to make statements like 'he seems a pretty ethnic sort of a guy' (at 11). The Court of Appeal dismissed the appeal, and directed strongly critical language at the Commission for Racial Equality.

Mandla v Dowell Lee (1983) (House of Lords)

The appeal was framed primarily as a battle between the narrow dictionary definition, where *ethnic* more or less meant 'race', and the broader socio-cultural and religious one, from the *OED Supplement* of 1972. The argument from the appellants was for a 'broad cultural construction' of the term. In their view an ethnic group was

> a distinct community of persons who regard themselves and are regarded by others as such as a distinct community by reason of such factors as a shared history, religion, language and literature, family, social and personal customs and manners, so that they have a separate ethnic or communal identity. (at 551)

On behalf of the appellant (the Sikh schoolboy), it was put to the House of Lords that the Court of Appeal had rendered 'nugatory and meaningless' the words *ethnic or national origins*. There was, however, one evident problem with the broader definition, namely, that it did not reflect the idea of common descent. It was argued on this point that the community was created through individuals being born into it, and even if someone left the faith, they were marked by their origin in it. In the case of converts, their children would be born into the community, and in this sense there was continuity over time. The racial concept of 'inherited physical attributes' was distinct from that of *ethnic group*. This connoted 'a complex of attributes which makes the group distinctive in character from those not in the group'. When the statute spoke of 'defined', it meant 'defined by society or socially defined' (at 549).

The respondent (the school) countered that if the narrow meaning was rejected and the broad meaning applied, the Act would cover not only Sikhs but also Benedictine monks (founded AD 529) and Freemasons (founded AD 1400). The use of *ethnic* or *national* origins was intended to include Jews, who were 'regarded by themselves as a religion, but regarded by many others as a race'. This category of *ethnic group* was included 'to cover groups which had an undoubted racial character, but which might be difficult to prove as constituting a clearly separate "race" biologically' (at 556).

In his judgment Lord Fraser noted that it was not being suggested that Sikhs were 'a group defined by reference to colour, race, nationality or national origins'. Rather, the issue at stake was whether they were a group defined by *ethnic origins* (at 560). The question therefore became how the word *ethnic* was to be understood. Reviewing the definitional debate, Lord Fraser went through a number of dictionary definitions of *ethnic*. The *Oxford English Dictionary* (1897) gave two meanings: 'Pertaining to nations not Christian or Jewish; gentiles, heathen, pagan'. This was evidently not the intended meaning, since it could not have been the case that Parliament would have intended protection that did not apply to Christians and, in particular, Jews. The second meaning was as follows: 'Pertaining to race; peculiar to a race or nation; ethnological'. Lord Denning had accepted the shorter definition, omitting 'peculiar to a race or nation', from the *Concise Oxford Dictionary* as the relevant one.

The term *ethnic* no doubt conveyed 'a flavor of race', but Parliament could have not have used the term 'in a strictly racial or biological sense'. It could not have been intended that 'membership of a particular racial group should depend upon scientific proof that a person possessed the relevant distinctive biological characteristics (assuming that such characteristics exist)'. This would make it almost impossible to provide such proof. Rather, the word must have been used in a 'some more popular sense' (at 561). There were few if any racial distinctions that were 'recognized scientifically as racial'. Lord Fraser quoted a statement from *Ealing London Borough Council v Race Relations Board* (1972) to the effect that *racial* was not a legal nor properly a scientific term of art (at 561): 'anthropologists would dispute how far the word "race" is biologically at all relevant to the species'. This was 'rubbery and elusive language' designed not to leave any loopholes (*Ealing*, at 362).

Lord Fraser then turned to a consideration of the broader definition of *ethnic* found in the *Supplement to the Oxford English Dictionary* (1972). This included the following: 'pertaining to or having common racial, cultural, religious, or linguistic characteristics, esp. designating a racial or other group within a larger system'. The enumerated features ('common racial, cultural, religious, or linguistic characteristics') were too imprecise, and might imply that any of the enumerated features would be sufficient. It might suggest that religion alone was sufficient, and this was too broad. Nor should the section be read so as to mean 'racial *or other group*' (emphasis in original): 'If that were the meaning of the word "ethnic" in the statute, it would add nothing to the word group, and would lead to a result which would be unacceptably wide' (at 562). In the search for the 'true meaning' of the term *ethnic*, the court was not tied to any particular dictionary definition. The main value of the 1972 definition was in demonstrating that the term was now 'commonly used in a sense appreciably wider than the strictly racial or biological'. It retained a 'racial flavor' but 'it is used nowadays in an extended sense to include other characteristics thought of as being associated with common racial origin' (at 562).

In this way, Lord Fraser moved social perception or recognition into the centre of his deliberations. It was not that a group had to have certain characteristics, but rather that it had to 'regard itself and be regarded by others' as having them. The key phrase above is 'thought of as being associated with'. There was no scientific or definitional fact to which the court could appeal. The essential characteristics at play here were:

(1) a long shared history, of which the group is conscious as distinguishing it from other groups, and the memory of which it keeps alive; (2) a cultural tradition of its own, including family and social customs and manners, often but not necessarily associated with religious observance.

Other non-essential but contributing or relevant characteristics included:

(3) either a common geographical origin, or descent from a small number of common ancestors; (4) a common language, not necessarily peculiar to the group; (5) a common literature peculiar to the group; (6) a common religion different from that of neighbouring groups or from the general community surrounding it; (7) being a minority or being an oppressed or a dominant group within a larger community, for example a conquered people (say, the inhabitants of England shortly after the Norman conquest) and their conquerors might both be ethnic groups. (at 562)

It would be possible to meet enough of these characteristics and still include converts, e.g. those who married in, and exclude apostates:

Provided a person who joins the group feels himself or herself to be a member of it, and is accepted by other members, then he is, for the purposes of the Act, a member. [...] In my opinion, it is possible for a person to fall into a particular racial group either by birth or by adherence, and it makes no difference, so far as the Act of 1976 is concerned, by which route he finds his way into the group. (at 562–63)

One could discriminate against someone on the basis of a mistaken belief that that person was of a particular race, even if that belief was 'from a scientific point of view, completely erroneous' (at 563). The Greek word *ethnos* simply meant 'a group' and was defined without reference to race. The original Greek meaning was not directly relevant to the statute, 'but the fact that the meaning of the latter was wide avoids one possible limitation on the meaning of the English word' (at 563).

This construction found strong support in the New Zealand Court of Appeal case *King-Ansell v Police* (1979), in which the Court found that Jews were a group with common *ethnic origins*. Lord Fraser quoted (at 564) a number of extracts from this judgment, in which one of the key themes was self-perception and the perception of others:

> The real test is whether the individuals or the group regard themselves and are regarded by others in the community as having a particular historical identity in terms of their colour or their racial, national or ethnic origins. That must be based on a belief shared by members of the group. (*King-Ansell v Police* (1979) at 542)

There was a strong element of subjective presumption in the definitional mix:

> [A] group is identifiable in terms of its ethnic origins if it is a segment of the population distinguished from others by a sufficient combination of shared customs, beliefs, traditions and characteristics derived from a common or presumed common past, even if not drawn from what in biological terms is a common racial stock. It is that combination which gives them an historically determined social identity in their own eyes and in the eyes of those outside the group. They have a distinct social identity based not simply on group cohesion and solidarity but also on their belief as to their historical antecedents. (*King-Ansell v Police* (1979) at 543)

The Sikh community, although originally defined by religion, had been accurately described by the judge in the county court (cited at 565):

> The evidence in my judgment shows that Sikhs are a distinctive and self-conscious community. They have a history going back to the 15th century. They have a written language which a small proportion of Sikhs can read but which can be read by a much higher proportion of Sikhs than of Hindus. They were at one time politically supreme in the Punjab.

Lord Fraser concluded that Sikhs were therefore 'a group defined by a reference to ethnic origins' within the meaning of the Act, 'although they are not biologically distinguishable from the other peoples living in the Punjab' (at 565). The other judges concurred, with Lord Templeman noting that

> the evidence of the origins and history of the Sikhs which was adduced by the parties to the present litigation disclosed that the Sikhs are more than a religion and a culture. And in view of the history of this country since the second world war I find it impossible to believe that Parliament intended to exclude the Sikhs from the benefit of the Race Relations Act and to allow

discrimination to be practised against the Sikhs in those fields of activity where, as the present case illustrates, discrimination is likely to occur. (at 568)

Key points in the House of Lords judgment

- The crucial phrase at issue was whether Sikhs were defined by reference to *ethnic origins*, since there was no possibility of defining them strictly as a *race*.

- Sikhs had begun as primarily a religious group, but their identity had widened to take on ethnic features.

- The dictionary definitions of *ethnic* cited by the Court of Appeal were either too narrow or too wide.

- If the narrow meaning were to be accepted then the Act would be impossible to implement, since *race* in this biological sense was no longer recognized by academic opinion.

- If the broadest meaning were to be accepted then the Act would potentially cover almost any group with a shared set of views, culture or identity.

- The key criterion was that the group in question must retain a 'flavour of race'.

- The 'flavour of race' was defined in relation to self perception of a common history, culture, beliefs and sense of community, as well as society's perception of the group.

Discussion

The use of the dictionary resulted in a choice between narrow and a broad definition. In the view of the Court of Appeal, *ethnic group* was to be defined primarily with reference to race, since the adoption of the second view threatened to include a potentially open-ended set of characteristics. Lord Denning included Jews under the narrow racial definition, but, as was implied by counsel in the House of Lords, he had failed to explain clearly why Jews were a race and Sikhs were not (see Love, 1985; Toolan, 2002: 174). On the Court of Appeal's own logic, Jews could be included only by adopting a wide understanding of race and ethnicity. Given the catastrophe of Nazism, it was unthinkable that such a law would exclude Jews. But this would seem to have made it impossible to exclude Sikhs. The inclusion of Jews opened up the law to religious groups which also, in some difficult-to-define sense, had an ethnic identity.

It was evident to both courts that there was not much help to be drawn from scholarly accounts of human diversity, and that Parliament must have intended a popular meaning of *ethnic group* rather than one based on physical anthropology or linguistic analysis. However, the Court of Appeal saw this popular meaning as evolving rapidly and acquiring meanings which went far beyond what they understood as the basic grounding of the statute, that is, the concept of race as involving inherited physical characteristics such as skin colour.

In this context, Lord Fraser's judgment made an important break with the idea that the question was to decide between a narrow and a broad meaning. Rather, drawing on the New Zealand case of *King-Ansell v Police*, he brought into the centre of discussion issues of self-understanding, recognition and social perception. If a group saw itself and to a degree was seen as a racial or ethnic community ('a flavour of race'), then it was potentially a protected group under the Act. It was not that the broad meaning was preferred to the narrow one; rather, social perception was used to identify the boundary between a racial or ethnic group and other kinds of social or cultural groups. However, the exact relation between self-perception and other-perception was not specified.

Mandla is an important example of the interaction between law and self-perception. The case created a context in which the pupil and his family, and Sikhs in Britain in general, had an interest in defining themselves as a racial or ethnic group. The question was posed in the context of the Race Relations Act, and it was presumably seen to be in the general interest of the Sikh community that their status as a protected category under this Act be recognized. This illustrates the paradox that law may be required to reify and support categories such as *race*, even while their scientific basis is not recognized and has been undermined in the wider intellectual culture.

Points for further consideration

One contentious issue in legal interpretation is the relation between linguistic categories and legal categories. Just because a tenancy agreement is called a *lease* by the parties does not mean that it is a *lease* (as opposed to a *licence*) in law. Labels do not define legal substance. But in legal interpretation, judges often ascribe distinct legal meanings to enumerated items in a list, as if each word picked out a different legal entity. This second strategy might be termed 'word magic'. What exactly is meant by this term? For some critics, the entirety of legal culture is permeated with magical thinking and word magic (Noonan, 2002).

Lord Denning is known as an advocate of purposive interpretation. But if we compare his judgment in the Court of Appeal in *Mandla* with that in *Re Rowland* (see Chapter 5), is not his position somewhat less than consistent?

In *Ozawa* the Court concluded that the category of *Japanese* was so clearly *non-white* or *non-Caucasian* that there was no need to investigate further the 'determination that the words "white person" are synonymous with the words "a person of the Caucasian race"'. The Court did, however, recognize that: 'Controversies have arisen and will no doubt arise again in respect of the proper classification of individuals in border line cases' (at 198). *Thind* was such a case, and the Court took the approach of stipulating that the relevant meaning of *Caucasian* was its narrow, popular meaning, which was equivalent to *white person*. Haney López (1996: 79) argues that in *Thind*, Justice Sutherland rejected the reliance on scientific racial classification to follow the logic of common speech. Weiner (1998), however, argues that the two decisions are not in opposition at all.

In *Thind*, the reliance on ordinary (rather than scientific) meaning led to civic exclusion in the form of loss of citizenship; in *Mandla*, the application of the ordinary or commonsense meaning of *race* ('a flavour of race') led to the inclusion of a group within the protection of the law. In *Thind*, the judge viewed race science as insufficiently certain for legal application; in *Mandla*, the House of Lords accepted that *race* was no longer a scientifically supported category. What does a comparison of these two cases tell us about law's construction of race, its relation to racial science and the role of ordinary language? Is law's construction of racial identities always anti-progressive? As noted in the Introduction, one can conclude that law has multiple discourses about categories and classification but 'no all-purpose theory of things' (Madison, 2005: 382).

CHAPTER 13

Defining Identity III: Transgender Identities

Introduction and background

Transgender identities are those that conflict psychologically and experientially with the sexual classification assigned officially at birth, and with the bio-social role associated with such assignments. In some cases, an individual will strongly affirm a sexual identity which is at odds with his or her bodily make-up: 'the person feels and believes that he or she is trapped in a body of the wrong sex' (*W v Registrar of Marriages* (2010) para. 14). The term *transsexual* is often used to refer to such individuals. Such a person may, if the option is available, seek to undergo medical procedures, including hormonal and surgical treatment, in order to achieve the desired identity. This is popularly called a 'sex change operation', but more formally (or correctly) it is 'sex reassignment surgery' (SRS). There is, however, no single procedure, and no definitive beginning and end point. More broadly, transgender identities may embrace a diverse range of sensibilities and self-labelling, including affirmed, asserted or aspired-to identities which do not confirm to normative assumptions about binary sex/gender identities. This has been termed the 'gender galaxy' (Vade, 2005).

There are broadly two classes of decisions in transgender cases. The first asserts that the boundary between *male* and *female* is set at birth, and that this distinction should be upheld in relation to the legal question before the court. The boundary is held to be reflected in human biology (XX versus XY chromosomes), anatomy, dictionary definitions of the words *man* and *woman*, and the ordinary meaning of these words as a matter of social usage. In the case of marriage, it is held that 'natural' heterosexual consummation and procreation are essential features. Such decisions may make reference to medical expertise or even religious belief. A second class of decisions makes reference to changes in the medical understanding of sexual identity, and also to social and institutional attitudes to gender in society. These decisions recognize so-called 'post-operative' transgender identities for the legal purpose at hand. In the case of marriage, it is held that the resulting marriage is not a same-sex marriage but a valid heterosexual union. In effect, the psychological reality of the transgender person's self-classification is given legal recognition, but crucially this must be reflected in a psychiatric evaluation and a completed course of medical treatment. In such cases, courts in effect recognize the medically created alignment of the body with the mind (see Sharpe, 2006).

Hong Kong's legal order

Hong Kong, a British colony from 1842 until 1997, is a common law jurisdiction within the People's Republic of China (PRC). In 1997, Hong Kong became a Special Administrative Region of the PRC, under a mini-constitution known as the Basic Law. This allows Hong Kong to retain its economic system and liberal socio-legal framework until 2047, under the policy framework of 'one country two systems'. The existing common law was preserved and carried over into the postcolonial order, but formal links to the United Kingdom and its legal evolution were severed. Appeals from the Hong Kong courts no longer go to the Privy Council in London for example. Hong Kong has its own Court of Final Appeal (CFA), on which senior judges from other jurisdictions may also serve as non-permanent members. Decisions of the UK House of Lords (now the Supreme Court) continue to have a substantial degree of persuasive authority. The definitive interpretation of the Basic Law, however, lies in a non-common law body, namely the Standing Committee of the National People's Congress of the PRC in Beijing.

Of special relevance to the case discussed here is Art. 37 of the Basic Law, which guarantees Hong Kong residents 'freedom of marriage' and the 'right to raise a family freely'. In addition, Hong Kong has a Bill of Rights that incorporates the International Covenant on Civil and Political Rights (ICCPR). Article 14(2) protects against 'arbitrary or unlawful interference' with, among other things, 'privacy' and 'family'; Art. 19(2) states that the 'right of men and women of marriageable age to marry and to found a family shall be recognized'.

Is a post-operative transgender woman a *woman* for the purpose of marriage?

W v Registrar of Marriages (2013)	Post-operative transgender woman	Woman	'the voluntary union for life of one man and one woman to the exclusion of all others' (Marriage Ordinance (Cap. 181), s. 40)	A post-operative transgender woman was a woman for the purpose of marriage

W v Registrar of Marriages (2010) (Court of First Instance)

This case involved judicial review of a decision of the Registrar of Marriages. The Registrar had determined that under the Marriage Ordinance, a post-operative male-to-female transgender woman could not marry in her affirmed gender, that is, as a woman. The Ordinance, originally enacted in 1875, provides in s. 1 that 'Every marriage under this ordinance shall be a Christian marriage or the civil equivalent of a Christian marriage'. Under s. 2 this implies 'a formal ceremony recognized by the law as involving the voluntary union for life of one man and one woman to the exclusion of all others'. This wording echoes Lord Penzance's statement in *Hyde v Hyde and Woodmansee* (1866, at 133), an

English case that concerned a polygamous marriage contracted in Utah. The Hong Kong Matrimonial Causes Ordinance (Cap. 179), s. 20(d) provides that a marriage is void if 'the parties are not respectively male and female'.

From the point of view of W (the applicant), it was her desire and her right to enter into a heterosexual marriage with a man. The Registrar (the respondent) took the birth certificate as the decisive document, which in W's case indicated that she was male. In terms of this document, the marriage would have been a same-sex marriage. Hong Kong has no provision for same-sex marriage or homosexual civil partnerships.

Medical procedures (SRS) are funded by the Hong Kong Government. On completion, the individual is issued with a medical certificate. It is also required that the Hong Kong identity card be changed to show the affirmed gender. The identity card is issued by the same government department (Immigration) that deals with marriages. The Government's position was that the identity document is changed for the convenience of the bearer (e.g. to allow W to use a woman's public toilet) and did not involve full official recognition of W's affirmed gender. The Government recognized the existence of what is referred to medically as 'gender identity disorder' (GID) or 'gender dysphoria', but the affirmed identity was not granted legal recognition for the purposes of marriage.

The judgment in the Court of First Instance in *W v Registrar of Marriages* opened with a discussion of transsexualism and marriage. The judge, Cheung J, noted that if sexual identity were to be defined as 'meaning biological sex determinable and determined at birth which cannot be changed subsequently' then the case raised the question of same-sex marriage (para. 7). In most individuals there was an alignment between physical appearance (i.e. secondary sexual characteristics such as body hair and breasts), anatomical features ('the presence or absence of male or female internal organs, such as ovaries, testes, prostate gland and uterus'), and XY chromosomes in males and XX chromosomes in females (para. 12). In some cases, however, there was a strong sense that 'psychological sex' was at odds with these biological indications: 'the person feels and believes that he or she is trapped in a body of the wrong sex' (para. 14). The question of sexual identity was therefore a definitional one (para. 15):

> Thus analysed, it is immediately apparent that what a person's sex is, whether a person is 'male' or 'female', and whether such a person, in adulthood, should be described as a 'man' or 'woman', are ultimately questions of definition. Put another way, the crucial issue is: whose definition?

Cheung J distinguished between transsexualism, which involved the desire for full transition to the affirmed sexual identity and was a defined medical condition, and the notion of transgender, which encompassed a broader set of identities and experiences (para. 27). He quoted medical expertise on the nature of surgical procedures used to treat transsexualism, but noted in conclusion (at 32):

> Surgery [...] however, cannot change the chromosomes of the person or establish fertility. Surgery can change the sex phenotype to suit the patient's

gender identity so that his or her distress can be relieved. Surgery can also enable the individual to feel better accepted as a member of the desired gender. Surgery, however, cannot change the genetic sex.

The relevant legislation concerning marriage in Hong Kong did not define the words *man, woman, male* or *female*. This matter was therefore 'left to the interpretation of the court' (para. 54).

Cheung J then analyzed the legal background. The English case of *Corbett v Corbett (otherwise Ashley)* (1971) had determined that for the purpose of marriage, only biological criteria, rather than a mixture of biological and psychological criteria, should be considered. The so-called '*Corbett* criteria' were (i) chromosomal (XX for a woman, XY for a man), (ii) gonadal (presence or absence of testes or ovaries), and (iii) genital (nature of the internal and external sexual organs). Factors such as psychological identity and secondary sexual characteristics (e.g. body hair, distribution of body fat) were not essential or determining criteria. The judge in *Corbett*, Ormrod J, had emphasized that the 'capacity for natural hetero-sexual intercourse' was essential to marriage. When considering what was meant by the word *woman* in the context of marriage (rather than the 'legal sex' as a general category), it was biological criteria that were determinative (*Corbett* at 105–06, cited para. 60),

> for even the most extreme degree of transsexualism in a male or the most severe hormonal imbalance which can exist in a person with male chromosomes, male gonads and male genitalia, cannot reproduce a person who is naturally capable of performing the essential role of a woman in marriage.

For Ormrod J, this had meant that the law should adopt the first three medical criteria, namely 'the chromosomal, gonadal and genital tests'. If these were congruent, this would 'determine the sex for the purpose of marriage accordingly'. No surgical intervention could alter this state of affairs. Following the decision in *Corbett*, the UK Parliament passed the Nullity of Marriage Act 1971; s. 1(c) of this Act was re-enacted as s. 11(c) of the Matrimonial Causes Act 1973. This declared void any marriage contracted where 'the parties are not respectively male and female'. In 1972 the same wording was added to the Hong Kong Matrimonial Causes Ordinance (s. 20(1)(d)), a move that has generally been understood as incorporating *Corbett* into Hong Kong law.

Cheung J then traced the reception of *Corbett* in common law courts around the world, including the United States. Many courts took the line that biological criteria were decisive: 'There are some things we cannot will into being. They just are.' (*Littleton v Prange* (1999) at 231) However, there had been some decisions, notably in Australia and New Zealand, which did not follow *Corbett*. For example, in *Re Kevin and Jennifer* (2001), the Australian court took a very broad view of the factors that might contribute to someone's sex/gender. These included 'biological and physical characteristics at birth', but also socialization, attitude, self-perception, social identity and profile, medical treatments and 'the person's biological, psychological and physical characteristics at the time of marriage', as well as, if possible, any features of the brain associated with a particular sex (para. 329). On appeal (*Attorney-General (Cth) v 'Kevin and Jennifer'* (2003)), the finding in *Re Kevin and Jennifer* (2001) that a post-operative transgender man was validly married to a woman was upheld (para. 70):

> Giving the words 'man' and 'woman' in the law of marriage their ordinary contemporary meanings according to Australian usage, the Court found that they included post-operative transsexuals as men or women in accordance with their sexual reassignment.

As far as the UK was concerned, both the Court of Appeal (*Bellinger v Bellinger* (2002)) and the House of Lords (*Bellinger v Bellinger* (2003)) had applied the *Corbett* criteria, holding that 'legal recognition of marriage is a matter of status and is not for the spouses alone to decide; it affects society and is a question of public policy for Parliament' (*Bellinger* (2002) para. 99). Cheung J noted, however, that there was a dissenting judgment in the Court of Appeal. Thorpe LJ had argued that major shifts in social and medical thinking since *Corbett* had undermined the rationale for the decision.

Before *Bellinger* reached the House of Lords, the European Court of Human Rights had decided in *Goodwin v United Kingdom* (2002) that UK law on transgender marriage violated Arts 8 and 12 of the European Convention on Human Rights (ECHR). The lead judgment in *Bellinger* in the House of Lords had been written by Lord Nicholls. Cheung J discussed the House of Lords' arguments in detail, as well as the decision in *Goodwin* and moves in the UK to change the law to 'allow transsexual people who could demonstrate that they had taken decisive steps towards living fully and permanently in the acquired gender to marry in that gender' (para. 84). However, Lord Nicholls had concluded that to give recognition to a transsexual person for the purpose of marriage would be to give the expressions *male* and *female* from the Matrimonial Causes Act 1973 'a novel, extended meaning: that a person may be born with one sex but later become, or become regarded as, a person of the opposite sex' (*Bellinger* (2003) para. 36, cited in *W v Registrar of Marriages* (2010) para. 85).

In particular, Cheung J emphasized the House of Lords' conclusion that this issue was a matter of social policy for the legislature, given the manifold policy implications in many areas of law. These policy issues needed to be addressed together, and not in piecemeal fashion. There was a need for certainty as regards which identities would be recognized, and it was far from self-evident where the line was to be drawn (*Bellinger* (2003) paras 41–43). The nature of marriage also needed to be addressed, as this case raised the wider question of same-sex marriage. This would involve 'a fundamental change in the traditional concept of marriage' (*Bellinger* (2003) para 48, cited in *W v Registrar of Marriages* (2010) para. 89). Lord Hope had stressed that the terms *male* and *female* were not technical terms. He had found no evidence that according to contemporary usage in the UK, these words included 'post-operative transsexual persons'. After referring to dictionary definitions, Lord Hope had concluded: 'The fact is that the ordinary meaning of the word "male" is incapable, without more, of accommodating the transsexual person within its scope' (*Bellinger* (2003) para. 62, cited in *W v Registrar of Marriages* (2010), para. 92). However, in view of *Goodwin*, the House of Lords had issued a declaration of incompatibility between Arts 8 and 12 ECHR and s. 11(c) of the Matrimonial Causes Act 1973. The UK Parliament in due course passed the Gender Recognition Act 2004, which provided in s. 9(1) that the affirmed gender of post-operative transsexuals was recognized 'for all purposes', subject to specific exceptions (e.g. in relation to peerages). The UK also passed the Civil Partnership Act 2004 that gave legal recognition to same-sex partnerships but did not recognize same-sex marriage.

The main part of the judgment in *W v Registrar of Marriages* (2010) is divided into two parts. The first (paras 104–62) involves statutory interpretation, specifically of the Hong Kong Marriage Ordinance and related legislation, with an emphasis on the meanings of the words *man* and *woman* in relation to marriage. The second (paras 163–258) considers the effect of constitutional provisions in the Basic Law and the Bill of Rights, and asks whether W's claim receives any support from the rights and freedoms laid out in these constitutional documents.

Cheung J first set out the principles underlying statutory interpretation in Hong Kong. The 'context and purpose' of the legislation must be considered within a purposive approach, 'especially in the case of general words' (para. 106). The context of the statute should be taken in its widest sense, including the state of the law as a whole and background materials preceding the enactment (para. 106). However, the judge should not 'distort or even ignore the plain meaning of the text and construe the statute in whatever manner that achieves a result which is considered desirable' (para. 107). The law regarding marriage in Hong Kong dated from the colonial era and provided 'for the celebration of Christian marriage or the civil equivalent thereof'. Marriage was a legal institution at the heart of 'most if not all civilized societies'; it was 'a social institution greatly affected by a society's culture, history and traditions' (para. 110). The Hong Kong law of marriage was 'to recognise, regulate and restrict marriages in our society' (para. 110). Among the restrictions was the requirement that marriage 'be the union of one man and one woman'. This meant that 'same sex marriage is prohibited' (para. 113). The colonial background reflected Church of England doctrine on marriage, and the centrality of procreation: 'And procreation is, by definition, a matter for members of the opposite biological sex' (para. 116). The law expressed the 'natural heterosexual aspect of Christian marriage (and its civil equivalent)'.

Further, the Matrimonial Causes Ordinance had by general consent incorporated *Corbett* into Hong Kong law, via the UK Nullity of Marriage Act 1971. Given the close relationship between the UK and the Hong Kong legal systems, it was 'unrealistic to suggest that *Corbett* did not represent the state of Hong Kong law prior to 1997 or, that it does not represent the present state of the law here, subject to any possible change thereto' (para. 121). Cases like *Re Kevin and Jennifer* and Thorpe LJ's dissent in *Bellinger* (2002) drew on changes in social attitudes and in medicine. Yet if one took as a premise the view that marriage was a voluntary union of two people of the opposite sex, 'one simply cannot escape from the conclusion that the ability to engage in natural heterosexual intercourse is an essential feature of marriage' (para. 122). Even though people 'past their child bearing age' or who were infertile were allowed to marry, procreation was nonetheless the 'central theme of marriage'. The judgment quoted from *Bellinger* (para. 123):

> Of course, it is not given to every man or every woman to have, or to want to have, children. But the ability to reproduce one's own kind lies at the heart of all creation, and the single characteristic which invariably distinguishes the adult male from the adult female throughout the animal kingdom is the part which each sex plays in the act of reproduction. When Parliament used the words 'male' and 'female' in section 11(c) of the 1973 Act it must be taken to have used those words in the sense which they normally have when they are used to describe a person's sex, even though they are plainly capable of including men and women who happen to be infertile or are past the age of child bearing. (Lord Hope, *Bellinger* (2003) para. 64)

There was nothing in the 'traditions, custom or societal practice either in the United Kingdom or in Hong Kong' to support the marriage of transsexual people in their 'preferred sex'. While the idea of 'updating construction was recognized', in that statutes were 'always speaking', there was a limit to this. 'Sex discrimination' could not be interpreted to mean 'sexual orientation discrimination' (*MacDonald v Advocate-General for Scotland* (2004)). In *R (Quintavalle) v Secretary of State for Health* (2003) para. 9, Lord Bingham had explained (cited, para. 127):

> There is, I think, no inconsistency between the rule that statutory language retains the meaning it had when Parliament used it and the rule that a statute is always speaking. If Parliament, however long ago, passed an act applicable to dogs, it could not properly be interpreted to apply to cats; but it could properly be held to apply to animals which were not regarded as dogs when the Act was passed but are so regarded now.

The lack of any definition in the statute gave support to the idea that an updating construction might be adopted 'in the light of moral, ethical and societal values as they are now' (para. 128). This had been the theme of Thorpe LJ's dissent in *Bellinger*, which tracked the radical changes in the nature of marriage since the modern common law definitions were laid down. It was not necessarily the case 'as a matter of logic, legal reasoning or practical reality, that the assigned sex is inviolable or otherwise immutable for the rest of the person's life' (para. 132).

The judgment in *W v Registrar of Marriages* then turned to the 'ordinary usage of language', which was ultimately the question in construing the text 'according to its plain meaning':

> Words used in a statute should be given their natural and ordinary meaning unless the context or purpose points to a different meaning. Here, one is

concerned with the contemporary meaning and usage of the relevant words and text. (para. 134)

Whereas the Australian courts had been able to conclude that 'in the English language *as used in Australia*, the words "man" and "woman" (and "male" and "female") include respectively a post-operative transsexual man and a post-operative transsexual woman', this was not the case in the United Kingdom. Further, under Hong Kong law (in contrast to Australia and New Zealand), non-consummation of marriage was a ground by which a marriage could be rendered void. That is, this was grounds to declare the marriage void if one of the parties so wished, but it did not automatically make it so (para. 136).

The definitional issue had been addressed by Lord Hope (*Bellinger* (2003) para. 62), who had cited the definition of *male* in the *New Shorter Oxford English Dictionary* (1993) as 'of, pertaining to, or designating the sex which can beget offspring'. There was no mention in the dictionary of transsexual persons. Similar conclusions had been reached in the United States, where courts had assessed common usage and consulted dictionaries. The *Shorter Oxford English Dictionary* (6th edn, 2007) defined the word *woman* as 'an adult female person' and the adjective *female* as 'of, pertaining to, or designating the sex which can beget offspring or produce eggs'. In the instant case, the relevant context was Hong Kong. 'Very little evidence' had been offered with respect to 'the ordinary, everyday usage of the relevant words in this jurisdiction', that is, 'whether and how the local usage and understanding differ from the UK or US usage described in the cases' (at 139). It was the court's understanding that 'post-operative transsexual people in Hong Kong are still, in ordinary, everyday usage and understanding, referred to as such'. Such an individual was generally referred to in English or Chinese as a transsexual person (i.e. 變性人, 變性男人 or 變性女人), 'rather than simply as a "man" (男人) or a "woman" (女人) in accordance with the post-operative gender acquired'. The fact that colloquially sex reassignment was referred to as a 'sex change operation' did not in ordinary usage 'represent a general understanding or acceptance that the person's "sex" (whatever one understands the word to mean) has really been "changed"' (para. 140).

Further to this, there was uncertainty, discussed in *Bellinger*, as to where the line could be drawn along a continuum

> which begins with the person who suffers from transsexualism but who has not chosen to cross-dress on a regular basis and has embarked on no program of hormonal modification or surgery, through to the person who has embarked on hormone therapy and perhaps has some minor surgical intervention such as removal of gonads, through to the person who undergoes complete reconstructive surgery. (para. 143)

There was even the technical possibility of medically reversing the assignment surgery. Given the complexity of the policy issues involved, this was a matter for the legislature acting 'in a comprehensive manner', not for a judge reflecting private views on social issues (para. 157). Sex for the purposes of marriage 'is and continues to be determined according to [an individual's] biological sex at birth' (para. 162).

The second part of the judgment concerned whether the court could declare the Hong Kong legal provisions relating to marriage unconstitutional in respect of W's claim. The focus of the arguments had been on the right to marry under Art. 37 of the Basic Law and Art. 19(2) of the Hong Kong Bill of Rights. Cheung J argued that the right to privacy could not yield a stronger result for the applicant than the right to marry itself, and that this latter right was therefore the proper focus. It was not the applicant's case that marriage should be interpreted to include same-sex marriage, rather it was her contention that her marriage would be heterosexual (para. 176). The right to marry was a 'strong right' in constitutional law terms, that is, a fundamental right that should not be injured or substantially impaired (para. 179). However, Cheung J felt that the argument in court had rightly focused on the question of definition, rather than being framed as a question about the proportionality of the restriction on transsexuals. If marriage was understood 'as a voluntary union between persons of the opposite sex, that is to say, a voluntary union between a man and a woman', then the definitional question became: 'What is a "man" or "woman" under the Basic Law?' (para. 181). He concluded that there could be no serious doubt about the meanings of the words *man* and *woman* as used in the drafting of the Basic Law. This had been promulgated in 1990, as the result of negotiations between China and Britain through the 1980s.

There were also no grounds to find different meanings in the ICCPR. This had been adopted in 1966, coming into force in 1976. The applicant's case therefore hinged on whether a 'generous' reading of the constitutional instruments as 'living instruments' could be justified. It was right that the law of marriage should not lag behind the evolving societal consensus. If the law of marriage were more restrictive than the societal consensus, 'the "essence" of the right would be impaired and the law would be unconstitutional' (para. 190). However, the court, unlike the legislature, could not go beyond that societal consensus (para. 192):

> [T]he versatility of the constitutional right to marry does not give the courts a judicial licence to engineer a fundamental social and legal reform of the institution of marriage.

While there was now a holistic approach to gender identity in medical science, this did not mean that the law's definition should follow that of the doctors: 'the law's definition of a person's sex serves a purpose that is not necessarily identical to that served by a medical definition'. Marriage law was not enacted for the purposes of reflecting the definitions adopted by medical science (para. 201). It remained the case 'that the ability to reproduce one's own kind still lies at the heart of all creation' (Lord Hope, in *Bellinger* (2003) para. 64). Nonetheless, the court recognized that there were important social changes underway in relation to marriage, from being an institution primarily for procreation to one 'affording mutual society, help and comfort' (para. 206).

However, if one followed this logic, then even a pre-operative transsexual could marry in his or her 'preferred sex' (para. 206).

Decisions of the European Court of Human Rights were based on an emerging consensus among contracting states. Hong Kong was not a party to the ECHR. In a 'predominantly Chinese society like Hong Kong', marriage originally 'had a lot to do with procreation and the continuation of the family line' (para. 206). Decisions of the European Court of Human Rights on similar rights might have persuasive authority, but it was for Hong Kong to decide the nature of the right to marry. There was no consensus among the contracting states to the ICCPR; the United Nations Human Rights Council had made no comment on this question in relation to Hong Kong. While fundamental rights were an exception to the principle of majority rule, it was not the case here that the majority was taking something away from a minority:

> Rather, one is here to discover the present day boundary of the social institution of marriage as is understood by society or a majority thereof, and to give the fundamental right to marry a contemporary context or meaning that conforms to the social institution as it is understood now. (para 217)

There was no evidence of an emerging societal consensus in Hong Kong. The fact that an identity card was issued in the acquired gender, or that SRS was publicly funded, did not come close to establishing 'a general change in understanding or an emerging societal consensus' (para. 226). The argument had been put that the law classified everyone as either male or female and that all residents enjoyed the right to marry; therefore, to classify a post-operative transsexual person according to biological sex denied that person the right to marry. This argument had merit as a general point about how the law might be reformed, but not as to the law as it actually was (paras 236–38). It was 'not for the Court, sitting in a constitutional challenge, to seek to engineer a fundamental social and legal reform' (para. 243).

Key points in the judgment

- The words *man* and *woman* were not defined in the legislation and were to be given their ordinary meaning, understood within a purposive framework.
- The Marriage Ordinance defined *marriage* as 'the voluntary union for life of one man and one woman to the exclusion of all others' (*Hyde v Hyde and Woodmansee* (1866)).
- This, in combination with the Matrimonial Causes Ordinance which enacted the decision in *Corbett v Corbett* (1971), meant that the parties to a marriage should be those born biologically male and female respectively.
- There had been significant medical and legal developments since *Corbett*, and the Hong Kong Government funded SRS and allowed ID cards to be issued in the affirmed gender; but this did not change the position in relation to marriage.
- There was no evidence of a societal consensus that the meanings of the *man* and *woman* had changed in Hong Kong to include transsexual identities.

- The *Corbett* criteria had been upheld in *Bellinger*, and the reasoning and dictionary definitions cited there remained persuasive for Hong Kong.

- Hong Kong was not a party to the ECHR, and should determine its own legal understanding of marriage, within which procreation remained a key conceptual element.

- Non-consummation was a ground for annulment in Hong Kong, unlike jurisdictions such as Australia and New Zealand where courts had rejected the *Corbett* criteria.

- The required social consensus was lacking to support a 'generous' constitutional claim that would include transsexual identities within the ordinary definition of *man* and *woman*.

- Marriage was a public institution which society was entitled to regulate.

- It was not within the court's remit to engineer social change in a complex area such as marriage; this was the proper duty of the legislature.

W v Registrar of Marriages (2011) (Court of Appeal)

The Court of Appeal upheld the judgment of the Court of First Instance in all its particulars. It agreed that when *Corbett* was adopted into Hong Kong law in 1972, 'the words "woman" and "female" (and "man" and "male") did not in their ordinary meaning include a transsexual woman (or transsexual man)'. The argument had been made that marriage in Hong Kong had become 'a vehicle for public demonstration of love and affection to a partner, to secure private law rights (such as inheritance and maintenance) and for access to public benefits (such as tax allowances and public housing)', and that it no longer existed 'primarily for the procreation of life'. However, the Court stressed that non-consummation remained a ground for annulling a marriage (s. 20(2)(a), Matrimonial Causes Ordinance). This suggested that 'the essential nature of marriage requires a partnership between two persons of the opposite sex, with the procreation of children remaining as one of its purposes and attributes' (para. 77). The Government's treatment of transsexualism did not lead to the conclusion 'that the ordinary meaning of "man" and "woman" should be treated as having been updated to include transsexuals' (para. 86). The Court concurred that 'there was no evidence of a societal consensus in Hong Kong' which could support a constitutional claim (para. 144).

W v Registrar of Marriages (2013) (The Court of Final Appeal)

The Court of Final Appeal reversed the decisions of the lower courts and found, by a majority of four to one, that a post-operative transgender woman was a *woman* for the purposes of marriage on Hong Kong. The lead judgment (by Chief Justice Ma and Justice Ribeiro, with Lord Hoffmann, sitting as a foreign judge, concurring) opened with a discussion of transsexualism. In summarizing the evidence of a psychiatrist, the Court stated that it was possible 'to regard the sexual identity of an adult individual as determinable by reference to psychological and biological factors'. The psychological aspects included 'gender identity (self perception of being male or female); social sex role (living as male or female); sex orientation (homosexual, heterosexual, asexual or bisexual); and sex of rearing (whether brought up as male or female)' (para. 6).

This set the tone for the judgment, which set out a sustained criticism of *Corbett* (and, less directly, of *Bellinger*). The first factor presented was that of self-perception. This reversed the commonly adopted mode of presentation beginning with the biological and ending with the psychological. In *Corbett*, 'psychological factors' are the fourth factor listed. Within the biological aspects of sexual identity, the list of 'biological aspects' of sexual identity presented by the court was more detailed and inclusive than in *Corbett*. These included (para. 6):

> the genetic (the presence or absence of the Y chromosome); the gonadal (the presence of ovaries or testes); the hormonal (circulating hormones and end organ sensitivity); internal genital morphology (the presence or absence of male or female internal structures such as the prostate gland and the uterus); external genital morphology (the structure of male or female external genitalia); and secondary sexual characteristics (body hair, breasts and fat distribution).

Whereas for the vast majority these 'indicia are all congruent', this was not the case for those suffering from gender identity disorder (para. 7). In a footnote, a dissenting judgment from the European Court of Human Rights decision in *Cossey v United Kingdom* (1990) was cited, noting that transsexual individuals experienced their plight in terms of a lack of full legal recognition, in addition to needing medical intervention (*Cossey*, para. 2.4, cited in fn. 8).

As in the previous decisions, the judgment considered, first, the question of statutory interpretation and, secondly, the constitutional position. While it took issue with the basis of *Corbett*, in particular on the issue of procreation being the essence of marriage, *Corbett* had been in effect adopted into Hong Kong law (para. 48). If *W v Registrar of Marriages* were to be decided as a matter of statutory construction alone, the appeal would have been denied. On that issue, the question of 'ordinary meaning' was raised (see paras 50–53). This had formed the second part of the Registrar's argument on statutory interpretation, where it had been asserted that there was no evidence that the ordinary meanings of words like *man* and *woman* in Hong Kong included transgender men and women.

It had frequently been asserted that since the word *woman* was not given 'a technical or special meaning', the question concerned the 'ordinary meaning' of the word. This was true up to a point, but the use of the term 'ordinary meaning' should not obscure 'the crucial importance of context and purpose' (para. 50):

> One is not concerned with asking whether a post-operative transsexual woman is 'a woman' in some abstract or general sense, but whether she is

'a woman' for the purposes of the law of marriage and so has capacity to marry a man.

The question at issue was not an abstract or general one; as Ormrod J in *Corbett* had said, it was not a question of determining the 'legal sex […] at large'. The 'context and purpose' was crucial, and in this case it concerned marriage. It was 'perfectly possible that as a matter of law, someone in W's position may qualify as a woman for some, but not all purposes' (para. 51). The Court therefore gave no weight to arguments relying on the ordinary meaning of the terms *man* and *woman*, current usage, dictionary meanings, and 'the existence of negative attitudes' in relation to whether or not in ordinary usage in Hong Kong *woman* encompassed a male-to-female transsexual person. Rather than rely on a textual 'ordinary meaning', the Court looked at 'the legislative intent' in Hong Kong following the *Corbett* decision (para. 53). The position of the law in relation to the consummation of marriage was also not considered relevant. There was in any event no legal impediment to a marriage with a post-operative transsexual woman being consummated (para. 55, referencing *S Y v S Y* (1963), which held that the 'artificiality' of a woman's genitalia was not an obstacle to consummation).

On the constitutional question, the Court discussed the possibility of a 'remedial interpretation' of the statute, in the light of the constitutionally recognized right to marry. This would fall short of the Court striking down a provision as unconstitutional, but go beyond a declaration of incompatibility. It consisted in modifying or **reading into** the provision particular constitutionally protected meanings (para. 62). The Court tracked the evolution of the issue in decisions of the European Court of Human Rights, noting that the Strasbourg Court eventually concluded in *Goodwin* that, given 'medical advances and social developments', the use of purely biological criteria was no longer sufficient (para. 77(b)). The Registrar argued that the relevant constitutional instruments – such as the ICCPR (1966), on which Art. 19(2) (right to marry and found a family) of the Hong Kong Bill of Rights was based, the Joint Declaration on the Future of Hong Kong (1984) and the Basic Law (1990) – all should be assumed to take a traditional approach to marriage, and there was no social consensus in Hong Kong or international consensus that the word *woman* had developed a different meaning in this context. Any change required a systematic legislative approach, not piecemeal action by the courts (para. 83). However, the Court argued that the framers of these documents would not necessarily have adopted the approach in *Corbett*. In any case, these were 'living instruments intended to meet changing needs and circumstances' (para. 84). Social and medical changes had been recognized by courts in a range of jurisdictions. The *Corbett* emphasis on biological factors alone and the idea that 'procreative sexual intercourse is an essential constituent of marriage' (para. 89) were no longer tenable (para. 95):

> Having had access to surgical, hormonal and psychiatric treatment of undoubtedly greater sophistication than available in Corbett's time, [W] may now properly be described as an individual who is psychologically,

medically and socially a woman living and having a physical relationship with a man, although a woman who is unable to bear children.

Of the three biological criteria identified in *Corbett*, the 'male genital and gonadal factors' had been eliminated by medical intervention: only the male chromosomal criterion remained. The Court took exception to the language used in *W v W* (1976) ('pseudo-type of woman') and in *Corbett* ('pastiche of femininity', 'female impersonator'). This betrayed 'a failure to recognize the fundamental importance and potency of the individual's psychological compulsion as a determinant of her sexual identity' (para. 99).

There was no meaningful sense in which W might marry a woman, given the irreversible nature of the surgery (paras 109–11). The argument had been that the European Court of Human Rights had waited until a Europe-wide consensus had emerged among the Contracting States, and there was no equivalent consensus among the signatories to the ICCPR. The Court rejected these arguments. It noted that the Court in Strasbourg was a very different kind of court, and in any case to rely on 'the absence of a majority consensus as a reason for rejecting a minority's claim' was 'inimical to fundamental rights' (para. 116). While as a matter of statutory construction the Registrar had been correct, in relation to the constitutional right to marry, the *Corbett* criteria did not permit 'a full and appropriate assessment of the sexual identity to be made' for the purposes of determining the right to marry (para. 118). Further, the provisions denied W 'the right to marry at all', and were therefore unconstitutional (paras 118–19). The Matrimonial Causes Ordinance (s. 20(1)(d)) and the Marriage Ordinance (s. 40) should be given a remedial interpretation, which required

> the references to 'woman' and 'female' to be read as capable of accommodating post-operative male-to-female transsexual persons for marriage purposes and as allowing account to be taken of the full range of criteria for assessing sexual identity, viewed at the date of the marriage or proposed marriage. (para. 123)

Someone who had undergone SRS should be included as a *woman* within the meaning of these sections: 'We leave open the question whether transsexual persons who have undergone less extensive treatment might also qualify' (para. 124). Ideally, the Hong Kong Government would enact legislation in relation to how the borderline should be drawn and other policy questions. The UK Gender Recognition Act provided an important point of reference (para. 138).

The dissenting judgment by Justice Chan, in contrast with the majority, laid emphasis on the ordinary meanings of the words *man* and *woman*. The meanings of these words argued for by W would amount to 'a radical change to the traditional concept of marriage' (para. 159). Those meanings referred

> respectively to a biological man and a biological woman capable of producing children. This accords with the common understanding of these words

and is also reflected in their meanings in the dictionary. These words do not include a post-operative transsexual man and woman [...] (para. 160)

There was no evidence that in Hong Kong 'these words have acquired any new contemporary meanings which are different from what is commonly understood by these words'. This had been true for the House of Lords in *Bellinger*, whereas in *Re Kevin and Jennifer* (2001), the Australian court had found such evidence: 'Obviously, the situation varies in each country, depending on its social and cultural conditions' (para. 161). There was also no evidence that the consensus as to the nature of marriage in Hong Kong had changed. Even if the *Corbett* criteria were unsatisfactory, it was for the legislature to redefine the nature of marriage (para. 168), as this was a 'change of social policy' (para. 192). There was a need for a 'comprehensive review of the relevant legislation' (para. 197).

A separate judgment by Justice Bokhary stressed that this was not a case of the law being changed to meet 'new expectations' (para. 220). What was at stake was an already existing and fundamental human right. It was one of the most important tasks of constitutions to protect minorities: 'The greatest and most urgent need for constitutional protection is apt to be found among those who form a minority, especially a misunderstood minority' (para. 220). While the expression 'post-operative transsexual' had been used, a person who had undergone SRS treatment was no longer a transsexual: 'In truth, such a person is a person of the sex brought about by such treatment' (para. 228).

Key points in the majority judgment

- An individual's sexual identity was a combination of psychological and biological factors, including self-perception.
- The *Corbett* decision, especially in relation to sexual identity and the definition of *marriage*, was no longer acceptable.
- As a question of statutory construction, Hong Kong law had incorporated the *Corbett* decision.
- Questions relating to the 'ordinary meaning' of the words *man* and *woman* in Hong Kong were not relevant, since the statute concerned marriage law, not an abstract legal identity.
- Questions of consummation of marriage were not of direct relevance, especially given the decision in *S Y v S Y* (1963).
- The constitutional question concerned the right to marry, as set out in the Hong Kong Bill of Rights and the Basic Law.
- The Court had the power to declare a law unconstitutional, or to adopt a remedial interpretation, in which it read specific meanings into the legal text.
- A range of jurisdictions, in particular those within the jurisdiction of the European Court of Human Rights, Australia and New Zealand, had adopted the view that post-operative transsexual persons could marry in their affirmed gender.

- Hong Kong's constitutional order involved 'living instruments'; there was no need to demonstrate a societal consensus for the protection of minority rights.

- W had no prospect of contracting a lawful marriage with either a man or a woman.

- There had been substantial medical, societal and legal changes since *Corbett*.

- As a matter of constitutional interpretation, a post-operative transsexual woman was a *woman* for the purposes of the relevant laws relating to marriage.

- Ideally the Government would enact legislation to lay down guidelines on this and related policy questions.

Discussion: self-classification and the law

In the line of cases discussed here, including the UK cases, those judgments that take the ordinary meaning of the words *man* and *woman* as legally determinative, tend to deny legal recognition to the affirmed identity of the transgender person. In the Court of First Instance and the Court of Appeal, the question of the ordinary meaning for purposes of statutory interpretation was carried over into the constitutional argument. The judges sought and failed to find a societal consensus for a change of the constitutional position. There was no evidence in Hong Kong that the words *man* and *woman* included transgender individuals, specifically post-operative transsexual individuals. In other words, the constitutional right still had to pass the filter of ordinary language.

In the Court of Final Appeal, the majority rejected the relevance of the ordinary meaning of these words for statutory interpretation, asserting that the issue was essentially a legal one. There was no question of carrying over this concern with ordinary meaning into the constitutional debate. The Court employed a strategy based on constitutional rights, rather than that followed in the Australian case *Re Kevin and Jennifer* (2001). In *Re Kevin and Jennifer*, the court asserted that the ordinary meanings of *man* and *woman* had changed; it followed an updating strategy, arguing that the statutory language now should be read in line with the widely accepted meanings. The evidence for this was usage by official bodies, and also the acceptance of transgender parties in their family and communities. There was no actual evidence presented in that case as to the general meanings of the words *man* and *woman* in Australian English. (It is worth noting that Australia has no Bill of Rights or constitutionally defined human rights law. The result is that courts must frame their judgments by reference to the ordinary meanings of statutory terms.)

Justice Chan, in his dissenting judgment on this point, remarked that 'the situation varies in each country, depending on its social and cultural conditions'. But if this was intended as a sociological or sociolinguistic generalization, it would be stretching the fiction of ordinary meaning to absurdity to imply that the word *woman* in Australia included transgender identities, whereas (at that time) in the United Kingdom it did not. The Court of Final

Appeal followed an alternative strategy, stressing that the protection of minority rights did not require the consensus of the majority. It in effect stipulated the meanings of the words *man* and *woman* in the relevant ordinances not as sociological fact, but as a reflection of constitutional law. Ultimately, the decision in *W v Registrar of Marriages* (2013) reflected the weight of medical and legal culture in comparable jurisdictions, especially the United Kingdom, more than any specific Hong Kong development. However, the fact that the case was brought at all without doubt reflects socio-cultural changes in Hong Kong, including government recognition in some domains of issues relating to sexual minorities. The fact that the Court of Final Appeal decided to ignore the question of ordinary meaning illustrates how legal questions can be formulated in terms of the meanings of words, or the nature of things (objects, events, people) or legal rights. There is another level to the linguistic question. The question posed in the Court of First Instance about the meanings of the words *man and woman*, 'Whose definition?', was indirectly answered at the beginning of the judgment of the Court of Final Appeal. Psychological factors were placed at the head of the factors determining sexual identity. Yet, paradoxically, self-perception must be validated by medical certification, a process that requires a long and difficult series of medical interventions. Self-perception can therefore achieve legal recognition through a form of trial by ordeal, that is, in virtue of the willingness to undergo a painful and complex medical procedure. In the end, the medical judgement that 'passes' the post-operative individual's body emerges as more significant than self-perception.

Judgments that deny and those that recognize post-operative transgender identities agree in affirming that self-classification cannot be regarded as a free-standing and autonomous factor (Hutton, 2011). Below is an illustrative quotation from each type of judgment:

> Individuals cannot choose for themselves whether they wish to be known or treated as male or female. Self-definition is not acceptable. That would make nonsense of the underlying biological basis of the distinction. (*Bellinger v Bellinger* (2003) at 5)

> The law could never countenance a definition of male or female which depends on how a particular person views his or her own gender. The consequence of such an approach would be that a person could change sex from year to year despite the fact that the person's chromosomes are immutable. (*R v Harris and McGuinness* (1988) at 11)

Sexual identity is generally understood as a continuum from 'hard' (or 'real') biology (chromosomes) to 'soft' (or purely 'subjective') self-perception. The Court of Final Appeal opened, however, by stressing the importance of psychological factors. While for many individuals this legal recognition is precisely what they are seeking, recognition of one category brings into focus a further, highly diverse set of marginalized categories of sexual identity. It sets up the medical verdict as the gatekeeper for law (Sharpe, 2006). Ironically, this replays in progressive form the underlying logic of the *Corbett* decision. A Hong Kong commentator, while welcoming the decision in *W*, argued that more profound legal reform was needed, following either the UK model or solutions from other jurisdictions. If surgery was set 'as a precondition for legal gender recognition' then this would be equivalent to saying that transgender women, to enjoy equality before the law, would have no choice but to go through the full SRS (Winter, 2013: A11):

> You want to live in dignity and respect? First strip out your genitals, rearrange your insides, and make sure you come back sterile. Then come back and ask.

Points for further consideration

The decision in *W v Registrar of Marriages* is of direct relevance to wider issues of how and why societies classify people. In addition, it opens up questions about the nature of personal identity, marriage, and the way law and medicine both reflect and drive social change. To what extent, if at all, did the Court in *W v Registrar of Marriages* recognize self-classification as valid for purposes of law? If we compare *Re Kevin and Jennifer* with the Court of Final Appeals decision in *W*, what conclusion might be drawn as to the role of ordinary language versus constitutional reasoning in the adjudication of transgender cases? It is also worth asking a truly fundamental question: What is the ultimate origin and nature of law's investment in the recognition of two discrete genders with stable, non-overlapping membership?

CHAPTER 14

Defining Identity IV: Personhood

Who or what is a *legal person*?

In the post-apocalypse TV drama *The Walking Dead*, small bands of humans struggle to survive in a world where flesh-eating zombies (known as *walkers*) roam. A person is transformed into a zombie by being bitten, but remains recognizable as his or her former self. In Season II (2011), a conflict arises among the survivors about the status of zombies, whether they are human beings who are ill, or simply a terrifying kind of non-human. The survivors argue about the rights and wrongs of depersonifying the zombies as *walkers*, and whether it is justifiable to kill them, definitively, for a second time. This is not entirely a fictional problem. In Haiti, at least for some, the zombie is a recognized social category, although extremely difficult for an outsider to encounter and define (Davis, 1985; Morris, 2011). In any case, *The Walking Dead* debate about the status of zombies is an easily recognizable one, in spite of its apocalyptic backdrop. The history of legal rights is a continual set of debates over the 'successive extension of rights to some new entity' (Stone, 1972: 453).

Categories of *legal person*

A full legal person is a 'natural person' (i.e. a human being) who enjoys the maximal autonomy that law can provide, with the complete set of rights available in the jurisdiction. These might include: citizenship, freedom of life, liberty and property, the right to form contracts, to consent to sexual intercourse, to marry, to vote, to stand for elected office, the standing to initiate legal action, and so on. A full legal person is also liable for his or her actions in respect of the criminal and civil law, and may be called to serve in respect of civic duties such as paying taxes, military service, jury duty, etc.

The list of categories that are or have been problematic in relation to the status of 'legal person' is very long and remains open-ended. For example, the monarch (e.g. the Queen of England) is in effect a 'hyper-person', in that the Crown and the monarch, as the personification of law, cannot be charged with a crime, nor sued in the courts. The monarch by convention does not vote and does not require a passport to travel. The Crown is also the ultimate and absolute owner of land.

A second problematic category, the members of which historically lacked full autonomy in respect of legal personhood, used to be *woman* (*De Souza v Cobden* (1891)). In *Minor v Happersett* (1874), the US Supreme Court ruled that the 'equal protection under the laws' extended by the Fourteenth Amendment to '[a]ll persons born or naturalized in the United States' did not automatically confer the right to vote: 'the constitutions and laws of the several states which commit that important trust to men alone are not necessarily void' (at 178). In *Edwards v A.G. of Canada* (1930), the Privy Council ruled that the statutory term *qualified persons* found in s. 24 of the British North America Act (1867) included women. This meant that women were eligible to be 'summoned to and become members of the Senate of Canada' (see Sharpe and McMahon, 2007).

A third, profoundly important category that has a long and complex legal history is that of *race*. The intertwining of racial categorization and the category *citizen* shaped the now notorious United States Supreme Court decision in *Dred Scott v Sandford* (1857).

At the cutting edge of legal debate, the status of animals within law raises increasingly complex ethical questions. In a recent case, the organization People for the Ethical Treatment of Animal (PETA) filed a lawsuit on behalf of plaintiff killer whales (orcas) held in captivity by the marine park SeaWorld in California. The suit alleged that these orcas were *slaves* within the meaning of the US Constitution and the Thirteenth Amendment. The Amendment forbids 'slavery' and 'involuntary servitude', without specifying that this applies only to human beings. The complaint was dismissed by a federal judge on 8 February 2012 (*Tilikum v SeaWorld* (2012)).

Examples of categories where full personhood, in the sense defined above, is, or has been or may become an issue include:

- Monarch ('corporation sole')
- Bishop ('corporation sole')
- Corporation (town, university, monastery)
- Temple
- Idol, sacred statute
- Company, incorporated business
- Woman
- Child
- Slave, former slave
- Foetus
- Conjoined twins
- Prisoner
- Association, group
- Member of a particular race or ethnic group
- Indigenous inhabitant
- Ship
- Prisoner

- Migrant, non-citizen, refugee, etc.
- Machine (robot, computer, …)
- Mentally ill person
- Mentally handicapped person
- Animal.

Who or what is a *corporation*?

A corporation is an organization that has been granted legal recognition of its identity or *personhood* ('personality'), independently of the individuals that constitute it. Historically, incorporation was a privilege granted by Royal Charter to religious, educational, trading and other institutions, and to political entities such as towns and colonies. In this section, the term *corporation* refers primarily to an incorporated business or company. Since corporations are legally *persons*, one rich vein of legal discussion is the question of how a legal person compares in rights, obligations, and potential civil and criminal liabilities with a natural person. In order be registered ('incorporated') as a legal entity, a business must submit to a complex regime of rules and regulations.

Corporations or incorporated companies can own assets in their own name, sue and be sued. As legal persons who are potentially immortal, they offer continuity of identity and of ownership of assets: 'a perpetual succession of individuals are capable of acting for the promotion of the particular object like one immortal being' (*Trustees of Dartmouth College v Woodward* (1819) at 636). Corporations generally provide limited liability for their members, whose private assets and persons are protected in legal actions against the company for debt, bankruptcy, and most criminal and civil acts. In traditional corporation law, 'one corporation cannot make another' (Sheppard, 1659: 112), but in the modern law of corporations (company law) the members of the company may themselves be other (subsidiary) companies. The fact that a company or a corporation is a *person* has fascinated but also confounded legal scholars and judges:

- 'Did you ever expect a corporation to have a conscience, when it has no soul to damn, no body to kick? By God, it ought to have both.' (attributed to Edward, First Baron Thurlow 1731–1806; Coffee, 1981)
- 'A corporation is an artificial being, invisible, intangible, and existing only in contemplation of law. Being the mere creature of law, it possesses only those properties which the charter of its creation confers upon it either expressly or as incidental to its very existence.' (*Trustees of Dartmouth College v Woodward* (1819) at 636)
- 'A corporation is a body aggregate – none can create souls but God; but the king creates them, and therefore they have no souls.' (Merewether and Stephens, 1835: 1521)
- 'A corporation is an imaginary, immaterial, legal entity, with certain powers, rights and duties. It is immortal, unless limited in duration, when created by a formal act.' (Eaton, 1902: 294)

- '[T]here are nowadays many who think that the personality of the corporation aggregate is in no sense and no sort artificial or fictitious, but is every whit as real and natural as is the personality of a man.' (Maitland, 1900: 335–36)
- 'That invisible, intangible and artificial being, that mere legal entity [...]' (Chief Justice Marshall, *Bank of the US v Deveaux* (1809) at 86)

It is unclear how seriously the *person* metaphor is to be taken (see Schane, 2006: 54–96). Corporations are 'legal fictions created by the states' and therefore 'necessarily lack human dignity and worth'; they are not 'real entities' but rather 'means of structuring financial transactions to the benefit of investors' (Bunker, 1995: 598). Corporations can sue in defamation even though 'they cannot experience the humiliation, emotional distress, and personal indignities that may be endured by a natural person' (Langvardt, 1990: 494); they 'cannot suffer physical pain, worry or distress', lying awake at night 'brooding about a defamatory article' (Phelps and Hamilton, 1979: 80). But they can protect their reputation in relation to business affairs: 'A corporation's interest in protecting its good name, often referred to as its goodwill, is solely economic' (Moll, 1978: 339).

While a corporation may be self-evidently an artificial creation, the autonomy of natural persons is also a psychological, theological and philosophical assumption. For some philosophers, the human self is no less a fiction than the personality of a company. The mystery about human identity is 'the remarkable way in which a complicated bundle of mental events, made possible by the brain, creates a singular thing underlying it' (Baggini, 2011: 123; Huenemann, 2011). From this perspective, a company and a person are similar, in that a company is also a bundle of events and processes (legal, social, psychological and economic events) that are attributed to an underlying single being. The notion of individual criminal responsibility relies on what is, from this point of view, a fiction about human behaviour.

Corporations as citizen or Frankenstein's corporate monster?

Citizens United v Federal Election Commission (2010)	A film funded by a corporation and attacking Hillary Clinton, then seeking nomination for President, which was intended to be advertised and broadcast on cable TV	Electioneering communication: 'any broadcast, cable, or satellite communication' which makes reference to 'a clearly identified candidate for Federal office' and is 'made for public distribution within 30 days of the primary election'	Bipartisan Campaign Reform Act (BCRA) of 2002 116 Stat. 81 s. 203, amending the Federal Election Campaign Act of 1971 (2 USC s. 441b)	The film was an electioneering communication but BCRA s. 203 in part violated the First Amendment

Citizens United v Federal Election Commission (2010) (US Supreme Court)

In the United States, a vexed question is the extent to which corporations have the same free speech rights as so-called *natural persons*. The First Amendment prevents Congress from 'prohibiting the free exercise' of, or 'abridging', freedom of speech. On one view, the participation of commercial corpora tions in the 'market-place of ideas' (Hutton, 2009: 118ff.) is essential to the functioning of democracy (*Bellotti v First National Bank of Boston* (1977)). Any distinction drawn between individuals and companies must not amount to the censoring of corporate speech. Set against this are: concerns about *quid pro quo* corruption (Tilman Act 1907; *Buckley v Valeo* (1976)), the distortion of public debate by powerful corporate interests (*Austin v Michigan Chamber of Commerce* (1990)), and the domination of popular democracy by a class of legally privileged, self-seeking and immortal beings. Dissenting in *Bellotti*, Justice Rehnquist pointed to the danger of economic power being translated into political domination (at 825–26):

> A State grants to a business corporation the blessings of potentially perpet-ual life and limited liability to enhance its efficiency as an economic entity. It might reasonably be concluded that those properties, so beneficial in the economic sphere, pose special dangers in the political sphere.

In *McConnell v Federal Election Commission* (2003), the ability of corporations to form Political Action Committees (PACs), which can solicit contributions from individuals, was held to give them adequate opportunities for express advocacy on behalf of political figures.

Citizens United concerned a film entitled *Hillary: The Movie* (2008). It consisted of a hostile polemic against Hillary Clinton. Senator Clinton was seeking the Democratic Party nomination for President. The film had been funded by a not-for-profit corporation, Citizens United (see <www.citizensu-nited.org>). Citizens United was funded primarily by individuals, but it also received funds from for-profit corporations. The law forbade such corporations from using their 'general treasury funds' to make direct contributions to candidates, or to advocate for or against a candidate for Federal Office by means of an *electioneering communication* within 30 days of the primary election.

The Court determined that the film met the specific statutory criteria for identifying an *electioneering communication*. This was true both in terms of content (the film was the 'functional equivalent of direct advocacy' for or against a specific candidate) and by virtue of being its being intended for public distribution on TV to at least 50,000 persons in the relevant state. The Court also upheld disclosure provisions relating to donors. But on the broader question of whether the provision fell foul of the First Amendment, the majority held that the statutory provision represented an unconstitutional violation of the corporation's right to free speech.

The long judgments in *Citizens United* cannot be analyzed in all their detail here; rather, the discussion will focus on the definition of *speech* itself and the analogy between an individual and a corporation.

Can the corporation speak? The judgment of Justice Kennedy

One of Justice Kennedy's prime concerns in the lead judgment was that there should be no 'chilling effect' on free speech, especially in the heat of an election battle (at 17):

> The decision to speak is made in the heat of political campaigns, when speakers react to messages conveyed by others. A speaker's ability to engage in political speech that could have a chance of persuading voters is stifled if the speaker must first commence a protracted lawsuit.

Justice Kennedy referred to 'the primary importance of speech itself to the integrity of the election process', without alluding to any distinction between the speech of an individual and that of a corporation. The word *speaker* was used as a general term covering all kinds of entities. If anything, the implication was that the massively complex regulatory schema governing political speech, which had 'separate rules for 33 different kinds of political speech' (at 18), represented in effect a form of censorship and operated as 'prior restraint' on corporate speech in particular. Any statute and any precedent decision which had the effect of chilling speech should be invalidated. Even though 'a PAC created by the corporation can still speak', this exemption 'does not allow corporations to speak' (at 21). In any case regulation and government supervision meant that PACs were highly burdensome to set up and administer (at 22):

> This might explain why fewer than 2,000 of the millions of corporations in this country have PACs. [...] PACs, furthermore, must exist before they

can speak. Given the onerous restrictions, a corporation may not be able to establish a PAC in time to make its views known regarding candidates and issues in a current campaign.

The statutory provision (s. 441b) represented 'a ban on speech' (at 22):

> If s. 441b applied to individuals, no one would believe that it is merely a time, place, or manner restriction on speech. Its purpose and effect are to silence entities whose voices the Government deems to be suspect. (at 23)

Speech was 'an essential mechanism of democracy, for it is the means to hold officials accountable to the people'. As the Court in *Buckley* had stressed: 'In a republic where the people are sovereign, the ability of the citizenry to make informed choices among candidates for office is essential' (*Buckley* at 14–15, cited at 23). Political speech was essential to the functioning of a democracy (at 23):

> The right of citizens to inquire, to hear, to speak, and to use information to reach consensus is a precondition to enlightened self-government and a necessary means to protect it.

Any law that restricted 'speech uttered during a campaign' should be subject to rigorous scrutiny under the First Amendment. In particular, the Government might not 'disfavor certain subjects or viewpoints', nor distinguish in terms of restrictions among different categories of speakers, nor identify 'certain pre-ferred speakers': 'Speech restrictions based on the identity of the speaker are all too often simply a means to control content' (at 24). The exemptions to this were generally justified by the prevention of interference with governmental functions, which was not a factor in this case.

The Government could not establish a category of disfavoured *speaker*, and the Court had long recognized that First Amendment protection extended to corporations and to political speech by corporations (at 25–26). This was the principle behind *Bellotti* (784–85, cited at 31): 'the legislature is constitution-ally disqualified from dictating the subjects about which persons may speak and the speakers who may address a public issue'. The decision in *Austin* had justified government limitation on corporate speech by pointing to the need to prevent

> the corrosive and distorting effects of immense aggregations of wealth that are accumulated with the help of the corporate form and that have little or no correlation to the public's support for the corporation's political ideas. (*Austin* (1990) at 660, cited at 31–32)

Justice Kennedy rejected the reasoning in *Austin*, arguing that the decision discriminated against the political speech of speakers simply because they were corporations. The Government had also suggested in oral argument that *Austin* might extend to 'all corporate expenditures for almost all forms of communication stemming from a corporation', though without stating its clear support for this view. In any case Justice Kennedy was unimpressed (at 33):

> This troubling assertion of brooding governmental power cannot be reconciled with the confidence and stability in civic discourse that the First Amendment must secure.

The rejection of restrictions based on a speaker's identity extended to limits 'based on a speaker's wealth', and the state could not restrict the free speech rights of corporations as a trade-off for the advantages of incorporation. There was no meaningful distinction to be drawn between an individual and a corporation (at 35): 'All speakers, including individuals and the media, use money amassed from the economic marketplace to fund their speech.' The judgment then attacked the underlying logic that exempted media corporations from these provisions (at 35–38). The decision in *Austin* interfered with the 'open marketplace' of ideas (at 38):

> It permits the Government to ban the political speech of millions of associations of citizens. [...] Most of these are small corporations without large amounts of wealth. [...] This fact belies the Government's argument that the statute is justified on the ground that it prevents the 'distorting effects of immense aggregations of wealth.' [...] It is not even aimed at amassed wealth.

The electorate was being deprived of the right to hear from those who represented 'the most significant segments of the economy' (at 38, citing Justice Scalia in *McConnell*, at 257–58). Smaller or non-profit corporations could not participate in the political process and 'raise a voice to object when other corporations, including those with vast wealth, are cooperating with the Government' (at 39). The argument about the possibility of *quid pro quo* corruption was also rejected: 'Limits on independent expenditures, such as s. 441b, have a chilling effect extending well beyond the Government's interest in preventing quid pro quo corruption' (at 41). Nor was the theory tenable that 'the appearance of influence or access' justified controls on corporate speech (at 44):

> The appearance of influence or access, furthermore, will not cause the electorate to lose faith in our democracy. By definition, an independent expenditure is political speech presented to the electorate that is not coordinated with a candidate. [...] The fact that a corporation, or any other speaker, is willing to spend money to try to persuade voters presupposes that the people have the ultimate influence over elected officials.

The judgment also examined and rejected the argument that control on corporate speech was justified as a means of protecting dissenting shareholders from in effect funding speech with which they disagreed. This problem could be dealt with by 'the procedures of corporate democracy'; in addition, the provision's time limitations and lack of distinction among different corporations made it both 'underinclusive and overinclusive' (at 46). Restrictions on free speech made relative to certain media were likely to fall foul of rapid technological change (at 49):

> Rapid changes in technology – and the creative dynamic inherent in the concept of free expression – counsel against upholding a law that restricts political speech in certain media or by certain speakers.

The Court upheld certain disclaimer and disclosure requirements (with Justice Thomas the lone dissent on this point), but reversed the lower court's decision with respect to the constitutionality of the statutory provision (s. 441b).

The concurring judgment of Chief Justice Roberts (joined by Justice Alito) is not analyzed here. The primary focus there was on the doctrine of *stare decisis*, and on the dangers implicit in the decision in *Austin*.

Justice Stevens' dissent

The dissent rejected the 'conceit that corporations must be treated identically to natural persons in the political sphere' and the equation of 'corporate with human speakers':

> In the context of election to public office, the distinction between corporate and human speakers is significant. Although they make enormous contributions to our society, corporations are not actually members of it. They cannot vote or run for office. (at 2)

Corporations might be controlled by non-residents; their 'financial resources, legal structure, and instrumental orientation of corporations raise legitimate concerns about their role in the electoral process'. There were compelling grounds for supervision, and the decision 'threatens to undermine the integrity of elected institutions across the Nation' (at 4). The majority had strategically widened the legal issue before it, in order to strike down precedents with which it was unhappy. There were narrower grounds on which the case could have been decided (at 6–17), and there was no justification in the doctrine of *stare decisis* for the overruling of *Austin* (at 17–23). The repeated talk of a 'ban' on corporate speech was 'highly misleading' (at 23); the mechanism of the PAC was available to finance electioneering communications:

> Like all other natural persons, every shareholder of every corporation remains entirely free under *Austin* and *McConnell* to do however much electioneering she pleases outside of the corporate form. The owners of a 'mom & pop' store can simply place ads in their own names, rather than the store's.

The restriction was highly specific and targeted; it left wide scope for the participation of corporations in the political process (at 27–28):

> In the case at hand, all Citizens United needed to do to broadcast *Hillary* right before the primary was to abjure business contributions or

use the funds in its PAC, which by its own account is 'one of the most active conservative PACs in America,' Citizens United Political Victory Fund [...]

It was incorrect that restrictions on free speech based on category of speaker were unconstitutional, and there were plenty of examples of this (at 29): 'the authority of legislatures to enact viewpoint-neutral regulations based on content and identity is well settled' (at 31). The 'distinctive potential of corporations to corrupt the electoral process [had] long been recognized'. In the domain of campaign finance, corporate spending was furthest away from the core interest of political expression, since it was derived indirectly, i.e. from those 'of their members and of the public in receiving information' (at 32). The difference between a natural speaker and a corporate one was crucial (at 32–33):

> Campaign finance distinctions based on corporate identity tend to be less worrisome, in other words, because the 'speakers' are not natural persons, much less members of our political community, and the governmental interests are of the highest order. Furthermore, when corporations, as a class, are distinguished from noncorporations, as a class, there is a lesser risk that regulatory distinctions will reflect invidious discrimination or political favoritism.

Turning to the historical background of the First Amendment, Justice Stevens argued that the framers of the Constitution 'conceived of speech more narrowly than we now think of it', and also viewed corporations as the recipients of legal privilege and therefore subject to heightened legislative scrutiny. There was the fear that the 'soulless' corporation would subvert the Republic (at 37):

> Unlike our colleagues, [the framers] had little trouble distinguishing corporations from human beings, and when they constitutionalized the right to free speech in the First Amendment, it was the free speech of individual Americans that they had in mind.

The idea that the First Amendment would apply to corporations would have been 'quite a novelty'. Individuals might 'join together to exercise their speech rights', but 'business corporations, at least, were plainly not seen as facilitating such associational or expressive ends' (at 37).

In a footnote, Justice Stevens analyzed dictionary definitions relating to the word *speech*, which in 'normal usage then, as now' referred to 'oral communications by individuals'. For example, Johnson's *Dictionary of the English Language* (4th edn, 1773) listed as the primary definition: 'the power of articulate utterance; the power of expressing thoughts by vocal words'; Webster's *American Dictionary of the English Language* (1828) had: 'The faculty of uttering articulate sounds or words, as in human beings; the faculty of expressing thoughts by words or articulate sounds. Speech was given to man by his Creator for the noblest purposes'.

Justice Stevens also quoted academic views to the effect that the concept of institutional speech was foreign to the period, and that 'free speech was individual and personal' (at fn. 55):

> Given that corporations were conceived of as artificial entities and do not have the technical capacity to 'speak', the burden of establishing that the Framers and ratifiers understood 'the freedom of speech' to encompass corporate speech is, I believe, far heavier than the majority acknowledges.

The argument for equality in free speech rights for corporate speakers was an implausible one. Justice Scalia's argument (see below), that 'because corporations are created and utilized by individuals' their electioneering 'must be equally protected by the First Amendment and equally immunized from expenditure limits', was illogical (at 40–41). The distinction between corporate and individual spending was deeply embedded in the law (at 42–74).

Drawing on *Austin*, Stevens returned to the theme of the distinction between human beings and corporations: 'The fact that corporations are different from human beings might seem to need no elaboration, except that the majority opinion almost completely elides it' (at 75). Corporations had limited liability, perpetual life, separation of ownership and control, and the ability to attract capital and deploy their assets. Their acquisition of resources did not reflect anything about 'popular support' for the corporation's political ideas; and the corporation's power did not necessarily bear any relation to the 'the power of its ideas' (at 76). Justice Stevens also reverted to classical descriptions of the corporation:

> It might also be added that corporations have no consciences, no beliefs, no feelings, no thoughts, no desires. Corporations help structure and facilitate the activities of human beings, to be sure, and their 'personhood' often serves as a useful legal fiction. But they are not themselves members of 'We the People' by whom and for whom our Constitution was established.

The protection of the individual's self-expression required the regulation of the 'derivative speech' of the corporation (at 76–77). It was unclear 'who' exactly was speaking 'when a business corporation places an advertisement that endorses or attacks a particular candidate'. It was not the customers or employees; the shareholders were too far removed from such decisions; it was more likely the 'officers and directors of the corporation' who were speaking, but 'their fiduciary duties generally prohibit them from using corporate funds for personal ends'. The individuals who took the decision on behalf of the corporation to place the advertisement might well be acting against their own private political convictions: 'no one's autonomy, dignity, or political equality has been impinged upon in the least' (at 77). Corporate domination of the election process might induce disillusion and cynicism in the electorate; the majority invocation of the rights of listeners was unrealistic. Justice Stevens then moved onto the question of shareholder protection (at 86–89).

The judgment concluded with these words (at 90):

> At bottom, the Court's opinion is thus a rejection of the common sense of the American people, who have recognized a need to prevent corporations from undermining selfgovernment since the founding, and who have fought against the distinctive corrupting potential of corporate electioneering since the days of Theodore Roosevelt. It is a strange time to repudiate that common sense. While American democracy is imperfect, few outside the majority of this Court would have thought its flaws included a dearth of corporate money in politics. I would affirm the judgment of the District Court.

Justice Scalia's commentary

Justice Scalia disputed the dissent's understanding of legal and linguistic history. It had failed to show how freedom of speech 'that was the right of Englishmen' did not include the freedom to speak 'in association with other individuals, including association in the corporate form' (at 1). Whether the framers liked or disliked corporations was only an issue in so far as their view 'can be thought to be reflected in the understood meaning of the text they enacted'. In fact their disapproval was directed primarily at state-granted monopolies, not the modern commercial corporation. The Constitutional text itself made no distinction between different kinds of speakers, and the idea of associations speaking was a familiar one in that period (at 5):

> The dissent offers no evidence – none whatever – that the First Amendment's unqualified text was originally understood to exclude such associational speech from its protection.

The right of an individual to free speech included the right to speak in association with others (at 7):

> Surely the dissent does not believe that speech by the Republican Party or the Democratic Party can be censored because it is not the speech of 'an individual American'. It is the speech of many individual Americans, who have associated in a common cause, giving the leadership of the party the right to speak on their behalf. The association of individuals in a business corporation is no different – or at least it cannot be denied the right to speak on the simplistic ground that it is not 'an individual American'.

The idea that 'since corporations are not human beings they cannot speak' was sophistry (at fn. 7):

> The authorized spokesman of a corporation is a human being, who speaks on behalf of the human beings who have formed that association – just as the spokesman of an unincorporated association speaks on behalf of its

members. The power to publish thoughts, no less than the power to speak thoughts, belongs only to human beings, but the dissent sees no problem with a corporation's enjoying the freedom of the press.

The claim that institutional speech was not recognized was historically inaccurate (at fn. 7). There was no justification for impeding the free speech rights of corporations, who were 'the principal agents of the modern free economy'. Indeed, we should 'celebrate rather than condemn the addition of this speech to the public debate'.

Key points on corporate free speech rights (Justice Kennedy)

- It was central to the democratic process that there should be no chilling effect on free speech during election battles.
- The massive regulatory schema in place verged on censorship and operated as a prior restraint, in particular on corporate speech.
- The regulatory burden in setting up a PAC was very high, and therefore corporations were not able to speak freely.
- Corporations should not be subject to restraints that would be unacceptable if placed on individuals.
- Restrictions on speech based on the identity, nature or wealth of the speaker in effect targeted the content of that speech.
- Restrictions targeting corporate associations of citizens deprived the electorate of the chance to hear from the most significant sections of the economy.
- There was no danger of *quid pro quo* corruption, and corporate sponsorship of political speech presupposed that voters made the ultimate decisions.
- Issues concerning dissenting shareholders were matters for corporate governance and democracy.
- The law should recognize the rapid evolution of media forms and the creative dynamic of free speech.
- Freedom of speech included the rights of individuals to associate with others to put forward their views.

Key points in Justice Stevens' dissent

- The distinction between corporate speakers and individuals was fundamental.
- Corporations were not members of society, though they made significant contributions to it.
- The resources, ownership, legal status and goal-orientated nature of corporations created compelling grounds for close supervision.
- The majority had taken the opportunity to strike down case law with which they were unhappy.
- The talk of banning corporate speech was highly misleading.

- Category of speaker was a legitimate and recognized ground for restrictions on speech.
- The danger of corporations subverting the electoral process was well recognized.
- The framers had a narrow definition of speech, and regarded corporations as privileged beings, naturally subject to scrutiny and regulation.
- Speech was primarily the personal expression of individuals.
- Corporate speech was a foreign concept to the framers, and there was no justification for treating corporations as equal to individuals.
- Corporations were legal fictions with limited liability, potentially immortal, with separation of ownership and control, and their assets did not reflect popular support for their ideas.
- Individuals' speech needed to be protected from the potential power of derivative speech by corporations. There was a danger of undermining the democratic process through the corrupt domination of corporations; the result would be cynicism and disillusion among the electorate.

Discussion: conservative postmodernists?

The majority argued that *corporate speech* was worthy of the same protection as individual speech. The idea that the more literal and more basic form of oral communication by a natural person was the true target (or prototype) of free speech protection was rejected. There was no policy distinction to be drawn between the speech of a human being and that of an artificial being. Rapidly evolving technology made distinctions based on medium undesirable. This position was defended on a number of grounds. First, corporate forms were associations of individuals governed by rules (see Ellis, 2011). Corporate democracy meant that the individual corporation speaks as the representative of those individuals and their interests. Alternatively, business corporations were part of the fabric of the republic, and key to its economic life and prosperity. This entitled them to a say in the political process. As corporate citizens they should have the same rights as any other citizen, and individual citizens benefited by the participation of the corporation in the 'market-place of ideas'. The Constitution made no distinction in respect of who was doing the speaking, and only in very special cases were any limits justified based on the category of speaker.

The dissent took the human being speaking orally as the prototype of speech, and the individual's free speech rights as the prime target of protection. In the case of the corporation, there was no clear way of identifying who was actually speaking. The corporation as a political agent might not represent the political views of its shareholders, nor those of its managers. It pursued self-interest, taking its own economic interest as primary. Artificial speech emanating from artificial associations was a form of speech, but it was anomalous in that it brought both dangers as well as benefits. It was derivative of natural speech, rather than a true form of it. The corporation was given its existence by the state, and the state had both a right and an interest in regulating it and in curtailing its position in relation to politics. This prevented corruption, distortion of the market place and rent-seeking, as well as maintaining a relatively level playing-field for political debate.

A more radical approach would be to reject the extension of the word *speech* to the corporation: *corporate speech* is not a kind of *speech* at all (Batchis, 2012). Batchis rejects the dissent's view that the speech of corporations is entitled to qualified protection under the First Amendment. He imagines a computer system designed with software that creates automatically electronic mails pertaining to candidates. This computer-generated political 'spam' would not be entitled to First Amendment protection, most would agree (2012: 8): 'Once one learns that the messages were produced randomly by a computer, the conclusion that they should constitute protected speech becomes suspect.' Even though there was human input into the design of the program, as with messages typed randomly by monkeys, this would not be *speech* (2012: 8):

> Speech is not merely that which resembles speech; to constitute speech, a communicative product must have, at its source, a 'speaker'. By the very first three words of the Constitution's Preamble, it is clear that 'We the People' are the objects of the Constitution's guarantees. The First Amendment should not be thought to protect computers or monkeys, no matter how eloquently they may string words together. Quite simply, they do not constitute speakers – or at least the kind of speakers the Framers of the Constitution had in mind.

There was little analysis in *Citizens United* about what constituted speech and what it meant to speak: 'By virtually ignoring this question, the Court implicitly accepts a conception of speech not unlike the computer-generated spam discussed above' (2012: 9). Batchis' argument rests on an equation of corporate speech with this kind of computer-generated political spam (2012: 9):

> Corporate communications do not represent the product of an individual mind; they are a complex consequence of multiple layers of collective action, highly constrained and narrowly tailored to achieve limited goals. Human beings certainly make this communication possible, but this does not make it their speech. It is as much their speech as are randomly generated political e-mail messages, derived in part from fragments of their ideas taken from personal data on their hard drive and patched together out of context. The ultimate result may communicate a message, but it merely simulates 'speech'.

Justice Stevens' dissent touched on the argument that corporate speech was not speech in the sense understood by the framers, but failed to press the point to its conclusion, in that he conceded that corporations were *speakers* and 'therefore potentially eligible for protections clearly designed by the Amendment's framers for human beings' (Batchis, 2012: 10).

It might seem that it is the conservatives on the Supreme Court who are in tune with postmodern ideas of speech, unconcerned as they are with the lack of a single agent or identifiable human consciousness behind the corporation. However, their argument was not an embrace of post-humanist accounts of the self; rather they emphasized that a corporation is an association or aggregation of individuals who act together. This served to downplay the artificiality of the corporation. Arguments critical of the *Citizens United* decision rely on a rejection of the metaphor implicit in the phrase *corporate speech*, that is, the extension of the meaning of the word *speech* to cover corporate communications. Compared to this core or prototype concept, other forms of so-called speech are to be regarded as derivative at best (Justice Stevens). On Batchis' more radical analysis, *corporate speech* is the artificial imitation of real speech, a false copy of the true original.

Points for further consideration

A common tension in legal interpretation is that between a focus on word meaning and an insistence on policy analysis. Is the prototype of speech as spoken utterances produced by a natural person the correct starting point for the legal analysis of metaphorical extensions of speech to include communications of corporate persons? Or would we be better off starting with a vision of the complex multi-domain nature of communications in modern societies? A recent blog posting (Bryant, 2012) suggested that proponents of a strong view of corporate personality use the argument opportunistically. Discussing a money-laundering case settled out of court between the United States Government and the banking giant HSBC, one commentator had argued that the bank should not be held responsible because 'banks don't commit fraud, people commit fraud.'

> Why is this so galling? Because in 2010, the American Supreme Court decided that corporations, unions, and various other groups are people and therefore have a right to free speech through their campaign contributions. In other words, the Supreme Court took a posthuman turn, recognizing the existence of other beings beyond the human (corporations, unions, activist groups, etc).

This raises the wider question of law's relation to categories. Since legal definitions and legal acts of classification are carried out in relation to particular contingencies, there is no overall coherence to law's definitions and no overarching system of legal classification. Legal analysis is never autonomous; it is in constant interaction with wider definitional, social and ideological pressures.

PART III

Concluding Remarks

CHAPTER 15

Word Meaning and Interpretative Authority

For the purposes of this book, the linguistic-interpretative culture of law is shaped by three major elements:

(a) decontextual meaning;

(b) ordinary meaning; and

(c) the judge's authority to determine interpretative meaning.

This last chapter briefly reviews the arguments in relation to each.

Decontextual (abstract) meaning

Decontextual meaning is generally understood as the grounding on which successful communication rests: 'Conventions of word meaning represent shared beliefs that users of a language rely on to communicate with one another' (Hanks, 2013: 105). The argument is commonly made that communication would be impossible without a set of form-meaning relationships shared by speakers of the same language. On this view, human communication is built on identities ('abstract meanings') that are established and maintained by the language itself. The meanings established by the language system are relatively stable and exist independently of the particular contexts in which they occur. The idea of a stable core with a fuzzy margin is one of the most widely accepted views of word meaning, and it is reflected in Hart's theory of adjudication. For Hart, interpretative meaning is reliant on abstract meaning, and classification of objects, processes and events for the purposes of law draws on this set of stable linguistic categories.

Given that law is understood to be concerned with the meanings of words, appeals to decontextual meaning inevitably play a central role. If the abstract meanings of ordinary words are crucial to law, then one argument is that law should use more professional methods to determine what those meanings are. These might include forms of analysis from outside law, such as linguistic description, corpus data, social surveys, etc. Law, it is argued, should assess formally the potential that a discipline like linguistics represents for law (Ainsworth, 2006). Even if linguists cannot resolve linguistic questions directly, they can act as semantic 'tour guides', allowing the linguistic issues to be clarified and presented objectively (Solan, 1999). In hard cases, 'judges may turn to empirical methodologies like corpus linguistics to improve the predictability and consistency of judicial decision making' (Mouritsen, 2011: 205).

The counter-argument would be that there is no 'superior concept of a language, to which only the language expert has access' and that it is the ordinary language-user who 'has the only concept of a language worth having' (Harris, 1980: 3). Academic linguistics begins with decontextual, abstract meanings, and takes language as an institution which escapes the will of individual speakers (Taylor, 1990). Mainstream linguistics is not an interpretative discipline, so it has no *prima facie* claim to be able to improve the interpretative practices of law (Campos, 1995; Hutton, 1996). Proponents of indeterminacy reject the idea that language provides a stable medium for law, as well as simultaneously a stable set of reference points outside law. Decontextual, abstract meanings can be characterized or framed in ways that are strategic for the case at hand. This frequently leads to a rejection of law's authority as grounded in a set of non-benign fictions or myths.

To describe decontextual meaning as a fiction of law brings these arguments into focus. It also highlights the fact that legal adjudication shifts unpredictably between treating interpretative problems as a matter of linguistic meaning and framing them in terms of social policy, morality or rights.

Ordinary meaning

The appeal to ordinary (non-legal) meaning by judges is an appeal to a specific sub-set of decontextual meanings. In the context of legal adjudication, this technique of adjudication suggests that, for the majority of cases, the linguistic intuitions of judges, supplemented by dictionaries, will be in tune with popularly understood meanings. A judge, as a member of the speech community, has access to the same decontextual linguistic prototypes as ordinary speakers. This gives the impression that law is as transparent to the lay observer as the technical requirements of law will allow, and therefore that its linguistic foundations are, as far as possible, democratic in spirit. The idea that law is framed by stable meanings to which all speakers within the jurisdiction have access offers reassurance that its categories are anchored in the experience of those who are subject to law, and offers a partial answer to criticism that law is arbitrary, coercive and alienated from society's 'lifeworld'. This implies the predictability of legal decision making, as part of the rule of law. If 'ignorance of the law is no excuse' then law should be formulated in terms that those subject to its jurisdiction can understand.

One argument made by academic linguists is that law is out of touch with the practices that make up ordinary communication. Academic linguists tend to discount the views of ordinary language users about the nature of language and linguistic meaning (McCawley, 1994): 'Laymen are generally lousy linguists'. Judges are lay linguists whose profession is interpretation: this suggests to some commentators that while linguists do not have much to learn from the way judges interpret language, 'judges may have a lot to learn from accurate descriptive linguistic theory' (Kelley, 2001: 114). Solan likewise argues that 'judges do not make good linguists' (Solan, 1993: 59–63). In many cases linguistic analysis can have 'a clarifying effect' (Solan, 1995: 1072). Since the legal system has 'decided to adopt linguistic principles as part of its repertoire of legal rules', it is necessary for lawyers 'to ask about the nature of legal constructs such as definitional meaning and ordinary meaning, which the courts use routinely' (Solan, 2010: 80–81). Similarly, for Shuy, linguistics, unlike law, 'offers the truth about the way language works and changes' (Shuy, 2002: 11). The 'linguistic thought experiment' would, on this view, be one manifestation of the opportunistic semantics of judges.

Objections to this might be of two kinds. The first accepts that ordinary language exists and its meanings can be described empirically, but points to the dangers intrinsic to what might be called 'populist adjudication'. This can lead to majoritarian racism or sexism, to social prejudices being simply incorporated into law without any filter or analysis. The apparent transparency involved in the use of ordinary language is misleading, since the appeal to everyday usage is part of the judge's interpretative 'bag of tricks'. There is no way of knowing in advance where the judge will choose to apply a meaning identified as 'ordinary'. The transparency involved is from this point of view illusory: it is better to know you do not understand the language of law than to be mistaken in thinking that you do. In terms of legal theory, law's pursuit of justice requires its alienation from ordinary language and everyday categories. Therein lies the essence of law's objectivity.

Once we have historical distance on a decision, what would have seemed uncontroversial aspects of the background may come into focus. Holmes in *McBoyle v US* (1931), in citing *US v Bhagat Singh Thind* (1927) almost as an afterthought, implicitly compares the popular classification of objects with the racial classification of people. Linguistic populism merges with racism. No one is likely to express outrage over the decision in the 'pigeon case' (*Hong Kong Racing Pigeon Association v Attorney General* (1994, 1995), but the implication is that linguistic categories do the thinking for the judges when it suits them. Where judges dislike the implications of recognizing an ordinary linguistic category as a legal category, they are liable to talk of 'word magic' (*Cherokee Nation v State of Georgia* (1831)) or 'magic words' *California v Carney* (1985), or appeal to science or majority social sentiment (*W v Registrar of Marriages* (2010)), or shift to arguments in terms of rights (*W v Registrar of Marriages* (2013)).

A second set of objections derives from the view that there is descriptively or empirically no such thing as 'ordinary language' or 'ordinary meaning'. The idea that there exists such a single, homogeneous, stable variety of language is an intuition of judges, who by their very nature are members of the educated middle class. They have undergone many years of formal education and training, and are members of a 'community of practice' (Wenger, 1998) or 'field of practice' into which they have been socialized (Fish, 1984: 1347). Their ability to discuss 'ordinary language' and intuit the 'ordinary meanings' of words is a professional skill, and in that sense the category itself and the practices around it are constructs of legal practice. To demonstrate an empirical fact about a word meaning we need to identify the limits of the word's circulation and the relevant speakers for whom this word is an ordinary word 'in their language'.

But that requires us to draw on the very commonsense categories and knowledge that we are attempting to scrutinize. Ordinary meaning, like many other fictions, is a form of organized forgetting or non-attention, prone to being unmasked and vulnerable to the pressures of interpretative controversy.

By contrast with linguists, literary critics are indeed primarily concerned with textual interpretation. Literary texts are analogous to legal texts in that they accumulate readings over time. Both literary and legal texts have institutionalized interpretations that may be subject to challenge, and contain words that create specific interpretative problems because of definitional uncertainty, contextual contingencies, and changes in society, ideology, background assumptions and usage that divide the reader from the world of the text. However, there is a <u>crucial distinction.</u> Unlike literary interpretation, legal interpretation adjudicates the status of a unique set of circumstances (the facts of the case) by reference to a text which is set out at a particular historical moment, in general terms in order to be applied to future events. There is no parallel to this in literary interpretation. One voice from the law has drawn the conclusion that literary criticism has nothing directly to say to law. Scholars of law and literature should 'abandon efforts, so far fruitless and likely to remain so, to apply principles of literary interpretation to statutes and provisions of the Constitution' (Posner, 2009: 550). But this implies that the only reason to interpret a legal case is to second-guess the legal decision-making process. Law cases are social texts, and there is no reason to restrict artificially the way they can be read and understood.

Whatever view one takes of these questions, it is important to recognize that the category ordinary meaning is itself a legal category. It plays a fundamental role in strategies of legal interpretation and is an integral part of the linguistic culture of law.

Authority over meaning and interpretation: which is to be master?

Legal interpretation always takes place against an aim or objective (or aims and objectives) (Fuller, 1940). This is true even if the objective is confused or muddled, not explicitly identified or perceived, is contested or changes over time as the rule is applied. Purposes are entangled inextricably in the fabric of law. When we are faced with a question about the interpretative meaning of a word, we ourselves are already placed in a particular context, within which a particular set of circumstances, standards, beliefs come into play. An interpretative task viewed purely through the abstract and ordinary meanings of the terms as they present themselves is one where the underlying assumptions and massive social and ideological scaffold of beliefs, commonsense assumptions, frames, intentions and ideologies are invisible or barely glimpsed.

Law is the master of its own domain. Judges define their interpretative task and choose the tools and sources of authority that they believe will yield the right answer. Law defines categories and classifies objects, people and events for its own purposes, sometimes drawing on, and at other times rejecting, external, non-legal systems of classification and frames of reference. Many of these decisions have only local significance and do not impact on the status of social categories or wider systems of classification. Whether Pringles are analogous to *potato crisps* in the eyes of the law might seem to be a matter of curiosity (and money) rather than profound social significance. Yet taxation works in such cases as a moral instrument, in that law is used to encourage certain eating habits and discourage others. Law applies analogous forms of reasoning in relation to categories such as race and gender, and these decisions impact radically on individual lives and collective social understandings.

The methodological autonomy of legal adjudication might seem to foreclose commentary or criticism by outsiders such as linguists, anthropologists or literary critics. But this book aims to show how legal interpretation and adjudication appear when scrutinized from the outside. It is not only lawyers who have the right to judge legal decisions; the methods and analytic tools of law are not the only framework within which they can be understood. The texts, procedures and interpretative practices of law cannot and should not be judged by law alone, since they are part of the socio-historical and cultural fabric of each society. However, any criticism of legal interpretation must come to terms with the interpretative autonomy of the judge. It is in any case not just lawyers who rely on fictions and whose authority dissolves on inspection into a complex, multidimensional balancing act between contradictory forces. The same is true of all forms of interpretation.

References

Bibliography

Ainsworth, Janet (2006) 'Linguistics as a knowledge domain in the law', *Drake LR*, 54, 651–69.

Albery, Michael (1963) 'Coincidence and the construction of wills', *Modern Law Review*, 26, 353–66.

Anderson, Jill (2008) 'Just semantics: the lost readings of the Americans with Disabilities Act', *Yale Law Journal* 117, 992–1069.

Anon (1989) 'Toys: soldier Boy, you're a doll', *Time Magazine* 134 (5), July 31 1989, <www.time.com/time/magazine>.

Aprill, Ellen (1998) 'The law of the word: dictionary shopping in the Supreme Court', *Arizona State Law Journal*, 30, 275–336.

Austin, John (1956) 'A plea for excuses', *Proceedings of the Aristotelian Society*, 57, 1–30.

Austin, John (1979) 'The meaning of a word' in James Urmson and Geoffrey Warnock (eds) *Philosophical Papers*, 2nd edn (Oxford: Oxford UP), 56–75.

Baggini, Julian (2011) *The Ego Trick. What does it mean to you?* (London: Granta).

Ball, Miner (1999) 'All the law's a stage', *Cardozo Studies in Law and Literature*, 11, 215–21.

Barak, Aharon (2007) *Purposive Interpretation in Law*, trans. Sari Bashi (Princeton, NJ: Princeton UP).

Barlow, Anne (2012) 'Family law and housing law: a symbiotic relationship', in Rebecca Probert (ed.) *The Changing Legal Regulation of Cohabitation: From Fornicators to Family, 1600–2010* (Cambridge: Cambridge UP), 11–26.

Baron, Jane (1992) 'Intention, interpretation, and stories', *Duke Law Journal*, 42, 630–678.

Batchis, Wayne (2012) '*Citizens United* and the paradox of "corporate speech": from freedom of association to freedom of *the* association', *New York Review of Law & Social Change*, 36, 5–55.

Bennion, Francis (2010) *Bennion on Statutory Interpretation*, 5th edn (London: LexisNexis Butterworths).

Berger, Peter and Thomas Luckmann (1966) *The Social Construction of Reality* (New York: Anchor).

Bernardin, Mark (1992) 'The law and politics of dancing: *Barnes v Glen Theatre* and the regulation of striptease dance', *University of Hawai'i Law Review*, 14, 925–48.

Bettenhausen, Julie (1998) 'The implications of *Bailey v. United States* on the rise of convicted criminal claims and the fall of 18. U.S.C. s. 924(c)(1)', *Drake Law Review*, 46, 677–715.

Black, Ryan and James Spriggs II (2013) 'The citation and depreciation of U.S. Supreme Court precedent', *Journal of Empirical Studies*, 10, 325–58.

Blatt, William (2010) 'Missing the mark: an overlooked statute redefines the debate over statutory interpretation', *University of Miami Law Review*, 64, 641–62.

Bloom, Lackland (2009) *Methods of Interpretation: How the Supreme Court Reads the Constitution* (Oxford: Oxford UP).

Bloor, David (1982) 'Durkheim and Mauss revisited: classification and the sociology of knowledge', *Studies in the History and Philosophy of Science*, 13, 267–97.

Borges, Jorge Luis (2001) 'The analytical language of John Wilkins' in Eliot Weinberger (ed.), *The Total Library. Non-Fiction 1922–1986* (London: Penguin), 229–32.

Burke, Joseph (1969) 'The Cherokee cases: a study in law, politics, and morality', *Stanford Law Review*, 21, 500–31.

Brown, Travis (1931) 'Notes and comments: criminal law, statutory construction, aeroplane as motor vehicle', *The North Carolina Law Review*, 9, 447–49.

Bryant, Levi (2012) 'Posthuman conundrums', posted 12 December 2012, *Larval Subjects*, <larvalsubjects.wordpress.com>, accessed 11 July 2013.

Bunker, Matthew (1995) 'The corporate plaintiff as public figure', *Journalism and Mass Communication Quarterly*, 72, 597–609.

Burnett, Graham (2007) *Trying Leviathan: The Nineteenth-Century New York Court Case That Put the Whale on Trial and Challenged the Order of Nature* (Princeton, NJ: Princeton UP).

Calvert, Clay (1999) 'And you call yourself a journalist? Wrestling with the definition of "journalist" in the law', *Dickinson Law Review*, 103, 411–51.

Campbell, Joseph, Michael O'Rourke and Matthew Slater (eds) (2011) *Carving Nature at Its Joints: Natural Kinds in Metaphysics and Science* (Cambridge, Mass: MIT Press).

Campos, Paul (1995) 'This is not a sentence', *Washington University Law Quarterly*, 73, 971–82.

Cardozo, Benjamin (1928) *The Paradoxes of Legal Science* (New York: Columbia UP).

Carr, David (2013) 'Journalism, even when it's activism', *International Herald Tribune*, Tuesday, 2 July 2013, p. 17.

Carroll, Lewis (2012) *Through the Looking Glass, or What Alice Saw There*. Available at <www.gutenberg.net>. First published, 1871.

Carston, Robyn (2013) 'Legal texts and canons of construction: a view from current pragmatic theory', in Michael Freeman and Fiona Smith (eds), *Law and Language: Current Legal Issues*, vol. 15 (Oxford: Oxford UP), 8–33.

Chomsky, Carol (2000) 'Unlocking the mysteries of *Holy Trinity*: spirit, letter, and history in statutory interpretation', *Columbia Law Review*, 100, 901–56.

Chomsky, Noam (1965) *Aspects of the Theory of Syntax* (Cambridge, Mass: MIT Press).

[CJR] (1927) 'Curiosities of the law: is a tomato a fruit or a vegetable?', *Notre Dame Lawyer*, 2, 123–27.

Coffee, John (1981) '"No soul to damn, no body to kick": an unscandalized inquiry into the problem of corporate punishment', *Michigan Law Review*, 79, 386–459.

Cooley, Thomas (1888) *Treatise on the Law of Torts* (Chicago, Ill: Callaghan).

Corbin, Arthur (1965) 'The interpretation of words and the parol evidence rule', *Cornell Law Quarterly*, 50, 161–90.

[CR] (2000) 'Medicare prescription drugs coverage, speech by representative Sherrod Brown of Ohio, Congressional Record', vol. 146, part 3, pp. 3068–69. Available online at <www.gpo.gov>.

Culler, Jonathan (1982) *On Deconstruction: Theory and Criticism after Structuralism* (Ithaca, NY: Cornell UP).

Cunningham, Clark, Judith Levi, Georgia Green, and Jeffrey Kaplan (1994) 'Plain meaning and hard cases', *Yale Law Journal*, 103, 1561–1625.

Darwin, Charles (1859) *On the Origin of Species by Means of Natural Selection* (London: John Murray).

Davis, Wade (1985) *The Serpent and the Rainbow* (New York: Simon & Schuster).

Deniker, Joseph (1900) *The Races of Man: An Outline of Anthropology and Ethnography* (London: Walter Scott; New York: Charles Scribner).

Dickens, Charles (1854) *Hard Times: A Novel* (New York: Harpers).

DiFonzo, J. Herbie (1997) *Beneath the Fault Line: The Popular and Legal Culture of Divorce in Twentieth-Century America* (Charlottesville, Va: University of Virginia Press).

Dorato, Jimena A. (2013) 'A jurilinguistic approach to legal education', *International Journal for the Semiotics of Law*, 26, 635–50.

Driesbach, Daniel and John Whaley (1999) 'What the wall separates: a debate on Thomas Jefferson's wall of separation metaphor', *Constitutional Commentary*, 6, 627–74.

Driesen, David (2013) 'Purposeless construction', *Wake Forest Law Review*, 48, 97–148.

Dumbauld, Edward (1944) 'Valedictory opinions of Mr. Justice Holmes', *Michigan Law Review*, 42, 1037–48.

Durant, Alan (2010) *Meaning in the Media: Discourse, Controversy and Debate* (Cambridge: Cambridge UP).

Durkheim, Emile and Marcel Mauss (1963) *Primitive Classification*, ed. Rodney Needham (London: Routledge; Chicago, Ill: The University of Chicago Press). First published, 1903.

Duszat, Michael (2012) 'Foucault's laughter. Enumeration, rewriting, and the construction of the essayist in Borges's "The analytical language of John Wilkins"', *Orbis Litterarum*, 67, 193–218.

Eaton, Amasa (1902) 'The origin of municipal incorporation in England and the United States', *Annual Report of the American Bar Association*, 25, 292–372.

Elbourne, Paul (2011) *Meaning. A Slim Guide to Semantics* (Oxford: OUP).

Ellickson, Robert (2011) 'Two cheers for the bundle-of-sticks metaphor, three cheers for Merrill and Smith', *Econ Journal Watch*, 8, 215–22.

Ellis, Atiba (2011) '*Citizens United* and tiered personhood', *Marshall Law Review*, 44, 717–49.

Empson, William (1953) *Seven Types of Ambiguity* (London: Chatto & Windus). First published, 1930.

Empson, William (1985) *The Structure of Complex Words* (London: Hogarth).

Endicott, Timothy (1996) 'Linguistic indeterminacy', *Oxford Journal of Legal Studies*, 16, 667–97.

Endicott, Timothy (2000) *Vagueness in Law* (Oxford: Oxford UP).

Ernst, Thomas, Georgia Green, Jeffrey Kaplan, and Sally McConnell-Ginet (2008) Brief of Professors of Linguistics as Amici Curiae in Support of Neither Party. Brief submitted in relation to *Flores-Figueroa v US* (2009), available at <epic.org/privacy/flores-figueroa/amicus>.

Eskridge, William (1994) *Dynamic Statutory Interpretation* (Cambridge, Mass: Harvard UP).

Eskridge, William (1998) 'Textualism, the unknown ideal?', *Michigan Law Review*, 96, 1509–60.

Eskridge, William, Philip Frickey and Elizabeth Garrett (2001) *Cases and Materials on Legislation: Statutes and the Creation of Public Policy*, 3rd edn (St Paul, Minn: West Publishing Co.).

Fairfield, Joshua (2013) 'Mixed reality: how the laws of virtual worlds govern everyday life', *Berkeley Technology Law Journal*, 27, 55–116.

Farber, Daniel and Suzanna Sherry (1994) 'The 200,000 cards of Dimitri Yurasov: further reflections on scholarship and truth', *Stanford Law Review*, 46, 647–62.

Ferguson, William (2008) '*Hatfill v. New York Times Co.*: from watchdog to attack dog – transforming the modern media into "big brother"', *Maryland Law Review*, 68, 724–54.

Firth, John (1957) *Papers in Linguistics 1934–1951* (London: Oxford UP).

Fish, Stanley (1984) 'Fish v. Fiss', *Stanford Law Review*, 36, 1325–47.

Fish, Stanley (1987) 'Still wrong after all these years', *Law & Philosophy*, 6, 401–18.

Fish, Stanley (2005) 'There is no textualist position', *San Diego Law Review*, 42, 629–50.

Flanagan, Brian (2010) 'Revisiting the contribution of literal meaning to legal meaning', *Oxford Journal of Legal Studies*, 30, 255–71.

Florestal, Marjorie (2008) 'Is a burrito a sandwich? Exploring race, class, and culture in contracts', *Michigan Journal of Race and Law*, 14, 1–59.

Foucault, Michel (1994) *The Order of Things: An Archaeology of the Human Sciences* (New York: Vintage). First published, 1966.

Friedman, Lawrence (2000) 'Lexitainment: legal process as theatre', *De Paul Law Review*, 50, 539–58.

Fuller, Lon (1940) *The Law in Quest of Itself* (Boston, Mass: Beacon).

Fuller, Lon (1957) 'Positivism and fidelity to law: a reply to Professor Hart', *Harvard LR*, 71, 630–72.

Fuller, Lon (1967) *Legal Fictions* (Stanford, Conn: Stanford UP).

Gage, Conolly (1980) 'Review of Lord Denning, *The Discipline of Law*, Butterworths, 1979', *Cambridge Law Journal*, 39, 194–95.

Gant, Scott (2007) *We're All Journalists Now: The Transformation of the Press and the Reshaping of the Law in the Internet Age* (New York: Simon & Schuster).

Garner, Brian (2003) 'Legal lexicography: a view from the front lines', *English Today*, 9, 33–42.

Geeraerts, Dirk (2008) 'Prototypes, stereotypes, and semantic norms' in Gitte Kristiansen and René Dirven, *Cognitive Sociolinguistics, Language Variation, Cultural Models, Social Systems* (Berlin: Mouton de Gruyter), 21–44.

Gellner, Ernst (1959) *Words and Things; A Critical Account of Linguistic Philosophy and a Study in Ideology* (London: Gollancz).

Giroux, Danielle (1999) 'My dictionary of yours? The Supreme Court's interpretation of "carrying" under 18 U.S.C. s. 924(c)(1) in *Muscarello v. United States*', 8, 355–86.

Goddard, Cliff (2012) 'Semantic primes, semantic molecules, semantic templates: key concepts in the NSM approach to lexical typology', *Linguistics*, 50, 711–43.

Gore, Stephanie (2003) '"A rose by any other name": judicial use of metaphors for new technologies', *University of Illinois Journal of Law, Technology & Policy*, 2003, 403–56.

Grandy, Richard (1990) 'Understanding and the principle of compositionality', *Philosophical Perspectives*, 4, 557–72.

Greenawalt, Kent (2010) *Legal Interpretation: Perspectives from other Disciplines and Private Texts* (Oxford: OUP).

Groves, Matthew (2010) 'Law, religion and public order in colonial India: contextualising the 1887 Allahabad High Court case on "sacred" cows', *South Asia: Journal of South Asian Studies*, 33, 87–121.

Hacking, Ian (1999) *The Social Construction of What?* (Cambridge, Mass: Harvard UP).

Hall, Livingston (1935) 'Strict or liberal construction of penal statutes', *Harvard Law Review*, 48, 748–74.

Hamilton, Walton and Douglas Adair (1937) *The Power to Govern: The Constitution – Then and Now* (New York: Norton).

Haney López, Ian (1996) *White by Law: The Legal Construction of Race* (New York: New York UP).

Hanks, Patrick (2013) *Lexical Analysis: Norms and Exploitations* (Cambridge, Mass: MIT Press).

Harris, Roy (1980) *The Language Makers* (London: Duckworth).

Harris, Roy (1981) *The Language Myth* (London: Duckworth).

Harris, Roy (1988) *Language, Saussure and Wittgenstein* (London: Routledge).

Harris, Roy (2006) 'Was Saussure an integrationalist?' in Louis de Saussure (ed.), *Nouveaux Regards sur Saussure* (Genève: Droz), 209–17.

Harris, Roy and Christopher Hutton (2007) *Definition in Theory and Practice* (London: Continuum).

Hart, Herbert (1958) 'Positivism and the separation of law and morals', *Harvard Law Review*, 71, 593–629.

Hart, Herbert (1994) *The Concept of Law*, 2nd edn (Oxford: Clarendon). First published, 1961.

Henly, Burr (1987) '"Penumbra": the roots of a legal metaphor', *Hastings Constitutional Law Quarterly*, 15, 81–100.

Hinkelman, Edward and Sibylla Putzi (2005) *Dictionary of International Trade: Handbook of the Global Trade Community*, 6th edn (California: World Trade Press).

Hobbes, Thomas (1651) *Leviathan, or, The Matter, Forme, & Power of a Commonwealth Ecclesiasticall and Civill* (London: Andrew Crooke).

Hoey, Michael (2005) *Lexical Priming: A New Theory of Words and Language* (London: Routledge).

Hoffman, Craig (2003) 'Parse the sentence first: curbing the urge to resort to the dictionary when interpreting legal texts', *New York University Journal of Legislation & Public Policy*, 6, 401–38.

Holmes, Oliver (1920) 'The science of law and law as science' in *Collected Legal Papers* (New York: Harcourt Brace and Company), 210–43.

Huenemann, Charlie (2011) 'I'm not myself', *Times Literary Supplement* **5664**, 21 October 2011, p. 25.

Hunter, Dan (2003) 'Cyberspace as place and the tragedy of the digital anticommons', *California Law Review*, 91, 439–519.

Hurst, D. (1983) 'The problem of the elderly statute', *Legal Studies*, 3, 21–42.

Hutchinson, Allan (2000) *It's all in the Game: A Non-Foundationalist Account of Law and Adjudication* (Durham, NC: Duke UP).

Hutton, Christopher (1990) *Abstraction and Instance: The Type-Token Relation in Linguistic Theory* (Oxford: Pergamon).

Hutton, Christopher (1996) 'Law lessons for linguists? Accountability and acts of professional classification', *Language and Communication*, 16, 205–14.

Hutton, Christopher (2009) *Language, Meaning and the Law* (Edinburgh: Edinburgh UP).

Hutton, Christopher (2011) 'Objectification and transgender jurisprudence: the dictionary as quasi-statute', *Hong Kong Law Journal*, 41, 27–47.

Hutton, Christopher (2012) '"I crave the law" *Salomon v Salomon*, uncanny personhood and the Jews' in Marco Wan (ed.), *Reading the Legal Case* (London: Routledge), pp. 29–46.

Huxley, Thomas (1863) *Evidence as to Man's Place in Nature* (New York: Appleton).

Jaffe, Peter (2009) 'Varieties of textualism: unit of analysis and idiom in the interpretation of 18 U.S.C. s. 924(c)', *The Georgetown Journal of Law & Public Policy*, 7, 305–31.

Jaworski, Adam and Nikolas Coupland (eds) (1999) *The Discourse Reader* (Routledge: London).

Johnson, Mark (1987) *The Body in the Mind: The Bodily Basis of Meaning, Imagination, and Reason* (Chicago, Ill: The University of Chicago Press).

Kaminsky, Alan (1982) 'Defamation law: once a public figure always a public figure?', *Hofstra Law Review*, 10, 803–30.

Kaplan, Jeffrey (2012) 'Unfaithful to textualism', *The George Journal of Law and Public Policy*, 10, 385–428.

Kaplan, Jeffrey, Georgia Green, Clark Cunningham and Judith Levi (1995) 'Bringing linguistics into judicial decision-making: semantic analysis submitted to the US Supreme Court', *Forensic Linguistics: The International Journal of Speech, Language and the Law*, 2, 81–98.

Katz, Jerrold (1964) 'Semantic theory and the meaning of "good"', *The Journal of Philosophy*, 61, 739–66.

Katz, Lewis (1986) 'The automobile exception transformed: the rise of a public place exemption to the warrant requirement', *Case Western Reserve Law Review*, 36(3), 375–430.

Keane, August (1899) *Man, Past and Present* (Cambridge: Cambridge UP).

Kelley, Patrick (2001) 'Objective interpretation and objective meaning in Holmes and Dickerson: interpretative practice and interpretative theory', *Nevada Law Journal*, 1, 112–37.

Kempton, Willett (1978) 'Category grading and taxonomic relations: a mug is a sort of a cup', *American Ethnologist*, 5(1), 44-65.

Kennedy, Duncan (1997) *A Critique of Adjudication (Fin de Siècle)* (Cambridge, Mass: Harvard UP).

King, Neil (2003) 'Fans howl in protest as judge decides X-Men aren't human: Marvel fought to have characters ruled nonhuman to win lower tariff on toys', *Wall Street Journal On-line*, <online.wsj.com>, 20 January 2003.

Kołakowski, Leszek (2012) 'Is God happy?', *The New York Review of Books*, December 2012, p. 16.

Kress, Ken (1989) 'Legal indeterminacy', *California Law Review*, 77, 283–337.

Labov, William (1973) 'The boundaries of words and their meanings', in Charles-James Bailey and Roger Shuy (eds), *New Ways of Analyzing Variation in English* (Washington, DC: Georgetown UP), 340–73.

Lakoff, George (1970) 'A note on vagueness and ambiguity', *Linguistic Inquiry*, 1, 357–59.

Lakoff, George (1990) *Women, Fire, and Dangerous Things: What Categories Reveal about the Mind* (Chicago, Ill: University of Chicago Press).

Lakoff, George and Mark Johnson (2003) *Metaphors We Live By*, rev. edn (Chicago, Ill: The University of Chicago Press).

Langvardt, Arlen W. (1990) 'A principled approach to compensatory damages in corporate defamation cases', *American Business Law Journal*, 27, 491–534.

Langville, Brian (1988) 'Revolution without foundation: the grammar of scepticism and law', *Queen's Law Journal*, 13, 112–67.

Laughlin, Gregory (2010) 'Digitization and democracy: the conflict between the Amazon Kindle license agreement and the role of libraries in a free society', *University of Baltimore Law Review*, 40, 3–52.

Lee, Penny (1996) *The Whorf Theory Complex: A Critical Reconstruction* (Amsterdam: John Benjamins).

Lemley, Mark (2003) 'Place and cyberspace', *California Law Review*, 91, 521–42.

Lévi-Strauss, Claude (2013) *Anthropology Confronts the Modern World*, trans. Jane Marie Todd (Cambridge, Mass: Harvard UP).

Levin, Abraham (1934) 'The varying legal meaning and effect of the word "void"', *Michigan Law Review*, 32, 1088–1115.

Lewis, Clive (1990) *Studies in Words* (Cambridge: Canto). First published, 1967.

Lieber, Francis (1839) *Legal and Political Hermeneutics*, 2nd edn (Boston, Mass: Little and Brown).

Llewellyn, Karl (1950) 'Remarks on the theory of appellate decision and the rules and canons of how statutes are to be interpreted', *Vanderbilt Law Review*, 3, 396–406.

Lo, Alex (2013) 'A storey of woe for our developers', *South China Morning Post*, 14 May 2013, p. A2.

Look, Jeffrey (1999) 'The virtual wild, wild west (www): intellectual property issues in cyberspace – trademarks, service marks, and domain names', *University of Arkansas Little Rock Law Review*, 22, 49–89.

Love, Nigel (1985) 'The fixed-code theory', *Language and Communication*, 5, 1–17.

Lovejoy, Arthur (1964) *The Great Chain of Being* (Cambridge, Mass: Harvard UP).

Lyons, John (1968) *Introduction to Theoretical Linguistics* (Cambridge: Cambridge UP).

Madison, Michael (2003) 'Rights of access and the shape of the internet', *Boston College Law Review*, 44, 433–507.

Madison, Michael (2005) 'Law as design: objects, concepts, and digital things', *Cape Western Reserve Law Review*, 56, 381–478.

Maitland, Frederic (1900) 'The corporation sole', *Law Quarterly Review*, 16, 335–54.

Manderson, Desmond (2012) *Kangaroo Courts and the Rule of Law. The Legacy of Modernism* (London: Routledge).

Manning, John (2003) 'The absurdity doctrine', *Harvard Law Review*, 116, 2387–2486.

Marble, John, Robert Norman and Debra Charles (2002) 'Recent developments in insurance coverage litigation', *Tort & Insurance Law Journal* 37: 521–42.

Marx, Karl (1962) *Das Kapital. Band I; Kritik der politischen Ökonomie; Erster Band; Buch I: Der Produktionsprozeß des Kapitals* (Berlin, GDR: Dietz Verlag). First published, 1867.

Marx, Karl and Friedrich Engels (2012) *The Communist Manifesto: A Modern Edition*, ed. Eric Hobsbawm (London: Verso). First published, 1848.

McCawley, James (1994) *Noam Chomsky, critical assessments*, vol. III, tome 1 (New York: Routledge).

Merewether, Henry and Archibald Stephens (1835) *The History of the Boroughs and Municipal Corporations of the United Kingdom from the Earliest to the Present Time*, vol. 3 (Stevens: London).

Merrill, Thomas and Henry Smith (2007) *Property: Principles and Policies* (New York: Foundation Press).

Mill, John Stuart (1859) *On Liberty* (London: J.W. Parker).

Moll, Nessa (1978) 'In search of the corporate private figure: defamation of the corporation', *Hofstra Law Review*, 6, 339–60.

Morris, Hamilton (2011) 'Letter from Haiti: I walked with a zombie', *Harper's Magazine*, November 2011, pp. 52–61.

Mouritsen, Stephen (2011) 'Hard cases and hard data: assessing corpus linguistics as an empirical path to plain meaning', *The Columbia Science and Technology Law Review*, 13, 156–205.

Mullins, Morell E., Sr (2003) 'Tools not rules: the heuristic nature of statutory interpretation', *Journal of Legislation*, 30, 1–76.

Munday, Roderick (2013) '*Fisher v Bell* revisited: misjudging the legislative craft', *Cambridge Law Journal*, 72, 50–64.

[NYT] (1887) 'A preacher from London', *New York Times*, 24 September 1887, p. 8.

Nash, Jonathan Remy (2013) 'Standing's expected value', *Michigan Law Review*, 111, 1283–1336.

Natelson, Robert (2006) 'The legal meaning of "commerce" in the commerce clause', *St John's Law Review*, 80, 798–848.

Noonan, John (2002) *Persons and Masks of the Law* (Berkeley, Cal: University of California Press).

[Occasional notes] (1914) 'Occasional notes', *The Canadian Law Times*, 23, 1–9.

Ogden, Charles and Ivor Richards (1923) *The Meaning of Meaning* (London: Routledge & Kegan Paul).

Onstott, Christopher (2007) 'Judicial notice and the law's scientific search for truth', *Akron Law Review*, 40, 465–91.

Opderbeck, David (2013) 'Does the Communications Act of 1934 contain a hidden internet kill switch?', *Federal Communications Law Journal*, 65, 1–46.

Pablé, Adrian (2009) 'The "dialect myth" and socio-onomastics. The names of the castles of Bellinzona in an integrational perspective', *Language & Communication*, 29, 152–65.

Pablé, Adrian (2010) 'Language, knowledge and reality: the integrationist on name variation', *Language & Communication*, 30, 109–22.

Padfield, Nicola (2011) 'Time to bury the custody "threshold"?', *Criminal Law Review*, 8, 593–612.

[PCBI] (1838) 'Note J, Penal Code of British India', *The Asiatic Journal and Month Register for British and Foreign India, China, and Australasia*, vol. 27 (Sept–Dec 1838) (London: Allen), pp. 87–88.

Pellisser, Hank (2012) 'The Ukrainian "Human Barbie Doll" – Valeria Lukyanova – is this the future of cosmetic enhancement?', <transhumanity.net>, accessed 10 July 2013.

Penner, J.E. (2005) 'The "bundle of rights" picture of property', *UCLA Law Review*, 43, 711–20.

Pennington, Shane (2009) 'Cases, controversies, and the textualist commitment to giving every word of the constitution meaning', *Texas Review of Law and Politics*, 14, 179–207.

Phelps, Robert and E. Douglas Hamilton (1978) *Libel: Rights, Risks, Responsibilities*, rev. edn (New York: Dover).

Phillips, Carl (2007) *Quiver of Arrows: Selected Poems 1986–2006* (New York: Farrar, Straus and Giroux).

Pieroni, Caroline Lynch (2009) 'Staying out of jail … sometimes maintaining a free press through journalist shield laws requires changes not only at the federal level but among the states', *University of Louisville Law Review*, 47, 803–24.

Poscher, Ralk (2012) 'Ambiguity and vagueness in legal interpretation' in Peter Tiersma and Lawrence Solan (eds), *The Oxford Handbook of Language and Law* (Oxford: Oxford UP), 128–44.

Posner, Richard (1983) 'Statutory interpretation – in the classroom and in the courtroom', *University of Chicago Law Review*, 50, 800–22.

Posner, Richard (2008) *How Judges Think* (Cambridge, Mass: Harvard UP).

Posner, Richard (2009) *Law and Literature*, 3rd edn (Cambridge, Mass: Harvard UP).

Price, Jeanne (2013) 'Wagging, not barking: statutory definitions', *Cleveland Law Review* 60: 999–1055.

Probert, Walter (1972) *Law, Language and Communication* (Springfield, Ill: Thomas).

Purvis, Jeffrey and Benjamin Greer (2012) 'Is mom's basement the newsroom of the 21st century?: an analysis of statutory protections for online news reporters', *Reynolds Court and Media Law Journal*, 2, 107–36.

Putnam, Hilary (1973) 'Meaning and reference', *The Journal of Philosophy*, 70, 699–711.

Radcliffe-Brown, Alfred (1965) *Structure and Function in Primitive Society* (New York: Free Press).

Radoff, Todd (2010) 'Statutory interpretation as a multifarious enterprise', *Northwestern Law Reveiw*, 104, 1559–86.

Raigrodski, Dana (2013) 'Property, privacy and power: rethinking the Fourth Amendment in the wake of *US v Jones*', *Public Interest Law Journal*, 22, 67–128.

Richards, Ivor (1962) *Coleridge on the Imagination* (London: Routledge & Kegan Paul).

Richardson, Megan, Michael Bryan, Martin Vranken and Katy Barnett (2012) *Breach of Confidence: Social Origins and Modern Development* (Cheltenham: Elgar).

Sapir, Edward (1962) *Culture, Language, and Personality: Selected Essays*, ed. David Mandelbaum (Berkeley, Cal: University of California Press).

Sapir, Edward (1994) *The Psychology of Culture: a Course of Lectures*, ed. Judith T. Irvine (Berlin: Mouton de Gruyter).

Saussure, Ferdinand de (1972) *Cours de Linguistique Générale* (Paris: Payot). Trans. and ed. by Roy Harris, *Course in General Linguistics* (London: Duckworth, 1983). First published, 1916.

Saussure, Ferdinand (2002) *Écrits de Linguistique Générale*, Simon Bouquet and Rudolf Engler (eds) (Paris: Gallimard). Trans. and eds by Carol Saunders and Matthew Pires, *Writings in General Linguistics* (Oxford: Oxford UP, 2006).

Scalia, Antonin (1997) *A Matter for Interpretation: Federal Courts and the Law: an Essay* (Princeton, NJ: Princeton UP).

Scalia, Antonin and Brian Garner (2012) *Reading Law: The Interpretation of Legal Texts* (St Paul, Minn: Thompson/West).

Schane, Sanford (2006) *Language and the Law* (London: Continuum).

Schauer, Frederick (1984) 'Public figures', *William and Mary Law Review*, 25, 905–35.

Schauer, Frederick (1991) *Playing by the Rules* (Oxford: Clarendon Press).

Schutz, Alfred (1962) *Collected Papers*, vol. 1 (The Hague: Martinus Nijhoff).

Schutze, Carson (1996) *The Empirical Base of Linguistics: Grammaticality Judgments and Linguistic Methodology* (Chicago, Ill: University of Chicago Press).

Sharpe, Alex (2006) *Transgender Jurisprudence* (Oxford: Cavendish).

Sharpe, Robert and Patricia McMahon (2007) *The Persons Case: The Origins and Legacy of the Fight for Legal Personhood* (Toronto: University of Toronto Press).

Sheppard, William (1659) *Of Corporations, Fraternities, and Guilds* (London: Twyford, Dring, and Place).

Shuy, Roger (2002) *Linguistic Battles in Trademark Disputes* (Basingstoke: Palgrave Macmillan).

Sirico, Louis (2011) 'Failed constitutional metaphors: the wall of separation and the penumbra', *University of Richmond Law Review*, 45, 459–89.

Slocum, Brian (2012) 'Linguistics and "ordinary meaning" determinations', *Statute Law Review*, 33, 39–83.

Smith, Peter J (2007) 'New legal fictions', *Georgetown Law Journal*, 95, 1436–95.

Soboleva, Anita (2013) 'Use and misuse of language in judicial decision-making: Russian experience', *International Journal for the Semiotics of Law*, 26, 673–92.

Solan, Lawrence (1993) *The Language of Judges* (Chicago, Ill: The University of Chicago Press).

Solan, Lawrence (1995) 'Judicial decisions and linguistic analysis: is there a linguist in the court?', *Washington University Law Quarterly*, 73, 1069–80.

Solan, Lawrence (1998) 'Law, language and lenity', *William and Mary Law Review*, 40, 57–144.

Solan, Lawrence (1999) 'Can the legal system use experts on meaning?', *Tennessee Law Review*, 66, 1167–99.

Solan, Lawrence (2005a) 'The new textualists' new text', *Loyola of Los Angeles Law Review*, 38, 2027–62.

Solan, Lawrence (2005b) 'Private language, private laws: the central role of legislative intent in statutory interpretation', *The Georgetown Law Journal*, 93: 427–86.

Solan, Lawrence (2010) *The Language of Statutes: Laws and Their Interpretation* (Chicago, Ill: The University of Chicago Press).

Solan, Lawrence (2012) 'Linguistic issues in statutory interpretation' in Peter Tiersma and Lawrence Solan (eds), *The Oxford Handbook of Language and Law* (Oxford: Oxford UP), 87–99.

Solum, Lawrence (1996) 'Indeterminacy' in Dennis Patterson (ed.), *A Companion to Philosophy of Law and Legal Theory* (Cambridge, Mass: Blackwell), 488–502.

Sprankling, John (1999) *Understanding Property Law* (Newark, NJ: LexisNexis).

Steyn, Johan (2001) '*Pepper v Hart*; a re-examination', *Oxford Journal of Legal Studies*, 21, 59–72.

Stone, Christopher (1972) 'Should trees have standing? Toward legal rights for natural objects', *Southern California Law Review*, 45l, 450–501.

Stout, Jeffrey (1982) 'What is the meaning of a text?', *New Literary History*, 14, 1–12.

Strong, Don (1989) 'Oil and Gas: *Ejusdem Generis*: Oklahoma's approach to the interpretation of "other minerals" after *Commissioners of Land Office v Butler*', *Oklahoma Law Review*, 42, 483–98.

Sumner, Leonard (2013) 'Review of Jeremy Waldron, *The Harm in Hate Speech*, Harvard UP, 2012', *Law & Philosophy* 32: 377–83.

Taussig, Frank W. (1891) 'The McKinley Tariff Act', *The Economic Journal*, 1, 326–50.

Taylor, John (1995) *Linguistic Categorization: Prototypes in Linguistic Theory* (Oxford: Clarendon Press).

Taylor, Talbot J. (1990) 'Which is to be master? The institutionalization of authority in the science of language' in John Joseph and Talbot Taylor (eds), *Ideologies of Language* (London: Routledge), 9–26.

Teubert, Wolfgang (2010) *Meaning, Discourse, Society* (Cambridge: Cambridge UP).

Threadgold, Terry (1997) *Feminist Poetics:* Poiesis, *Performance, Histories* (London: Routledge).

Thumma, Samuel and Kirchmeier, Jeffrey (1999) 'The lexicon has become a fortress: the United States Supreme Court's use of dictionaries', *Buffalo Law Review*, 47, 227–301.

Tiersma, Peter (1999) *Legal Language* (Chicago, Ill: The University of Chicago Press).

Tiersma, Peter (2001) 'A message in a bottle: text, autonomy, and statutory interpretation', *Tulane LR*, 76, 431–482.

Tiersma, Peter (2007) 'The textualization of precedent', *Notre Dame Law Review*, 82, 1187–1278.

Tiersma, Peter (2010) *Parchment, Paper, Pixels: Law and the Technologies of Communication* (Chicago, Ill: University of Chicago Press).

Toolan, Michael (1996) *Total Speech. An Integrational Linguistic Approach to Language* (Durham, NC: Duke UP).

Toolan, Michael (2002) 'The language myth and the law' in Roy Harris (ed.), *The Language Myth in Western Culture* (Surrey: Curzon), 159–82.

Toolan, Michael (2006) 'Integrational corpus linguistics' in Nigel Love (ed.), *Language and History: Integrationist Perspectives* (London: Routledge), 172–87.

Townsend, Gregory (1999) 'Cardboard castles: the Fourth Amendment's protection of the homeless's makeshift shelters in public areas', *California Western Law Review*, 35(2), 223–42.

Ullmann, Stephen (1966) *Language and Style* (Oxford: Blackwell).

[US Senate] (1911) *Dictionary of Races or Peoples. Reports of the Immigration Commission*, Senate Document 662, 61st Congress, 3rd Session (Washington, DC: Government Printing Office).

Vade, Dylan (2005) 'Expanding gender and expanding the law: toward a social and legal conceptualization of gender that is more inclusive of transgender people', *Michigan Journal of Gender and Law*, 11, 253–316.

Varzi, Achille, 'Boundary', *The Stanford Encyclopedia of Philosophy* (Winter 2012 Edition), Edward N. Zalta (ed.), <plato.stanford.edu>, accessed 4 July 2013.

Veitch, Scott, Emilios Christodoulidis and Lindsay Farmer (2012) *Jurisprudence: Themes and Concepts*, 2nd edn (London: Routledge).

Vermeule, Adrian (2010) 'Legislative history and the limits of judicial competence: the untold story of *Holy Trinity Church*', *Stanford Law Review*, 50, 1833–96.

Vilinbakhova, Elena (2013) 'The notion of stereotype in language study', *History and Philosophy of the Language Sciences*, <http://hiphilangsci.net>.

Wagner-Ott, Anna (2002) 'Analysis of gender identity through doll and action figure politics in art education', *Studies in Art Education*, 43, 246–63.

Wan, Marco (ed.) (2012) *Reading the Legal Case: Cross-Currents between Law and the Humanities* (London: Routledge).

Warren, Samuel and Louis Brandeis (1890) 'The right to privacy', *Harvard Law Review*, 6, 193–220.

Watkins, Dawn (2012) 'The (Literal) Death of the Author and the Silencing of the Testator's Voice', *Law and Literature*, 24, 59–79.

Watt, Gary (2013) 'Rule of the root: proto-Indo-European domination of legal language' in Michael Freeman and Fiona Smith (eds), *Law and Language: Current Legal Issues*, vol. 15 (Oxford: Oxford UP), 571–89.

Weaver, Russell (2013) 'Privacy in an age of advancing technology', *Mississippi Law Journal*, 82, 975–96.

Weiner, Mark (1998) '"Naturalization" and naturalization law: some empirical observations', *Yale Journal of Law and the Humanities*, 10, 657–66.

Weinstein, Jacob (2004) 'Against dictionaries: using analogical reasoning to achieve a more restrained textualism', *University of Michigan Journal of Law Reform*, 38, 649–81.

Wenger, Etienne (1998) *Communities of Practice* (Cambridge: Cambridge UP).

Werbach, Kevin (1994) 'Looking it up: dictionaries and statutory interpretation', *Harvard Law Review*, 107, 1437–1453.

White, G. Edward (2010) *The Marshall Court and Cultural Change, 1815-1835* (New York: Cambridge UP).

Wierzbicka, Anna (1996) *Semantics: Primes and Universals* (Oxford: Oxford UP).

Wilberforce, Edward (1881) *Statute Law: The Principles which Govern the Construction and Operation of Statutes* (London: Stevens & Sons).

Williams, Glanville (1945) 'Language and the law', *The Law Quarterly Review*, 61, 71–86; 179–95; 293–303; 384–406; 62: 387–406.

Wilson, James (1804) *Lectures on Law*, vol. 3 (Philadelphia, Pa: Lorenzo).

Winstead, Lizz (2011) 'Is pizza a vegetable? Well, Congress says so. What does childhood nutrition matter next to the frozen food industry's wishes?', *The Guardian On-Line*, Friday, 18 November 2011, <guardian.co.uk>.

Winter, Sam (2013) 'Gender justice', *South China Morning Post*, 17 May 2013, p. A11.

Winter, Steven (2008) 'What is the "color" of law?' in Raymond Gibbs Jr (ed.), *The Cambridge Handbook of Metaphor and Thought* (Cambridge: Cambridge UP), 363–79.

Wisotsky, Steven (1999) 'How to interpret statutes – or not: plain meaning and other phantoms', *The Journal of Appellate Practice and Process*, 10, 321–46.

Wittgenstein, Ludwig (1978) *Philosophical Investigations*, trans. G. Anscombe (Oxford: Blackwell). First published, 1953.

Wolf, George (1999) 'Quine and the segregational sign', *Language and Communication*, 19, 27–43.

Zander, Michael (2004) *The Law-Making Process*, 6th edn (Cambridge: Cambridge UP).

Cases cited

677 New Loudon Corporation v State of New York Tax Appeals 19 NY3d 1058 (2012)

Ali v Federal Bureau of Prisons 552 US 214 (2008)

American Guaranty and Liability Insurance Co. v Ingram Micro, Inc. Civ. 99–185 (D Ariz April 19, 2000)

Anheuser-Busch Association v US 207 US 556 (1908)

Asda Stores Ltd v Commissioners for Her Majesty's Revenue and Customs 2009 WL 3447997

Attorney-General (Cth) v 'Kevin and Jennifer' (2003) 172 FLR 300

Austin v Michigan Chamber of Commerce 494 US 652 (1990)

Bailey v US 516 US 317 (1995)

Bank of the US v Deveaux 9 US 61 (1809)

Barnes v Glen Theatre, Inc. 501 US 560 (1991)

Bellinger v Bellinger [2002] Fam 150

Bellinger v Bellinger [2003] 2 AC 467

Bellotti v First National Bank of Boston 435 US 765 (1977)

Berkey v Third Avenue Railway Company 155 NE 58 (NY 1926)

Branzburg v Hayes 408 US 665 (1972)

Brock v Wollams [1949] 2 KB 388

Brutus v Cozens [1973] AC 854

Buckley v Valeo 424 US 1 (1976)

Cabell v Markham 148 F2d 737 (1945)

California v Carney 471 US 386, 105 SCt 2066 (1985)

California v Greenwood 486 US 35, 108 SCt 1625 (1988)

Cannan v Earl of Abingdon [1900] 2 QB 66

Carroll v US 267 US 132, 45 SCt 280 (1925)

Chambers v Maroney 399 US 42 (1970)

Cherokee Nation v Georgia 30 US (5 Peters) 1 (1831)

Chevron, USA, Inc. v Natural Resources Defense Council, Inc. 467 US 837 (1984)

Chrysler Corporation v Smith 297 Mich 438, 298 NW 87 (1941)

Church of the Holy Trinity v US 143 US 457 (1892)

Citizens United v Federal Election Commission 558 US 310 (2010)

Clapper v Amnesty International USA 133 SCt 1138 (2013)

Commissioner of Internal Revenue v Acker 361 US 87 (1959)

Commissioners for Her Majesty's Revenue & Customs v Proctor & Gamble UK [2008] EWHC 1558 (Ch)

Commissioners for Her Majesty's Revenue & Customs v Proctor & Gamble UK [2009] EWCA Civ 407

Coolidge v New Hampshire 403 US 443 (1971)

Cooper v Stuart 14 App Cas 286 (1889)

Corbett v Corbett (otherwise Ashley) [1971] P 83

Corkery v Carpenter [1951] 1 KB 102

Cossey v United Kingdom (1990) 13 EHRR 622

Curtis Publishing Co. v Butts, Associated Press v Walker 388 US 130 (1967)

Customs and Excise Commissioners v Ferrero UK Ltd [1997] STC 881

Customs and Excise Commissioners v Quaker Oats Ltd [1987] STC 683

Danesh v Kensington and Chelsea Royal London Borough Council [2006] EWCA Civ 1404

Davidson v New Orleans 96 US 97 (1878)

De Souza v Cobden [1891] 1 QB 687

District of Columbia v Heller 554 US 570 (2008)

Doe ex rel. Hansen v Thorin 2012 WL 2866042 (Wis App)

Dred Scott v Sandford 60 US 393 (1857)

Dyson Holdings Ltd v Fox [1976] QB 503

Ealing London Borough Council v Race Relations Board [1972] AC 342

Edwards v A.G. of Canada [1930] AC 124

Edwards (Inspector of Taxes) v Clinch [1982] AC 845

Entick v Carrington 95 Eng Rep 807 (CP 1765)

Erickson v Crookston Waterworks P&L Co. 100 Minn 481 (1907)

Figas v Horsehead Corporation 2008 WL 4170043 (WD Pa)

First Health Group Corporation v BCE Emergis Corporation 269 F3d 800 (7th Cir.2001)

Fisher v Bell [1961] 1 QB 394

Fitzpatrick v Sterling Housing Association Ltd [2001] 1 AC 27

Flores-Figueroa v US 556 US 646 (2009)

Frigaliment Importing Co. v BNS International Sales Corporation 190 F Supp 116 (SDNY 1960)

Fully Profit (Asia) Ltd v The Secretary for Justice [2011] HKCFI 268

Fully Profit (Asia) Ltd v The Secretary for Justice [2012] HKCA 44

Fully Profit (Asia) Ltd v The Secretary for Justice Final Appeal No. 17 of 2012 (2013)

Gammans v Ekins [1950] 2 KB 328

Gertz v Robert Welch, Inc. 418 US 323 (1974)

Goldman v US 316 US 129 (1942)

Goodwin v United Kingdom (2002) 35 EHRR 447

Hardwick Game Farm v SAPPA [1969] 2 AC 31

Hasbro Industries, Inc. v US 703 F Supp 941 (CIT 1988)

Hasbro Industries, Inc. v US 879 F2d 838 (CIT 1989)

Hatfill v New York Times Co. ('*Hatfill III*') 532 F3d 312 (4th Cir.), cert. denied, 129 SCt 765 (2008)

Helby v Rafferty [1979] 1 WLR 13

Heydon's Case (1584) 3 Rep 7b

Hong Kong Racing Pigeon Association v AG [1994] 2 HKLR 309

Hong Kong Racing Pigeon Association v AG [1995] HKLY 1182

Hyde v Hyde and Woodmansee (1866) 1 P&D 130

In re Arzberger 27 CCPA 1315, 112 F2d 834 (1940)

In re Ho King 14 FedRep 724 (D Or 1883)

Investors Compensation Scheme Ltd v West Bromwich Building Society [1998] 1 WLR 896

John Pimblett and Sons Limited v Customs and Excise Commissioners [1988] STC 358

Jones v US, US Supreme Court, Docket no. 10–125 (2012)

Katz v US 389 US 347 (1967)

King-Ansell v Police [1979] 2 NZLR 531

Knox v Massachusetts Society for the Prevention of Cruelty to Animals 425 NE2d 393 (Mass App Ct 1981)

Kyllo v US 533 US 27 (2001)

Lines v Lines (1963) 107 SJ 596

Liparota v US 471 US 419 (1985)

Littleton v Prange 9 SW3d 223 (1999) (Texas)

Liversidge v Anderson [1942] AC 206

Lock v State 2012 WL 3043160

Lukhard v Reed 481 US 368 (1987)

MacDonald v Advocate-General for Scotland [2004] 1 All ER 339

Mack Oil Company v Mamie Lee Lawrence 389 P2d 955 (1964)

Maine State Board of Education v Cavazos 956 F2d 376 (1992)

Mandla v Dowell Lee [1982] 3 All ER 1108

Mandla v Dowell Lee [1983] 2 AC 548 HL

Margate Pier Co. v Hannam (1819) 3 B & Ald 266

Mattison v Hart and Anor (1854) 14 CB 357

Maughan v The Free Church of Scotland (1893) 3 TC 207

Maurice v Judd (1818) in the Mayor's Court of New York. Reported in William Sampson, *Is a Whale a Fish? An Accurate Report of the Case of James Maurice against Samuel Judd* (New York: Van Winkle, 1819)

McAllister v California Coastal Commission 169 Cal App 4th 912 (2009)

McBoyle v US 43 F2d 273 (1930)

McBoyle v US 283 US 25 (1931)

McConnell v Federal Election Commission 540 US 93 (2003)

McCollum v Board of Education 333 US 203 (1948)

McGilley v Chubb & Son, Inc. 369 Pa Super 547 (1987)

Miller v US 357 US 301 (1958)

Minor v Happersett 88 US 162 (1874)

Modavox, Inc. v Tacoda, Inc. 607 F Supp2d 530 (SDNY 2009)

Morris v Revenue and Customs Commissioners [2006] EWHC 1560 (Ch); [2006] RTR 37

Muscarello v US 524 US 125 (1998)

National Organization for Women v Scheidler 510 US 249 (1994)

New York Times Co. v Sullivan 376 US 254 (1964)

Ng Ka-ling v Director of Immigration Final Appeal No. 14, 15, 16 of 1998 (CIVIL) (1999)

Ni v Slocum (2011) 127 Cal Rptr 3d 620 (Cal App 1 Dist 2011)

Nix v Hedden 149 US 304 (1893)

Olmstead v US 277 US 438 (1928)

Omychund v Barker (1745) 1 Atk, 21, 49; 26 ER 15

Park v Appeal Board of Mich. Employment Sec. Commission 355 Mich 103 (1959)

Pennsylvania v Labron 518 US 938 (1996)

People v Blood 207 NYS 210 (1924)

People v Carney 117 Cal App 3d 36, 172 Cal Rptr 430 (1981)

People v Carney 34 Cal3d 597 (1983)

People v Kloosterman 2012 WL 1862331 (Mich App)

People v Ruggles 8 Johns 290, 5 Am Dec 335 (1811)

People v Thomas 38 Cal App4th 1331 (1995)

Pepper v Hart [1992] UKHL 3

Perrin v Morgan [1943] AC 399

Proctor & Gamble (UK) v Commissioners for Her Majesty's Revenue and Customs [2003] UKVAT 18381

Proctor & Gamble (UK) v Commissioners for Her Majesty's Revenue and Customs 2007 WL 1729910 (VAT Tribunal)

Queen-Empress v Bandhu (1886) ILR 8 All 51

Queen-Empress v Imam Ali and Anor (1888) ILR 10 All 150

Queen-Empress v Nalla (1888) ILR 11 Mad 145

R v Caldwell [1982] AC 382

R v Harris and McGuinness (1988) 17 NSWLR 158

R v Ireland [1998] AC 147

R v Judge of the City of London Court [1892] 1 QB 273

R v Parker (1895) 59 JP 793

R (Quintavalle) v Secretary of State for Health [2003] 2 AC 687

R v R [1992] 1 AC 599

R v Wong Sik Ming [1996] HKCFI 447

Re Kevin and Jennifer (2001) 165 FLR 404, [2001] FamCA 1074

Re Pringle [1946] 1 Ch 124

Re Rowland [1963] 1 Ch 1 (CA)

Robertson v Salomon 130 US 412 (1889)

Roman v CIA 297 F3d 1363 (CA Fed 2002)

Romesh Chunder Sannyal v Hiru Mondal and Anor (1890) ILR 17 Cal 852

Rosanova v Playboy Entertainments, Inc. 411 F Supp 440 (SD Ga 1976)

Rosenbloom v Metromedia, Inc. 403 US 29 (1971)

Rowland v California Men's Colony 506 US 194 (1993)

Russ Berrie & Co. v US 417 F Supp 1035 (Cust Ct 1976)

Sabritas v US 22 CIT 59, 998 F Supp 1123 (1998)

Salomon v A Salomon & Co. Ltd [1897] AC 22

Savoy Hotel Co. v London County Council [1900] 1 QB 665

Seaford Court Estates v Asher [1949] 2 All ER 155

Sher v Lafayette Ins. Co. 988 So2d 186 (La 2008)

Silverman v US 365 US 505 (1961)

Simpson v Teignmouth and Shaldon Bridge Co. [1903] 1 KB 405

Skanska Rashleigh Weatherfoil Ltd v Somerfield Stores Ltd 2006 WL 3327771

Smith v US 508 US 223 (1993)

South Dakota v Opperman 428 US 364 (1976)

South Eastern Electrical Plc v Somerfield Stores Ltd 2001 WL 753311

State v Reynolds 265 P3d 22 (Or App 2011)

State Auto Property and Casualty Insurance Co. v Midwest Computers and More 147 F Supp2d 1113 (WD Okla 2001)

State ex. rel. Miller v Claiborne 505 P2d 732 (Kan 1973)

Stradling v Morgan (1560) 1 Plowd 199, 75 ER 305

S Y v S Y (otherwise W) [1963] P 37

Takao Ozawa v US 260 US 178 (1922)

Taylor v Goodwin (1879) 4 QBD 228

Tea Trade Properties Ltd v CIN Properties Ltd [1990] 1 EGLR 155

Tektrol Ltd v International Insurance Company of Hanover Ltd & Anor [2005] EWCA Civ 845

The Queen v Sit Yat Keung [1985] HKCFI 154

Tilikum v SeaWorld Case No. 11cv2476 (WMC) (Southern District of California) (2012)

Towne v Eisner 245 US 418 (1918)

Toy Biz, Inc. v US 248 F Supp2d 1234 (CIT 2003)

TOYS "R" US, Inc. v Abir 45 USPQ2d 1944 (SDNY 1997)

Trustees of Dartmouth College v Woodward 17 US 518 (1819)

United Biscuits (UK) Ltd v Commissioners of Customs and Excise (1991) (Tax Tribunal)

United Biscuits (UK) Ltd v Commissioners for Her Majesty's Revenue and Customs 2011 WL 5105709 (Tax Tribunal)

US v Bhagat Singh Thind 261 US 204 (1923)

US v Carey 172 F3d (1999)

US v Chadwick 433 US 1 (1977)

US v Craig (1886), 28 Fed 795

US v Downing 201 US 354 (1905)

US v Gole 158 F3d 166 (2d Cir.1998)

US v Great Northern Railway Co. 287 US 144 (1932)

US v Johns 469 US 478 (1985)

US v Jones 308 F3d 748 (2002)

US v Kirby 74 US 482 (1868)

US v Knotts 460 US 276 (1983)

US v Nelson 459 F2d 884 (6th Cir.1972)

US v On Lee 193 F2d 306 (1951)

US v Palmer 16 US 610 (1818)

US v Rector of the Church of the Holy Trinity 36 F 303 (CCSDNY 1888)

US v Ross 456 US 798 (1982)

US v Williams 630 F2d 1322, 1326 (9th Cir.1980)

US v X-Citement Video, Inc. 513 US 64 (1994)

Updegraph v Commonwealth 11 Serg. & Rawle 394 Pa

W v Registrar of Marriages HCAL No. 120/2009 (2010)

W v Registrar of Marriages CACV No. 266/2010 (2011)

W v Registrar of Marriages FACV No. 4/2012 (2013)

W v W (Physical Inter-sex) [2001] Fam 111

Weeks v US 232 US 383 (1914)

White City Shopping Center, LP v PR Restaurants, LLC dba Bread Panera 2006 WL 3292641 (Mass Super)

Williams v Ellis (1880) 5 QBD 175

Wingrove v Secretary of State for Communities and Local Government 2009 WL 1725569

Wood v Lucy 118 NE 214 (NY 1917)

Yemshaw v London Borough of Hounslow [2009] EWCA Civ 1543

Yemshaw v London Borough of Hounslow [2011] UKSC 3

Index

Meanings of words and phrases